The Murder of
Richard Jennings

The Murder of Richard Jennings

The TRUE Story of New York's First Murder for Hire

Michael J. Worden

SISU BOOKS

Library of Congress Control Number: 2013950158

10 9 8 7 6 5 4 3 2 1

Printed in the United States of America.

Ordering Information:
Special discounts are available to booksellers, historical societies, schools, and on quantity purchases by corporations, associations, and others. For details, contact the publisher at:

Sisu Books
PO Box 421
Sparrowbush, New York 12780

www.sisubooks.com
sales@sisubooks.com

Cover & Book Design by Michael J. Worden
Crime scene tape photo © Can Stock Photo, Inc./bradcalkins

TABLE OF CONTENTS

LIST OF ILLUSTRATIONS

PREFACE

The idea for this book was born during a long drive home from Buffalo, New York, with Linda Zimmermann. It was the fall of 2009 and we had been talking about a crime from 1827 which had occurred at historic Cherry Hill in Albany. The murder there had led to the last public hanging in Albany. The details of the crime were quite salacious, and it was interesting to me both historically and as a law enforcement officer. Linda and I had previously visited the site of this murder (Cherry Hill) while researching a book she was writing, and I had some thoughts on the scene and the particulars of the crime, which led Linda to suggest a book on true crimes. Specifically, a look at historical crimes from my unique perspective as both a writer and police officer. Needless to say, I liked the idea.

I began to research the Cherry Hill murder and thought I would find a few other historical cases which I could wrap up into one nice book. One of the documents I obtained during that initial research was a legal decision rendered in the Cherry Hill case regarding the testimony of an accomplice being introduced at trial. In that case, a young woman had seduced a hired hand into killing her husband. He was convicted, and when the prosecution went to introduce him as a witness at her trial, the defense objected and the judge rendered a rather interesting opinion and prevented him from taking the stand (which, of course, led to her acquittal – isn't love grand?) In the decision, the judge made reference to a case from Orange County involving a murder trial in 1819, where four men had been tried for the murder of a man named Richard Jennings, with two of them later executed on the gallows.

How could I live in Orange County my entire life and never have heard about this? The brief particulars of the crime related in the decision were fascinating, so I decided to dig a little deeper. This was the start of a condition I have since referred to as *historical research attention deficit disorder,* which causes a person to easily get distracted while working on one project by the fascinating details of another! At one time I was managing (or, should I say, juggling) research on no less than six historical crimes! My kids told me I needed an intervention!

The information I began to uncover on the Jennings murder fascinated me: Attorney General Martin Van Buren assisting the prosecution and declaring it the first murder for hire in New York; stories on how the men hanged for murder were buried outside of the walls of the cemetery with locust stakes driven into their graves; the others condemned were spared the noose moments before they were to die in a dramatic reprieve read from the scaffold; and a story of redemption for one of the murderers who escaped the gallows and ended up living a pious life in Canandaigua, New York, where he resided in the home of Samuel S. Seward (nephew of the murdered man) and had a monument in his honor erected at his grave. There were even tales of families changing names and obscuring the record to cover the deed and protect their image years later. It was all sensational and, in many cases, conflicting. It was apparent that the version of events in one source was not always the same as in another source. So what was the truth? What was fact and what was fiction? Those were questions I wanted to answer.

Any notion that I would write one book about many crimes was discarded, and I opted instead to focus on one crime per book. I needed the space to do more because I wanted this to be much more than a true crime book. I wanted to delve into the case as no one had before and find the crime scene, the cemetery, and the graves. I wanted to know who the people were and find out every piece of factual information that I could in order to produce a historically accurate account of the case.

I also wanted to explore the legends and lore surrounding this case. There were some pretty fantastic stories connected to the incident, aftermath, and people involved. Questions such as: were two of the men really buried outside of the walls of a cemetery? Were locust stakes actually driven into their graves? Did one of the killers really live in the home of a future Secretary of State? Did local families make a concerted effort to conceal and obliterate references to the crime and trial?

This book would have been done a couple of years earlier if I were not so stubborn. Tracking down sources and materials became an obsession. If I learned about a document or publication that had (or could have) relevant information, then I wanted it! I recall one particular pamphlet that took me two years to track down - the execution sermon delivered at the hangings. I began trying to get my hands on that document in 2009 and finally got it in October 2011! I was persistent and it paid off.

I wanted to make the book accurate, interesting, and entertaining. Until I had been satisfied with the research and the content, the book would have to wait. And I am glad that I stuck to that. I hope that, as you read this book, you will feel the passion and thirst for knowledge that I felt as I researched and wrote it.

Some of the topics in this book warrant their own book to explore more completely. For example, the trials of the murderers could easily occupy a book (the transcript does!). This is not that book! The trials, for example, are discussed and reviewed, but not examined in minute detail. So too is the life of Jack Hodges. A book has been written about him, so again, the goal in this book is to apply his life to this case

I hope that you also find this book to be a valuable resource for genealogical research. There are many people included in this book, for example, as members of the jury, with family names that are still living in and around Orange County today. What a great discovery to find an ancestor of yours who sat on the jury, or perhaps was an attorney or witness in the case! It's very likely that for many readers they will be surprised!

Michael J. Worden
September 2013

LANGUAGE DISCLAIMER

A s you read through this incredible story, you will notice some words which are misspelled, used out of context, or are just plain 'politically incorrect.' To maintain historical accuracy, I have not changed grammatical or spelling errors when quoting from sources. In some instances, you will read quotes which are laden with errors. I have refrained from using [Sic.] as much as possible (generally only when there is one error in a quote – so you don't think it was bad proofreading!), so keep in mind as you read this book that errors which are in direct quotes or block quotes are original to the source. You may also see some alternate spellings, such as *colour* (instead of color) and *defence* (instead of defense), which are used in this book based upon the use of that word in the original source document.

There is also a fair share of language and words reproduced in the book which today are considered racist and offensive. I have not censored any of the language quoted – to do so would diminish the historical accuracy of this work. Much of the primary and secondary source documents pre-date the American Civil War, and the primary sources are, for the most part, contemporary to the crime and aftermath. This places the language and terminology into context. As much as I want this work to be enjoyable to read, I also want it to stand as an historically accurate work.

So this is my disclaimer: there is language and wording quoted or cited in this book which is now considered racist, bigoted, insensitive, or just plain offensive. There has been no editing or censorship or changing of this language. If you are easily offended, you may not want to read this book. You have been warned (so no negative or nasty e-mails or letters). Read at your own risk (of being offended!)

ABOUT TRANSCRIBED DOCUMENTS AND TEXTS

I had some difficult decisions to make while writing this book, one of them being how to handle some of the more lengthy passages that I felt needed to be transcribed and printed in the book. Reproducing pages of lengthy text is often frowned upon in historical writing, and I understand that.

Trust me, I debated this issue with myself and even tried rewriting chapters to exclude the more lengthy transcripts. They just didn't feel the same. The information contained in the quoted passages and transcripts is too important to exclude.

I have envisioned this book as immersing you – the reader – into the case – and presenting factual information which will allow you to develop your own theories and conclusions. Access to some of the statements, confessions, and testimony transcribed verbatim will give you an additional insight into the case and make that process easier.

INTRODUCTION

On the morning of December 21, 1818, seventy-year-old Richard Jennings walked from the small village of Sugar Loaf, New York, towards a plot of land of which a court had recently granted him possession. He had been battling his own nephew, James Teed, and Teed's brother-in-law, David Conkling, in the courts for years over this section of land. Bitter court fights had become the norm and even though Jennings had prevailed at the most recent session of court, he still couldn't take possession of the land until after the New Year.

The court battles had put a financial strain on James Teed, and David Conkling (who had been the most recent 'owner' of the land) was set to suffer financially from the loss. For James Teed, the loss was even grimmer: he and his family faced certain eviction from their home. This could be the foundation for what will become the first murder for hire in New York.

That cold December morning, Jennings would meet a horrific and brutal end. Jack Hodges, an ill-tempered former sailor employed by David Conkling, and a tenant farmer of Teeds, David Dunning, murdered the old man as he stood on the land he had recently regained. The pair had allegedly been hired by Teed and Conkling to kill old Dick Jennings. The price of the murder: $1000 to be split between Hodges and Dunning.

A week after the murder, the cold, stiff body of Richard Jennings was found lying in his lot, and after an inquest, Teed, Dunning, and Conkling were arrested. A few days later, Jack Hodges was arrested in New York (city), followed by the arrest of Teed's wife, Hannah. Five persons stood accused of plotting to murder Jennings, and the penalty, if convicted, was swift and certain: death by hanging.

Sensational trials followed in the early months of 1819, with Attorney General Martin Van Buren aiding in the prosecution. Thousands of people gathered in the village of Goshen to attend the court sessions, which often began at 9:00 A.M. and lasted until midnight or longer! Those who couldn't get a seat in the court room could read the details in the press, and news of the murder and trials spread throughout the still young United States.

By the end of the proceedings, all four men had been found guilty and sentenced to hang, with only Hannah Teed escaping the gallows. Two of them, Hodges and Conkling, would avoid their date with the hangman after being pardoned by the state legislature. Teed and Dunning would die at the end of a rope on April 16, 1819, before a crowd estimated to be as high as 20,000.

The drama didn't end on the scaffold. Local lore held that no cemetery would accept the bodies of Teed or Dunning, and, finally, the owner of a small private cemetery in Sugar Loaf agreed to allow the bodies to be buried on his property, provided that they were buried outside of the walls of the cemetery. It was said that later that night, a group of local men drove sharpened locust stakes into each of the graves. What a grisly and macabre scene that must have been!

David Conkling would serve more than ten years in prison before being pardoned and returning to Orange County. It was alleged that he changed his name to Daniel Conklin, and when he died, the year of death on his gravestone was recorded as *1810* to distance his family from the shame of his crime and conviction.

Jack Hodges may have been the first inmate in American history to find God and religion in prison. He served less than ten years of his sentence before he was pardoned and left prison for life as a free man. He lived for a time in Auburn, New York, in the home of Samuel S. Seward, future Secretary of State under Abraham Lincoln and a nephew of the murder victim. Jack later relocated to Canandaigua, New York, where he became a well-respected and admired member of the community. There is a large monument in his honor in the cemetery where his body now lies.

But what you have just read is not entirely true. The passage of time has muddied this case with half truths, legends, and inaccurate information. Facts have become distorted, events have become intermingled, and some things have all but been forgotten. We can take a protracted glance back into time, however, and piece together a definitive and accurate narrative of the crime.

The complete story of the murder of Richard Jennings is now revealed. You are about to read it. You are about to be let in on a long forgotten and often misunderstood part of our history. What really happened on the morning of December 21, 1818? What events led up the murder? What happened in the months and years after? After more than four years of research, I have formed my own conclusions- what will yours be?

Chapter 1

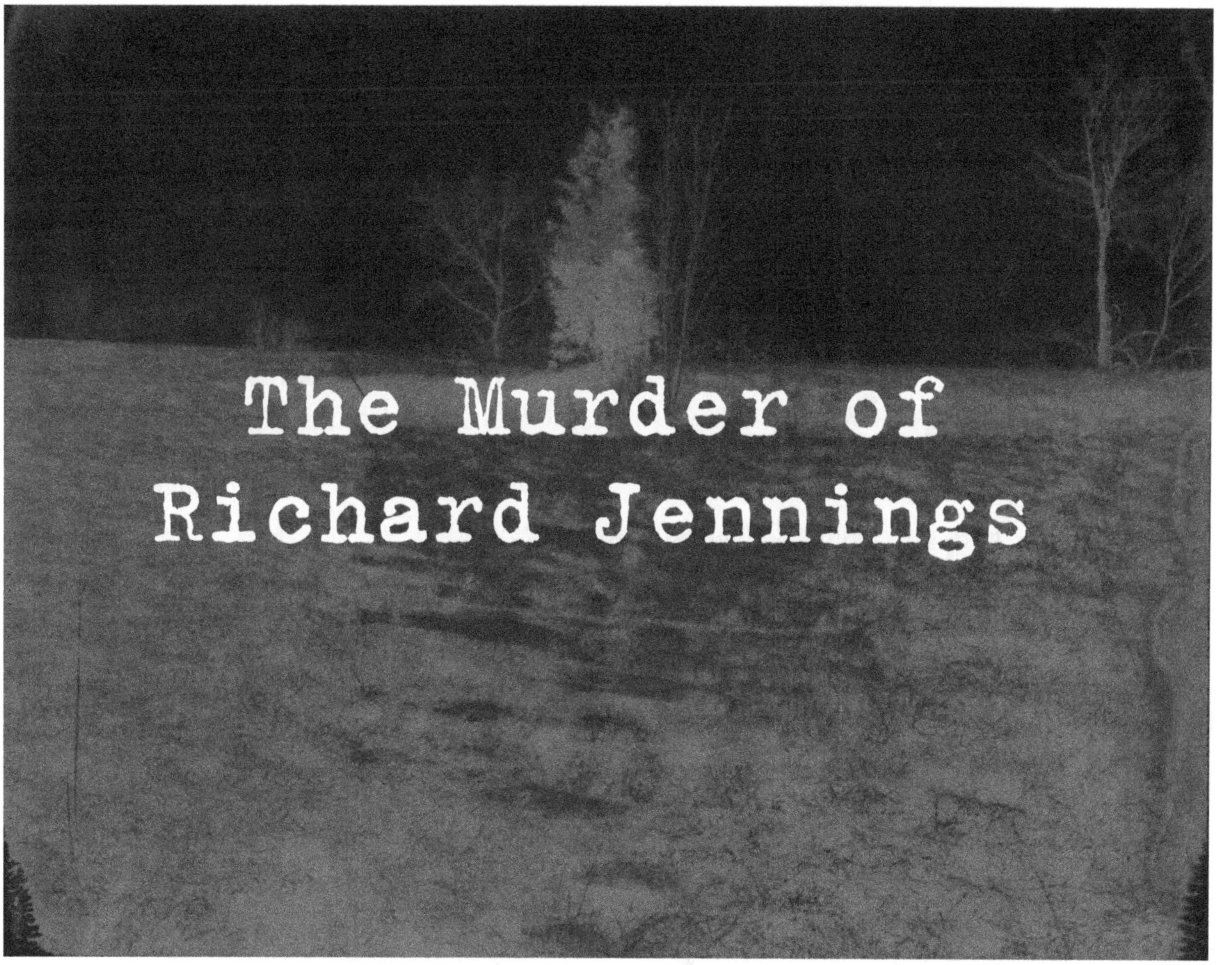
The Murder of
Richard Jennings

MEET THE MAIN PEOPLE

T here are essentially six people who are central to this entire event, and their names are referenced throughout this book, as are their relationships to one another. In some cases, one or more names may be used to reference the same person. Trust me, it can be confusing. I needed to make a diagram to refer to at times during my research. To spare you that trouble, this brief summary of the main cast of characters will help you understand who they are and who they are related to. If more than one name is used for a particular person, that name is also included below.

RICHARD JENNINGS

At the center of the story is Richard Jennings. A man in his seventies, he was involved in a dispute with his nephew, James Teed, over a piece of land which Teed's mother had inherited. Teed's mother and Richard were siblings. The property had recently been awarded to Jennings in court, and he was waiting to take possession of the property at the time of the murder. He is sometimes referred to as Dick Jennings.

JAMES TEED

A nephew to Richard Jennings (James' mother was Richard's sister), James Teed had been in a dispute with Richard over a plot of land that his mother had inherited. Teed had subsequently signed the land over to David Conkling who was in possession of the land in late 1818. James was married to Hannah Conkling.

HANNAH TEED

Hannah Teed was married to James Teed. She had come from a respectable Orange County family, the Conklings. Her brother was David Conkling, who had become embroiled in the land dispute with Jennings.

DAVID CONKLING

David Conkling was from a good family in Orange County and had been involved in a land dispute with Richard Jennings, siding with his brother-in-law, James Teed. David's sister, Hannah, was married to James Teed. David employed a former sailor named Jack Hodges to work for him. David was married to Fanny Knight, who was from a very well-respected Monroe, New York family. His last name is often given as Conklin, so both surnames, Conklin and Conkling, are used interchangeably in the book.

DAVID DUNNING

Not much is known about Dunning's life before his involvement in this event. In 1818, he was working with Teed and resided in the Teed home.

JACK HODGES

An African American sailor with a taste for alcohol and indulging in all manner of vices, Hodges resided in the home of David Conkling. It is Hodges who the conspiracy hinged upon, as well as the later prosecutions. He was also known as John Hodges, as well as Jacob Hodges and Black Jacob.

IT BEGAN WITH A WILL

T he story of the first murder for hire in New York doesn't begin with the terrible act that was committed in a woodlot on December 21, 1818. Rather, the single event that can be identified as the seed of the crime goes back to 1806 with the will of James Teed (this is James Teed's father – I'll refer to him as the "elder Teed" to keep everyone's names straight.) Elder Teed was married to Phoebe Allison Jennings and had moved to Orange County from Long Island. Phoebe and Richard Jennings were siblings.[1]

In 1806, elder Teed died and, in his will, left the majority of his land to his wife. A clause in the will, however, set aside 50 acres of land that was to be inherited by his namesake, the young James Teed, upon the death of elder Teed's wife.[2] Here is the seed which would slowly grow into a brutal homicide.

The will was something of an insult to James Teed. His father had accumulated a significant amount of debt while alive, and James had worked hard to satisfy his father's debts, paying them off and ensuring that his family would maintain possession of their property.[3] He probably expected that the land would end up in his possession and never predicted the terms of his father's will.

The events that follow are still clouded by time; however, based upon my research, I believe that these are the circumstances that unfolded. The young James Teed had acquired some debts after the death of his father and, seeking to pay them off, entered into an agreement with his mother to transfer ownership of the fifty acre parcel of land to him. However, the historical record is unclear as to whether or not ownership of the land was ever even legally transferred to James Teed.[4]

Keep in mind that this is a parcel of land that he was going to *legally* inherit at some point in the future, and his mother was the legal *owner* of that land. So this should not have been a difficult transaction. But enter Richard Jennings into the affair. Richard Jennings had persuaded his sister not to follow through with the land transfer and actually convinced her (allegedly through deceit) into signing over all rights to the "use and improvements" of the property.[5]

I am at a loss to explain his motives for interfering in this transaction between a mother and her son. Richard had no legal interest in the property, nor any financial stake in the use of the land. But for reasons that are long forgotten, he, well to put it colloquially, put his nose into other people's business and ended up paying for it with his life. I am certainly not trying to blame Richard Jennings for his own murder. He was the victim. But I can't help but feel some empathy for James Teed, who was simply trying to take possession of a piece of land which he was going to end up legally owning upon the death of his mother. And he was doing it with the cooperation and agreement of his mother – the legal landowner! Understanding this unwanted and seemingly unnecessary interference will help you understand Teed's hatred of his Uncle Richard.

What followed was a complicated mess of court cases, with James Teed eventually signing over the parcel of land to his brother-in-law, David Conkling (even though Teed's ownership of the land was still highly questionable).[6] This land transfer dragged Conkling into the mess, and he and Jennings began their own long-term battle. While the ownership of the land was being fought in the courts, David Conkling enjoyed escalating the conflict by purchasing debts and obligations against Jennings, often paying more than the value of the debt in order to demand immediate payment.[7] At a time when debtors could still be legally imprisoned, this leverage had allowed David Conkling to obtain warrants against Jennings and have him detained in the County Jail.[8]

"Mr.
Conkling
had·locked
him up in
jail, and
kept him
twenty four
hours
without
meat or
drink."[13]

In the fall of 1818, Jennings had served notice on Conkling that he was suing him at the fall term of the Circuit Court.[9] His intent was to regain the land and estate of his sister and to evict the Teed family and their tenant, David Dunning.[10] The outcome of that fall Circuit Court proceeding was in favor of Richard Jennings, and he was awarded legal title to the property, which included a house and land[11] and would receive his writ of possession in January of 1819.[12] This victory would be short-lived and prove to be the proverbial straw which broke the camel's back.

A MOST HORRIBLE AND DREADFUL TRANSACTION

Years of bitter rivalry had evolved into a deep-rooted hatred. The Teed and Dunning families now faced inevitable eviction from the land they had been living upon and cultivating, and only one course of action seemed to be left: cold-blooded murder! And the seeds of that crime had already been planted.

In the fall of 1818, prior to the Circuit Court, Jack Hodges was with David Conkling, plowing, when Jennings personally served Conkling with court papers. When Jennings had left, Conkling had an angry outburst, which would later come back to haunt him during his trial. Hodges would later recall that outburst, saying that "[Conkling] wished they had murdered him, and thrown him into the brook."[14] The reason why Conkling didn't go through with that idea was, according to Hodges, because the murder would have been on Conkling's own land.[15]

Later that same night, Conkling had offered Hodges a sum of four or five hundred dollars to kill Jennings (and said that Teed may match that; however, he had no money to do so), and explained to Hodges that he was the best one to carry out the crime. After all, Richard Jennings had caused the ruin of James Teed and was about to ruin Conkling as well. The talk of murder escalated during the court proceedings. One evening, it was reported that Conkling returned home, proclaiming that Jennings was going to win the suit, and that they needed to devise a plan to "make way of him."[16] Ultimately, Jack would claim that Conkling had offered him one thousand dollars to split between himself and David Dunning if they would kill Jennings.[17]

James Teed was also involved in these pre-murder plans. At Teed's trial, Hodges testified to statements that Teed had made to him about Jennings. Interestingly, his testimony that implicated Teed nearly mirrored the testimony that he had given against Conkling. Since we haven't even gotten to the murder, let alone the trials, I'll save this for the chapter about the trials. It is just interesting to me that Hodges would testify that Teed had said that Jennings was going to win the suit against Conkling, and that Jennings had ruined him [Teed] and was about to ruin Conkling. Hodges would also claim that Teed had said that if he [Hodges] killed Jennings, Conkling would give him four or five hundred dollars.[18]

Hannah Teed would contribute to the cause by supplying Hodges with copious amounts of alcohol and urging him to go through with the act. She repeatedly had said to him that it "was time the old savage, Jennings, was out of the way," all while keeping Jack inebriated with a seemingly never-ending supply of whiskey.[19] Hannah Teed's support and encouragement to commit murder would, on the morning of December 21, 1818, be the final piece of a fatal puzzle that would leave one man dead and forever change the lives of many others.

COLD-BLOODED MURDER

On Thursday, December 17, 1818, David Conkling, James Teed, and Jack Hodges met in what has been called the *hovel* to discuss the details of the murder.[20] It was agreed that Hodges would go to the Teed residence to assist James Teed and David Dunning in killing Jennings, and that he and Dunning were to receive one thousand dollars for the deed. The plan that was hatched was simple: David Dunning was to walk with Jennings (if the opportunity arose), and Hodges was to sneak up from behind and shoot Jennings to death.[21]

On the morning of Saturday, December 19, 1818, in the cellar of his home, David Conkling loaded his musket with powder and shot, handed it to Hodges, told him that it was a pretty good load, and to kill him if possible.[22] Hodges then proceeded to go to the Teed home where he met up with David Dunning, who asked Jack if he was there to help murder Jennings. Hodges affirmed that he was. Home at this time was Dunning, his wife, and Hannah Teed.[23] James Teed had gone to New York that day and would not be back home until later the following week.[24] On that day, Jack and Dunning agreed that they were going to kill Richard Jennings at the first available opportunity.[25]

That same night, Hannah Teed used her influence to encourage Jack to go through with the murder plan, telling him that it was (in her words as later related by Jack) "a pity but that he [Jennings] was out of the way."[26] The following day, Sunday, was spent with more talk between Hodges and Dunning about the impending murder, and Hannah encouraged Jack to carry out the deed and kept him supplied with ample amounts of liquid courage.[27]

The events that were to follow the next day would spill an old man's blood and be hotly contested in the trials of the murderers. Discrepancies between the accounts of Hodges and Dunning would illustrate two very different versions of the crime. In the following section, I have presented the murder as history has recorded it. It is the version that was affirmed numerous times by Jack Hodges and would ultimately lead him and three other men to be sentenced to hang.

Light snow had fallen the morning of Monday, December 21, 1818.[28] Jack Hodges had started the day early because Hannah Teed had asked him to drive one of the cows to a Mr. Weaden's property along with her son, Charles.[29] Once back at the Teed home, Jack indulged in consuming more whiskey and sat down to eat breakfast.[30] In the meantime, Richard Jennings, wearing blue pantaloons and a dark great coat,[31] had set off on what would be his last walk to check on the disputed lot. Although he had won in court, he still did not have possession of the land, and Teed and Dunning had been using this to their advantage by cutting wood from the lot. Jennings had thus gotten into the habit of personally inspecting the property to see what was being done to it. Unfortunately for Jennings, the road to the disputed lot took him past the Teed residence and to his own demise.[32]

While Jack had been eating, Dunning came into the room and said, "The old savage is going along the road."[33] Jack seized the opportunity to act. He grabbed the gun from behind the door, and Hannah handed him powder and shot. Jack asked for another drink, helping himself to some more whiskey. Looking for guidance or approval, Jack asked Hannah one last time if Jennings needed to be killed. She replied, "It is highly necessary that he should be destroyed, as he has been the cause of my ruin."[34] Having the affirmation he needed, Jack left the Teed house and set off after his prey.[35]

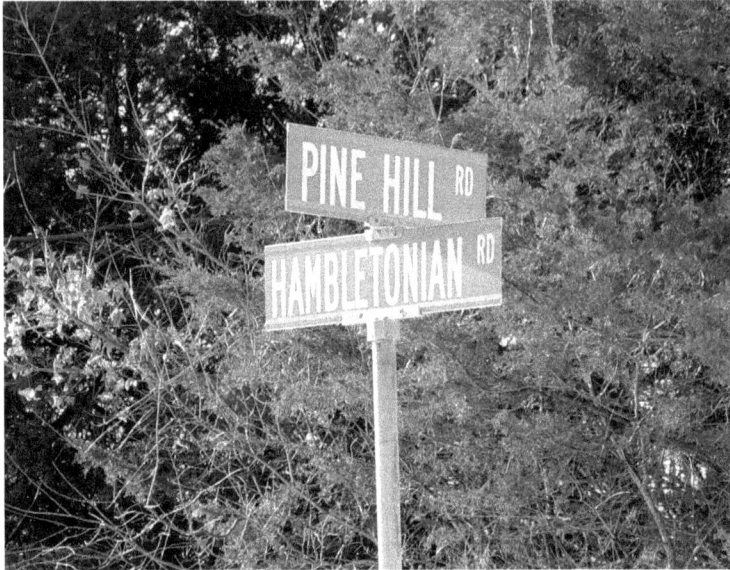

The murder took place in the vicinity of the intersection of Pine Hill Road and Hambletonian Road, near Sugar Loaf, New York.

As planned, Dunning had left the Teed residence ahead of Hodges and caught up with Jennings. The two – conspirator and victim – walked side by side up the road towards the disputed property. In the meantime, Jack crossed the Teed property and stealthily moved towards his unsuspecting prey. At the lot, Dunning was standing with Jennings about 140 feet away from the road as the hunter approached them, musket in hand.[36]

Seeing Hodges, Jennings pointed to some of the wood and asked him if he had assisted in cutting timber from the lot. Jack said that he had, turned his back to the old man, and cocked the musket. Jennings, hearing the clicking sound of a musket being readied to fire, walked towards Jack and asked if it was loaded. Jack said, "No, it isn't," as he turned around and leveled the musket directly at Richard Jennings' head. Dunning, who had been standing next to Jennings, stepped quickly off to one side as Hodges squeezed the trigger and a loud report cracked the cold morning air. The nearly point blank shot struck Richard Jennings on the side of his face near the eye, tearing through part of his eye and face, and taking off a good portion of his ear. The impact to the man's head knocked his hat off (tearing part of the hat) and threw him backwards onto the ground, where it was readily apparent that he wasn't dead.[37]

Seeing the brutal reality of his deed, Hodges froze. He had intended to kill him, but watching Jennings bleeding on the ground and moaning in pain gave him second thoughts. But there was no going back. Dunning realized that Hodges was paralyzed with fear and said to him, "The damned old rascal is not dead yet, why would you undertake to do a thing and not finish it, if you are going to do anything do it."[38] With that, Dunning grabbed the musket out of Jack's hands and began to repeatedly strike Jennings in the head with the butt end. Each blow produced groans of pain, and, after three or four hard blows, Richard Jennings lay dead in the woodlot he had so stubbornly fought for. The fatal blows to the head were so brutal that the musket broke, leaving pieces (such as the lock) behind as damning evidence. Hodges was given the barrel and breech of the gun to take away and dispose of before the murderers went their separate ways. The body of Richard Jennings was left in the field, where he had fallen. But the apparently dead Jennings wasn't quite dead enough! After his assailants had left, he managed to muster a little strength and crawl several feet away from where he had been shot and beaten, before he finally succumbed to his injuries. His body would lay face down on the frozen earth for a week before it was found.[39]

THE DEED IS DONE

Hodges and Dunning left the crime scene by way of different directions. Once back at the Teed home, Hodges informed Hannah Teed that he believed Jennings was dead. He and Dunning then went off to Dunning's room where the two of them agreed to never reveal any details of the murder and certainly not to inform against one another. The rest of the day and evening for Jack consisted of indulging in copious amounts of whiskey.[40]

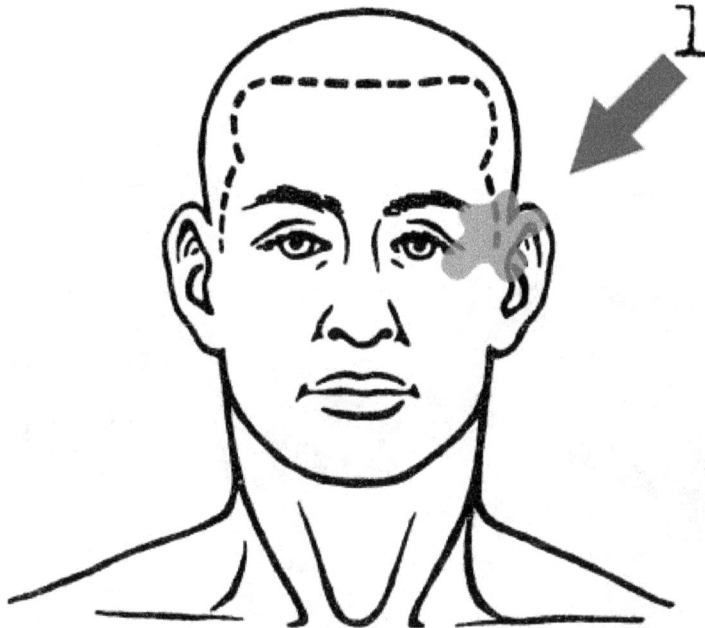

Diagram showing the approximate location of the gunshot wound (1) to the head. There is nothing in the available records to indicate which side the wound was on. I have chosen the left side because to me it seems the most likely location of the injury.

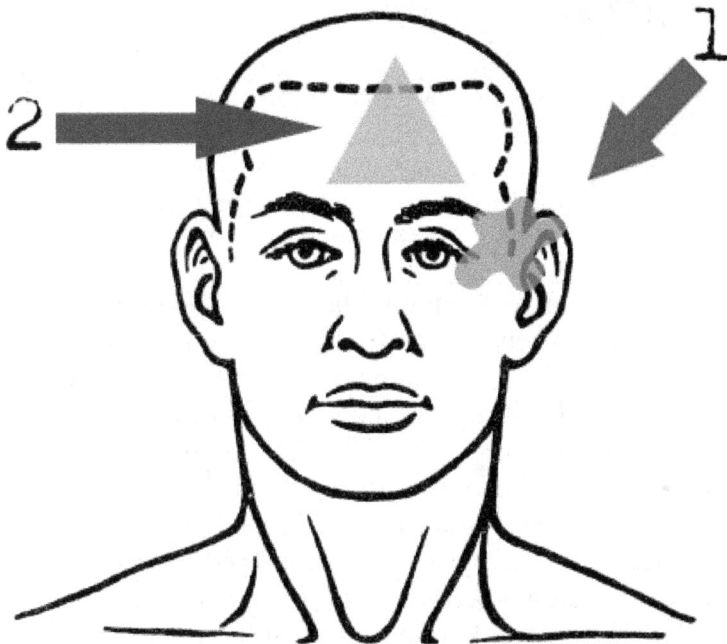

Shown above is the approximate area of the forehead where a large, triangular wound was found (2). The wound was about 1½ inches deep and most likely caused fracturing of the skull and was attributed as the cause of death [the musket wound (1) was not thought to have been a fatal injury].[41]

Early on the morning of Tuesday, December 22, 1818, Jack collected the pieces of the broken gun and left for home (Conkling's residence) before daylight. He arrived shortly after sunrise, hid the broken gun under his bed and woke up David Conkling to give him the news.[42]

David Conkling wanted to know if Jack had done what he had set out to do, but was not about to hear any of the gruesome details. Jack had begun describing the intricate details of the crime up to the point of when he shot Jennings. Conkling cut him off, telling him that he didn't want to know anymore.[43]

The intersection of Pine Hill Road and Hambletonian Road, near Sugar Loaf, New York. The site of the murder was described as being on a small knoll and in plain view of the road, and the view to Sugar Loaf obscured by a hill.[44] While certain areas have purported to be the location of the murder, the exact spot has been lost to time.

The broken pieces of the musket were given to Conkling later that Tuesday, and he immediately noticed that the lock was missing. When he pointed this out to Jack and asked where the lock was, Jack was stumped and said that he didn't know. He hadn't even realized that it was missing. This oversight didn't seem to bother either man too much, and Conkling simply told Jack that he would handle it and set the pieces off to the side. The rest of the day, Jack indulged in alcohol, slept, and stayed around the Conkling residence and farm.[45]

Wednesday, December 23, 1818, two days after the murder, Jack had gone to Conkling's barn to do some threshing when he was approached by Conkling, who had developed doubts about the murder. He confronted Jack, telling him that he did not believe that Jennings was dead because there had been no notice of it in the village. He urged Jack to leave so that he could avoid being discovered (so he must have believed him). Hodges told him that he would be caught anyhow and that murder couldn't be kept a secret. Conkling, revealing his underlying motives, said to Jack that he would rather that Jack not be apprehended at his home (perhaps Conkling was more afraid that he would be implicated in the crime and arrested if that were the case.)[46]

The following day, Christmas Eve, Thursday, December 24, 1818, was a busy one, with Conkling and Hodges cleaning up grain and putting it into bags for delivery to Goshen. While together, Conkling expressed some concern to Jack that he had not heard from Teed, and that he was going to send his son to deliver a message asking that James Teed come as soon as he arrived back from New York. He then offered to give Jack forty or fifty dollars if he would leave, to which Jack said that he was confident that he was going to be caught.[47]

This undated photograph from the collection of the Chester Historical Society purports to depict the location where Richard Jennings was murdered. The caption supplied with the photograph stated, "Scene of the Jennings murder, the rock ledge was four or five feet high then, covered with bushes and the cedar tree was a scrub oak." Photo courtesy the Chester Historical Society.

Friday morning, December 25, 1818, was Christmas, which, as a holiday, was not celebrated the way we do today, and work had to be done. Conkling sent Jack with a man named Hendershot to drive a cow to a Captain Howell's place, while he delivered bagged grain to Goshen. He also had sent his son to the Teed residence with a message for Teed to come to his farm. Teed was still not back from New York, and Mrs. Teed sent her nephew back to Conkling's to tell her brother that she would have James come as soon as he returned. Later that evening, Conkling gave Jack a jug of whiskey and sent him with a Mr. Howell to spend Christmas night with the Howells.[48]

By Saturday, December 26, 1818, people were beginning to notice that Richard Jennings had not been seen in nearly a week. Initially, his absence was overlooked, as Jennings was known to wander off for short periods of time without telling his family where he was going.[49] But by this time, some concern was growing that Jennings may have been the victim of foul play, and suspicions were cast toward Hodges.[50] That afternoon, Teed, Conkling, and Hodges met at Conkling's barn, and the two men prevailed upon Jack to leave for New York.[51]

THE GREAT ESCAPE AND A MURDER REVEALED

J ack changed his clothes, and Conkling gave him ten dollars with the promise that he and Teed would meet him in New York and pay him the reward [for murdering Jennings]. Conkling also gave Jack a note addressed to a friend of his in New York. This note, Jack was told, would help him find employment:[52]

Mr. James Adair,

Jack, the bearer, has some notion of shipping if he can get a chance, and as I have had some acquaintance with you, I wish you would try to get him in some business, until he gets a chance. I can recommend him to be a smart good man for business.

I am yours respectfully,

December 26th, 1818.   DAVID CONKLING.

Directed To Mr. James Adair, No. 18, Sixth Street, New York. [53]

Jack left the house, crossed the fields near Conkling's farm, and waited near a spring for Conkling to meet him. When he arrived at the spring, Conkling instructed Jack to leave by way of East Division, and that he or Teed would come to New York in a few days and bring him cloth for a coat and pantaloons, as well as money. Hodges left and traveled on foot to Chester and stayed the night at the home of Isaac Hallok. The following morning (Sunday, December 27, 1818), Jack set off for New Windsor and Newburgh, and at around sunset, he arrived near Newburgh and stopped near a brick kiln. It was here that Jack observed someone approaching on horseback and thought that he recognized who that person was: James Teed. Teed had arrived on one of Conkling's mares, and when he met up with Jack, asked him why he had taken so long; after all, Teed had only left for Newburgh earlier that day, while Jack had a day head start and should have been across the North River (Hudson River) by now. There was a growing concern that Jack would be caught, and Teed urged him to get across the river as soon as he could. Teed told Jack that he and Conkling had determined that Hodges should go northward, but Hodges countered that it didn't matter where he went, as he did not have enough money to sustain himself. Teed instructed Jack to follow him at a distance (keeping him in sight) and set off for Newburgh, ending up at a tavern run by Joshua Terry. Teed kept a distance from Hodges inside the tavern, and Jack stayed a short while before leaving (after he was refused alcohol – it was the Sabbath). Hodges went on from there to the home of a Josiah Peterson, where he spent the night.[54]

Jack Hodges met up with James Teed the next morning (December 28, 1818) on the road opposite the ferry on the North River. Teed was anxious that Hodges get moving and was still upset that it had taken him so long to leave the area. He told Jack to get to New York, promising to meet him there, and then he waited as Jack boarded the ferry and, as if making sure Jack didn't try to slip away, stood and watched as the boat pulled away from the dock and began crossing to the opposite side of the river.[55]

While Teed was busy aiding Jack's escape, the people of Sugar Loaf were in a state of alarm. Richard Jennings had last been seen on the morning of December 21 in Sugar Loaf, and it had been presumed that he had gone to check on the disputed parcel of land. Seven days later, about fifteen of his neighbors gathered to search for the missing man. One of the members of the search party was a man named Samuel Pitts, and he had set out to search the disputed lot. An hour into the search, Pitts made the shocking discovery of Jennings' body. He was quickly joined by Noble Howell, who stood by with the body until it could be moved to Sugar Loaf.[56] Fortunately for us, their observations allow us to envision what the crime scene looked like nearly 195 years ago:

> I was the first person who saw the body; it was lying in open sight on his stomach, his head turned on his right cheek, there was a quantity of blood a short distance from the body, I then supposed that the deceased had crawled after he had been wounded. I observed several marks of violence on the head and face, but did not examine them particularly.
> *– Testimony of Samuel Pitts.*[57]

> After we had been in search about one hour, Mr. Pitts discovered the body; I was a little distance from him; I immediately came up, and remained with the body the most of the time till it was taken to the village of Sugar Loaf. I discovered a gun lock, and some broken pieces of a gun stock, near a quantity of blood, a few feet from the body; it appeared that he had been knocked down and beat there, and had crawled a short distance before he died.
> *– Testimony of Noble Howell.*[58]

THE CORONER'S INQUEST

As was customary during this time period, Coroner John Curtice convened an inquest over the body of Richard Jennings in order to determine how he had met his fate.[59] One of the witnesses called to testify before the Coroner's Jury was David Dunning, who readily told of what he knew about the death of Richard Jennings. His version of events is starkly different than that of Jack Hodges. As I mentioned earlier in the chapter, I have related the murder as history has memorialized it. But David Dunning's story is not easily dismissed and, as you will see in Chapter 2, raises some very interesting, and disturbing, questions. David Dunning testified at the Coroner's Inquest as follows:

> Says, that on Monday morning, the 21st of December, he saw Jennings pass his house alone, that Jack Hodges soon followed with his gun, that he heard a gun discharged, that Jack returned to his house, with the broken pieces of the gun in his hands, and said that old Jennings never would be seen alive again, that he had shot him dead, and then beat him with the breech of the gun; he said he did it because Jennings had abused Conkling so much, and threatened, that if I told of him, he would kill me, and all my family. Jack said, that when he got to Conklings he should have money enough, and should be well taken care of the rest of his days. Dunning further said, that Jack, on the Saturday night before, told him that he came to Sugar Loaf for the purpose of killing Mr. Jennings; Dunning

also said, that he was cutting wood near the spot where the body was found, on the Saturday after the murder, and saw a hat, but did not see the body.[60]

David Conkling would also testify as a witness at the coroner's inquisition. Dr. Samuel S. Steward, a prominent surgeon and member of the community, took the examination:

The voluntary examination of David Conkling, taken in Sugar Loaf, before a Coroner's inquisition, upon the view of the body of Richard Jennings, then and there lying dead, on the twenty eighth of December, 1818.

Says that when he returned from Goshen on Saturday evening before Christmas, the family told him that Jack had taken the gun and was gone off; Jack returned on Tuesday morning very early, but had not the gun; did not account for the manner in which he had disposed of the gun; staid at home until Saturday, when he, Conkling, paid him three dollars, and he went off; Jack said he had been at Sugar Loaf; Jack had worked for Conkling ever since last march a year; lost no time except when in liquor; when he was sober was civil, and when intoxicated, vicious, and calculated to do almost any thing. Conkling had not had any conversation with David Dunning since the first of last court.

JOHN CURTICE, Coroner.[62]

"I put my thumb into the wound, and was certain that the skull was broken."[61]

Dunning also described more details to the Coroner's Jury of Jack's actions on the day that Richard Jennings had been murdered:

Says, that on Monday morning, the 21st of December, he saw Jennings pass his house alone, that Jack Hodges soon followed with his gun, that he heard a gun discharged, that Jack returned to his house, with the broken pieces of the gun in his hands, and said that old Jennings never would be alive again, that he had shot him dead and then beat him with the breech of the gun; he said he did it because Jennings had abused Conkling so much, and threatened, that if I told of him, he would kill me and all my family. Jack said, that when he got to Conkling's he should have money enough, and should be well taken care of the rest of his days. Dunning further said, that Jack, on the Saturday night before, told him that he came to Sugar Load for the purpose of killing Mr. Jennings, Dunning also said, that he was cutting wood near the spot where the body was found, on the Saturday after the murder, and saw a hat, but did not see the body.[63]

Thanks to a physical examination of the body by Dr. Samuel S. Seward, we can ascertain certain details about the condition in which Richard Jennings' body had been found:[64]

1. There was a triangular shaped wound on the forehead, which was as deep as a thumb. The skull was believed to have been shattered.
2. The wound on the forehead had produced a significant amount of bleeding.
3. There was a wound on the face near the eye, which had been produced by the shot.
4. A portion of the ear had been taken off.
5. The skin was cut in several places on the side of the face.
6. The eye near the shot was swollen.
7. The injuries produced by the shot were not sufficient to cause death.
8. Death was caused by the wound on the forehead, which had been inflicted by a severe blow.

The verdict of the Coroner's inquest was that Richard Jennings "had been murdered by John Hodges, a black man, and others as accessories."[65] A different source provides a more specific verdict, stating that not only was Jennings murdered by Hodges, but that David Conkling and David Dunning were accessories.[66] Either way, the end result was the same. Richard Jennings was dead, and the conspiracy had unraveled and the true depth of the crime would soon be revealed.

THE CONSPIRATORS ARE ARRESTED

The conspiracy to kill Richard Jennings had been exposed. David Conkling and David Dunning were immediately arrested and committed to the Orange County Jail. James Teed was arrested two days later, on December 30, 1818, and also sent to the county jail.[67] Hodges, however, had already escaped the area. After he crossed the North River at Newburgh on December 28, he made his way to a Lobdell's Tavern, where he was told that he could get passage to New York on a sloop at Cold Spring Landing. On Tuesday, December 29, 1818, as the conspiracy was crumbling back in Sugar Loaf, Jack boarded a wooden sloop and worked his passage to New York. He arrived in New York on Wednesday, December 30, 1818, by which time Teed, Dunning, and Conkling had all been taken into custody back in Orange County.[68]

Hodges became the focus of a massive manhunt, which, to me, is quite spectacular. In 1818, there were no real organized police forces, no radios, no teletype machines, no telephones, and no photographs to put on a wanted poster. It fell to the citizens of the area to organize and discover where Hodges had gone and to take him into custody. And looking back at what they did, I am very impressed.

On Tuesday night, December 29th, just hours after the terrible plot had unraveled, four men set off from Chester in pursuit of Jack Hodges. They were Charles Durland, Jonas Seely, John Banker, and Ezra King. They arrived in Newburgh later that evening and waited until the following morning when, sometime between eight and ten o'clock, they took the ferry across the North River and made their way to Fishkill. They, then, followed a stage coach road towards New York, stopping at Lobdell's Tavern, where they learned that a black man fitting the description of Jack Hodges had been there two days earlier and was purported to have gone to Cold Spring Landing. Hot on the fugitive's trail, the four men followed Hodges to Cold Spring and learned that a subject fitting Jack's description had taken a sloop to New York. Undaunted, the men travelled on to Peekskill where they hired teams to make the rest of the journey to New York.[69] Jack Hodges' flight was about to come to an end.

Early on the morning of New Year's Eve, Durland and his compatriots arrived in New York. Once there, Durland went to the Spring Street wharf, where the sloop had been docked (it had arrived the previous evening). There would be no difficulty in finding Jack. There, standing on the sloop near the cabin door, was Jack Hodges, and Durland recognized him immediately. Realizing that he would need assistance, Durland left the wharf so that Jack would not see him and attempted to find some men to assist him. When that plan failed, Durland knew he needed to act. He returned to the wharf and found that Jack was coming ashore. Using the element of surprise to his advantage, Durland quickly seized Hodges and informed the startled murderer that he was now his prisoner![70]

Jack, having been caught off guard and being unprepared for this moment, asked, "For what?"

"For murdering Richard Jennings!" Durland told him.

The murderer's spontaneous denial to this charge was, "I murder Richard Jennings? No I never did."[71]

That morning, Durland delivered Jack to the police. En route, he told Hodges that there was no reason to deny his involvement in the murder, and that David Dunning had testified before the Coroner's Jury that Jack "had killed Jennings and a better man."[72] Jack was brought to the Bridewell, New York's old prison, where a search of his person uncovered $6.76 (recall that he had been given ten dollars when leaving a few days earlier) and a letter. Later that evening, Durland and the other three fugitive hunters started back towards Orange County with their prisoner.[73]

JACK CONFESSES

A new year was dawning as Jack Hodges boarded a sloop with his captors for the journey toward an uncertain future. He had steadfastly denied any involvement in the murder of Richard Jennings, but Charles Durland was not buying it. Durland's persistence

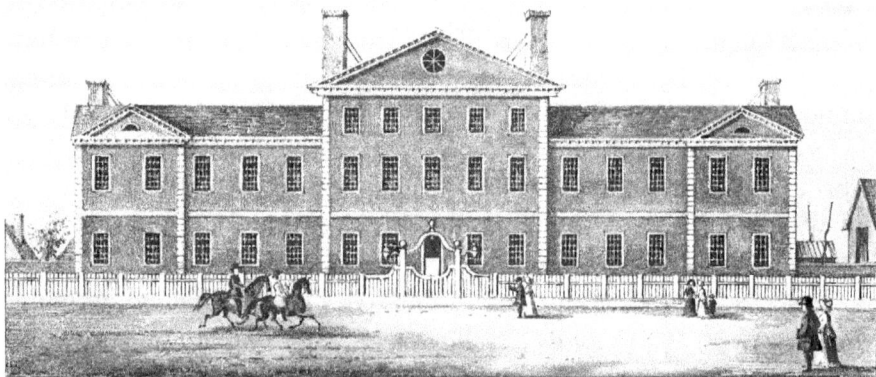
The Bridewell in New York where Jack was detained following his arrest at the wharf.[74]

in getting Jack to confess would later become an issue at the trials. Did he induce Jack to confess with a promise of a pardon? Did he give Jack the important details of the crime, such as the condition of the body, which aided Jack in concocting his confession? These are questions that would come to be examined during the trials in February and March of 1819.

While on the boat, Jack appeared distressed whenever the subject of the murder was brought up, and he would sweat profusely. In the early morning hours of January 1, 1819, Jack was escorted up to the deck for fresh air. Durland observed that Jack was very agitated and sweating more than he had been, and he seemed to be in a state of great emotional distress.[75]

Jack, perspiring and apparently anxious, said, "Durland, I know you, and I know that the truth must and will come out."[76] Durland assured him that it would and encouraged Jack to go and rest. The following day, Jack was again brought up to the deck for air and made his shocking confession. He finally admitted to his participation in the crime and related the details to Durland, including the roles that the others had played in the criminal transaction. On Saturday morning, January 2, 1819, Hodges was back in Goshen and confined in the county jail.[77]

AN INSECURE JAIL

The arrests of the five conspirators revealed a severe deficiency in the security of the county jail. Local residents chipped in and organized groups of guards from amongst themselves![79]

During the day on January 2, Jack was examined by Coroner Curtice and local magistrates Samuel S. Seward, Jesse Wood, Jr., Horace W. Elliot, Samuel J. Wilkin, and Samuel G. Hopkins, Esquires.[78] He made a detailed, complete confession regarding the murder plot. I had initially planned on extracting portions of his statement which I felt were more relevant than others; however, I have found that his statement, taken as a whole, is vital to understanding this case. It forms the core for the subsequent prosecution of the conspirators and ultimately spares Jack from a public death on the gallows. In view of this, the complete confession of Jack Hodges is printed in the following chapter on pages 36-39.

ONE LAST ARREST

The last of the conspirators at liberty, Hannah Teed, who had encouraged Jack with moral support and liberal amounts of whiskey, was arrested on Monday, January 4, 1819, and committed to the county jail. Five persons now stood accused of participating in the terrible and brutal murder of Richard Jennings.[80] As the details of the murder filtered out into the community, Jack Hodges stood out amongst the conspirators as a penitent but ignorant man, who had been manipulated into murder by the actions of the others.

The fate of James and Hannah Teed, David Dunning, David Conkling, and Jack Hodges would soon be handed over to a Grand Jury, who would evaluate the evidence and hand up indictments, and then to a jury of their peers who would decide their fate. The penalty for murder (as well as for accessory to murder) was death by hanging. All five had something big to lose: their lives.

Chapter 2

The Conspirators on Trial

INDICTMENTS

T he arrests of James and Hannah Teed, David Dunning, David Conkling, and Jack Hodges for the murder of Richard Jennings was only the beginning of the judicial process which would bring the defendants to trial and allow a jury to decide their fates. On Tuesday, February 23, 1819, the first step of that process, Grand Jury evaluation of the incident, would begin at the courthouse in Goshen.

The Honorable William W. Van Ness, a Justice of the Supreme Court of judicature, convened a Grand Jury along with Commissioners of the Oyer and Terminer[1] (the court which would have trial jurisdiction over the murder case). Twenty-two grand jurors were sworn in and, in the course of the day, given the appropriate charges by Judge Van Ness regarding the crime of murder, as well as being an accessory to murder both before and after the fact.[2]

On the afternoon of February 24, the Grand Jury handed up indictments against the accused murderers of Richard Jennings. At 3:00 P.M., the five defendants were brought before the court for arraignment:[3]

THE PEOPLE
vs.
JOHN, alias JACK HODGES

Indictment: 1. Murder.

Plea: Jack stood mute and refused to offer a plea. The court entered a plea of *not guilty* on his behalf. Attorney Henry Wisner was assigned as counsel.

THE PEOPLE
vs.
DAVID DUNNING

Indictment: 1. Murder.
              2. Accessory to murder before the fact.
              3. Accessory to murder after the fact.

Plea: Attorney Jonas Storey entered a plea of *not guilty* on behalf of Dunning, and reserved the right to withdraw that plea at any time before trial.

THE PEOPLE
vs.
JAMES TEED

Indictment: 1. Accessory to murder before the fact.
              2. Accessory to murder after the fact.

Plea: Attorneys Jonathan Fisk and William Price entered a plea of *not guilty* on behalf of their client.

THE PEOPLE
vs.
HANNAH TEED

Indictment: 1. Accessory to murder before the fact.
2. Accessory to murder after the fact.

Plea: Attorneys Jonathan Fisk and William Price entered a plea of *not guilty* on behalf of their client

THE PEOPLE
vs.
DAVID CONKLING

Indictment: 1. Accessory to murder before the fact.
2. Accessory to murder after the fact.

Plea: Attorneys Jonathan Fisk and William Price entered a plea of *not guilty* on behalf of their client.

After arraignment, the defendants were remanded back to the custody of the Orange County Sheriff. The courtroom had been packed with spectators, and there was some concern that the trials would commence later that day. Both sides – prosecution and defense – were unprepared for trial, however, and Judge Van Ness assured the onlookers that there would be no trial that date.[4]

An illustration depicting Goshen around the year 1820 – giving us a glimpse into what the village looked like at the time of the trials.[5] The county jail and courthouse were in the building depicted to the far left side of the print. The court room was located on the second floor, and the prisoners held in the county jail located on the third floor.[6]

The excitement and desire to see the proceedings would become the norm at the courthouse over the next weeks. People wanted to see and hear the trials and be a part of something so sensational and historic. Our fascination with big trials really hasn't changed. Today, the difference is how we obtain the information. Trials can be watched on television thanks to live coverage and the twenty-four hour news cycle, as well as online. Our ravenous appetite for these cases is certainly something we share with our ancestors.

THE PEOPLE VS JACK HODGES

The first trial began on Friday, February 26, 1819, barely two days after the indictments had been handed up. Jack Hodges was the first of the five defendants to be placed at the bar, which, for the prosecution, was a necessary step. In order to try and convict the Teeds and Conkling (as well as Dunning on two of the three counts of his indictment) as accessories, there needed to be a murder. Having made a full, detailed confession, Hodges was not only the first to stand trial, but he would become the state's star witness in the other proceedings.

The prosecution of the accused murderers was assisted by then New York State Attorney General Martin Van Buren. Van Buren would later go on to achieve a much higher elected office – the Presidency of the United States.[7]

The trial was opened by Orange County District Attorney (D.A.) Samuel R. Betts, who explained to the Jury that Hodges stood accused of murder, and that two different counts of murder were before them. The first charged that Hodges fired a gun at Jennings and then beat him to death with that gun. The second count alleged that David Dunning had murdered Jennings, and Hodges had been present and had aided in the crime. According to Betts, the one who aids and abets in murder is as guilty as the person who committed the deed, and the trial and punishment were the same.

D.A. Betts also prepped the jury for Jack's confession and told them in his opening that the confession may seem to diminish Jack's role in the crime. He urged them, however, to remember their only concern in the trial was whether or not the prisoner, Jack Hodges, was guilty of the crime.[8]

The prosecution presented their first witness, Jesse Wood, who testified that he had last seen Jennings alive on the morning of December 21, 1818, and that he had participated in the search for him a week later. Wood described the discovery of the body, his observations of the wounds, and the pieces of the broken gun.[9]

```
        THE PEOPLE                          TRIAL QUICK FACTS¹⁰
            VS
        JACK HODGES
```

THE PEOPLE VS JACK HODGES		TRIAL QUICK FACTS[10]
Hon. William Van Ness	}	Presiding
Nathan H. White	}	
Samuel S. Seward	}	Commissioners
Isaac Belknap	}	
Stephen Jackson	}	
Martin Van Buren	}	
Samuel R. Betts	}	Prosecution
John Duer	}	
Henry G. Wisner	}	Defense
Nicholas Bogart	}	
John Brown	}	
Stedman Chapman	}	
Samuel Corwin	}	
Henry Cuddeback	}	
Benjamin Hulse	}	Jurors
Peter Hulse	}	
William Lockwood	}	
Hezekiah Loring	}	
Samuel Palmer	}	
Nathan H. Sayre	}	
Montgomery Stevens	}	
February 26, 1819	}	Trial Began
February 26, 1819	}	Trial Ended
Verdict	}	Guilty

    Dr. Samuel S. Seward testified to his examination of the body on December 28, 1818. It was his opinion that the shot to the side of the head was not a fatal wound, and Dr. Seward believed that a blow to the forehead was the cause of death. Interestingly, when he was asked if the shot had struck the left or right side of the head, Dr. Seward could not recall.[11] Imagine such testimony today!

THE VOLUNTARY CONFESSION OF JACK HODGES

Samuel L. Wilkin, attorney and Orange County Magistrate, was perhaps the most anticipated witness of the trial. Wilkin had been present when Hodges was examined at the jail on January 2, and he was called to the stand to introduce the written confession as evidence against Hodges:[12]

> The voluntary examination of John Hodges, commonly called Jack Hodges, charged with the murder of Richard Jennings, taken in writing January 2d, 1819, before Samuel S. Seward, Jesse Wood, jun. Horace W. Elliott, Samuel J. Wilkin, and Samuel G. Hopkins, Esquires, Justices of the Peace in and for the county of Orange, and John Curtice Esq. Coroner.
>
> Who saith, that he has resided with David Conkling in Goshen, in said county two years since last March; that he, the prisoner, was at Sugar Loaf; on today fortnight, Saturday December 19th, and was employed to go there by David Conkling with a loaded gun; that said gun was loaded by Conkling; that about two weeks before the last circuit court, David Conkling requested the prisoner to take the life of Richard Jennings, and the prisoner made no answer; that twice, or three, or several times, during said court, David Conkling and James Teed made the same propositions to him, the prisoner, and about the close of court again applied to him concerning his, the prisoner's, murdering Richard Jennings; that in every conversation they, Conkling and Teed, offered money to the prisoner; that $1000 was mentioned as sufficient to maintain him during life; that on the Thursday before the prisoner went to Sugar Loaf; David Conkling, James Teed, and prisoner were together at said D. Conklings, at a hovel, by the side of the road; that Conkling and Teed then proposed to him, the prisoner, to go to Teed's at Sugar Loaf, on Saturday, and assist David Dunning and Teed to kill Jennings, and he, the prisoner, and Dunning, were to have $1000; that the plan fixed upon was for Dunning to walk out with Jennings, if he could get an opportunity, and prisoner was to follow and shoot him; that the gun was loaded by Conkling on Saturday, and given by him to the prisoner; that Conkling treated the prisoner when he gave him the gun, and told him to go across the fields; that prisoner went across the fields; that Conkling loaded the gun with shot, in his cellar kitchen, and that no others were present; that prisoner went to James Teed's and David Dunning's, who live in the same house; that Teed was not at home, but that Dunning and their wives were; that Dunning asked prisoner if he had come to assist him, Dunning, to destroy Jennings, that prisoner replied he had at the request of Conkling, and that Dunning said he was ready; that prisoner and Dunning agreed and determined to kill Jennings, the first opportunity, whenever they could find him; that no other person was present in any conversation between prisoner and Dunning concerning the murder; that their conversation

Samuel J. Wilkin was one of the men who examined Jack Hodges on January 2, 1819. Wilkin was an esteemed member of the Orange County Bar, and would later serve in the New York State Senate and Assembly, and as a Member of Congress. He also served as Orange County District Attorney for two days in May of 1835, having declined an appointment to the position.[13]

was out of doors; That prisoner lodged and boarded with Mrs. Teed; that on Saturday evening, prisoner asked Mrs. Teed, if he should not execute the Deed; that she replied, it was a pity but that he was out of the way, this in Mrs. Teed's room and Dunning present; that prisoner conversed with Dunning on Sunday, on the same subject, and also with Mrs. Teed; that Mrs. Teed repeatedly said to prisoner and Dunning, that it was time the old: savage, Jennings, was out of the way, and hoped that he, the prisoner, would execute his business; that Mrs. Teed treated prisoner often with spirits; that Dunning several times invited the prisoner to eat in his, Dunning's, room, but that prisoner did not go; that Mrs. Teed went to meeting on Sunday, and told prisoner to help himself to whiskey during her absence, from a two gallon jug left standing on the floor in the room; that he, the prisoner, went early on Monday morning, after taking his bitters, at Mrs. Teed's request, to drive her cow to Mr. Weaden's; that when he returned his breakfast was ready; that while prisoner was eating his breakfast, Dunning came into the room and told prisoner, that the old man, or savage, Jennings, was going bye; that he, prisoner, had eaten about half his breakfast; that he, prisoner, immediately arose and asked Mrs. Teed to give him some spirits, and that she immediately gave him some; that he, prisoner, took his gun and asked Mrs. Teed where his powder and shot were, that she told him; that he, prisoner, when he took his gun asked Mrs. Teed if he should execute his business, and thought she replied it was time the old savage was out of the world; that prisoner immediately went out with his gun, and saw David Dunning walking along the road following after Jennings, or together with Jennings, just at the turn of the road above the house about ten rods, prisoner went across the fields, and crossed the road which leads to Mr. Jonas Seely's, and passed into the woods by the side of the buckwheat fields, about half way between said road and a pine tree in said fields; that they, Dunning and Jennings, were standing discoursing together; prisoner went directly to them, that Jennings asked prisoner if he, the prisoner, lent a hand, or assisted, in cutting that timber, pointing to some, prisoner answered he did; that prisoner turned his back towards them, and that he, prisoner, cocked his gun, Jennings came towards prisoner and asked him if his gun was loaded; that prisoner replied it was not, and immediately levelled and fired; that when Jennings approached towards prisoner, and prisoner cocked his gun, Dunning, was abreast of Jennings, and stepped one side about three lengths of his gun, but was nearer Jennings than to prisoner; that he, prisoner, was about ten feet from Jennings; that when prisoner cocked his gun, levelled, and fired, Dunning faced him, the prisoner, and said nothing; that he, prisoner, took aim at Jennings head, intending to kill him, and believes he hit him there; that Jennings immediately fell on his seat; that after he fell, Dunning took the gun from the prisoner's hands, saying damn him he is not dead yet, and struck deceased three or four times about the head, or breast, and broke the breech of the gun, that Jennings's hat fell off when he was shot, that Dunning brought the pieces of the gun to prisoner, and they both went their own ways saying nothing; the gun broke at the lock, and the lock was left on the ground: Dunning went back towards the road, through the buckwheat field, and prisoner returned the way he came; they met again in the house, when prisoner returned to Mrs. Teed's he told her that he believed the old man was gone, SHE SMILED AND TREATED HIM; she invited him to eat, but he refused, the breakfast still waiting; had eaten about half his breakfast; when Dunning came to the house, prisoner went into his, Dunning's, room, and prisoner and Dunning agreed never to divulge the fact of killing Jennings, and that they would not expose each other; prisoner stayed at Mrs. Teed's through the day, and until just before day on Tuesday morning, and drunk freely of Mrs. Teed s liquor; that Mrs. Teed put the pieces of the gun under the bed up stairs, in which prisoner slept; that there was no blood on the gun, as he, prisoner, saw; that when he got up to go away on Tuesday morning, he asked Dunning what he intended to do that day, Dunning said he was going to thrashing at East division, that he' also asked Mrs. Teed where the pieces of the gun, she told him they were under his bed, prisoner went up and got them, and took them away with him: that Dunning advised him not to be seen there the next day, Tuesday, nor in going home, and that therefore he, prisoner, went before light; when prisoner arrived at David Conkling's, none of the family had arisen, prisoner put the pieces of the gun under his, the prisoner's bed, went up stairs, made a fire in Conkling's bed room, and asked him to get up; Conkling arose, and came down into the kitchen, and asked prisoner if he had executed the business he went to do. Prisoner replied he had. Prisoner then gave Conkling the pieces of the gun, together with the powder horn and shot bag; the shot bag made of tow cloth, and that the horn separate as to be put in the pocket. Conkling said he would make way with the pieces of gun, and treated prisoner with spirits. Prisoner has not seen the gun since. Prisoner began to describe the manner in which he had killed Jennings, and Conkling replied he did not wish to hear it, and advised prisoner to lay down or take a walk (as understood) that he is not discovered. Prisoner lay down, slept about two hours, arose, ate his breakfast, and lay down again, and stayed about the house all that day. On Wednesday morning prisoner went to the barn to think. Conkling told him, that he, Conkling, was afraid the murder would be found out, and wished him, prisoner, to go away; that prisoner replied, that he might as well be found out there, as any where; that Conkling frequently urged him to go away, until he did go; that the last conversation which prisoner, Teed, and Conkling had, was on Saturday last, Dec. 26th, about the middle of the day; that at that time the letter, or communication, signed David Conkling, and directed to James Adair, was given him; that at the same time Conkling paid him, prisoner, $10, and both Conkling and Teed said they would meet prisoner in New York, and pay him his wages, and his reward; that the $10 was not given him as a part of his wages; that he, prisoner, left all his clothes, excepting one suit, and they, Conkling and Teed, were to bring them to him at New York. Prisoner left Conkling's on Saturday about noon, went from them to Isaac Hallock's, a black man, in West Chester, and stayed there that night, was at Mr. Roe's tavern in Chester, at about nine o'clock, A.M. on Sunday, stayed there a few minutes, and then went down the turnpike, through New Windsor to Newburgh; that about sun set on Sunday, while just entering the village of Newburgh, he, prisoner, met James Teed on David Conkling's mare – no other one present; that Teed asked prisoner, why he had delayed so long on the road? and said, that he, prisoner, had left Conkling's on Saturday noon, and he, Teed, on Sunday, and that prisoner ought to hurry, and get across the river as soon as possible; that Teed told prisoner to walk after, and keep in sight of him, Teed, until he put up his horse. Prisoner did so, and went into the same tavern, a yellow house on the east side of the street; prisoner staid there a few minutes, and then went out to the house of Josiah Peterson deceased, a colored man, and stayed there that night; that on Monday morning prisoner saw Teed, at the ferry stairs, there were several people on the dock; that Teed said to him, prisoner, that if he did not hurry on board he would be suspected; that after he, prisoner, was on board he, Teed said that he would meet him, prisoner, in New York, and reprimanded him for delaying, and directed him to go immediately to New York. Prisoner crossed in a sail boat, went across the mountains to Lobdell's tavern, and was there directed to a wood sloop at Cold Spring landing, stayed that, Monday night with a black man, went on board Tuesday, arrived in New York on Wednesday, and was there apprehended on Thursday, by Mr. Durland, and others. In answer to questions, prisoner said further, that every time David Conkling and James Teed saw him after the commission of the murder, they both urged him to be off; that after prisoner fired, Jennings fell backward on his seat, and his head nodded forwards, prisoner heard him groan at every stroke Dunning gave him; that Conkling and Teed gave as a reason for wishing Jennings killed, that he was about to ruin Conkling in his law suits.

Signed, SAMUEL G. HOPKINS.[14]

The prosecution rested their case after calling a total of four witnesses, which was four more than the defense would offer. Defense counsel Henry Wisner gave an eloquent and well-planned closing argument, which was an attempt to spin Jack's own words into an acquittal. There was no attempt at denial: Jack's own words had already done enough damage. Wisner, instead, threw Jack at the mercy of the jury, explaining that Jack was guilty of discharging the gun at Jennings, but that the death was from blows inflicted by David Dunning. He told the jury that Jack was guilty of "assault with intent to murder," and "accessory to murder after the fact," but was not guilty of murder.[15] Wisner dismissed the allegations that Jack had shot, then beaten, Jennings to death and expressed his disbelief that this charge had even been made. The second count, however, he could not dismiss. He readily told the jury that after Jack had fired the shot he was "alarmed and confused" and had begun to walk away when Dunning seized the gun from him and beat Jennings in the head.[16]

As he began to conclude his argument to the jury, Wisner tried to paint a sympathetic image of Hodges:

> He was alarmed and shocked! Well might he be! He beheld his friend, (for friends Jennings and Jack had been,) weltering in blood. He thought he saw him in the agony of death; the groans of the sufferer pierced his soul; the feelings of nature overwhelmed him; the strong arm of conscience laid him low, and for a season, his power to act, nay, his power to will, was paralized.[17]

But Wisner's description of Jack near the end of his summation certainly didn't leave a very good impression:

> The prisoner at the bar, gentlemen, is an interesting object; the badge of his degradation covers his body; born and reared in poverty and ignorance; a friendless stranger. . .[18]

With such a vivid image of Jack having been made by Wisner, the prosecution didn't need to work very hard to convince the jury of his guilt. Having worked on this case for over four years now, I tend to believe that Wisner made a very smart, tactical move in the trial. I don't believe he was going for an acquittal, as he knew that, based upon the confession and weight of the evidence, Jack would be found guilty. I think that Wisner was setting the stage for a pardon by portraying Jack as an ignorant man who was easily manipulated by Teed and Conkling, and who had admitted his guilt and role in the crime. That Jack would later testify on behalf of the prosecution in the subsequent trials of his co-conspirators only would serve to strengthen any appeal for leniency. Wisner knew he couldn't spare Jack the guilty verdict, but he did believe he could spare him from the gallows.

Attorney General Martin Van Buren summed up the People's case against Hodges. He reminded the jury that Richard Jennings was a man who was more than seventy years of age and had met his death in a very violent manner. The details of the agreement between Jack and Dunning were mentioned, as was Jack's role in the crime wherein he shot Jennings in the head with the intent of committing murder. He dismissed the defense's argument that Hodges had realized his wrongdoing and attempted to turn and walk away when Dunning seized the musket from him, stating that, if this were true, why didn't Jack prevent Dunning from taking the gun from him? And why didn't he intervene to stop Dunning from inflicting the fatal blows? Van Buren urged the jury to render a verdict of guilty.[19]

Judge Van Ness then charged the jury with the law and informed them that it was the guilt of Hodges alone that was in question, and the conduct of any other participants in the crime was not to be considered. An interesting statement that Judge Van Ness gave the jury about this issue was, ". . . though they might or might not be acquitted, in consequence of the acquittal of Jack

Hodges. . . that consideration should have no influence upon their minds."[20] Did the wording of this statement influence the jury? An acquittal may have resulted in the other trials (of the accessories) ending in acquittals as well, so was the judge here making a subtle suggestion to the jury that they needed to vote for a guilty verdict? We can't get into the mind of Judge Van Ness, but it is, to me, a bit of a suggestive statement. The level of influence, if any, on the jury is unknown.

The jury deliberated one hour before returning to the court to pronounce their verdict: guilty. The exact count for which he was convicted is not specified, but it is reasonable to conclude that it was the charge that he had acted with David Dunning in the murder of Jennings.[21]

THE PEOPLE VS JAMES TEED

T he trial of Jack Hodges had occupied most of February 26, 1819, and at a time before the eight hour work day and collective bargaining agreements, there was not set hours of the court. At 3:00 P.M., the trial of James Teed began.[22] Unlike the trial of Hodges, the case against Teed would be more challenging for both the prosecution and the defense.

Jury selection began with a pool of around forty potential jurors. By the end of that process, only eleven had been selected and the Sheriff, Moses D. Burnet, picked the twelfth juror from amongst the spectators in the courtroom.[23] Most people already dread getting picked for jury duty, so imagine being selected for a jury just because you happened to be in the courtroom!

In opening for the prosecution, the District Attorney explained the charges to the jury and announced that Jack Hodges would be called as a main witness. He stressed that Hodges would not receive any pardon in exchange for his testimony, and that Jack would be executed regardless of his cooperation.[24]

During his opening statement, Betts declared that Teed's guilt was "incalculably beyond that of

Attorney John Duer assisted the prosecution at the trials of the accused murderers. In 1821, he was elected as a delegate from Orange County to the State Constitutional Convention.[25]

the wretched instrument he employed." After all, Teed was "a man of influence and respectability in life" who had "beguiled an ignorant and friendless negro [Hodges]."[26]

It was the District Attorney who, in his opening to the jury, would make a statement which would later come to be strongly associated with the murder of Richard Jennings, and be wrongly attributed to Martin Van Buren: "This is the first instance, in the criminal records of our state, of murder, by a hired assassin."[27] This reinforced to the jury the serious nature of the accusation against Teed and the others, and it was a reminder that not only was the trial about this particular murder, but it was an opportunity to send a message to prevent similar crimes in the future.

```
          THE PEOPLE                              TRIAL QUICK FACTS²⁹
             VS
          JAMES TEED
```

Hon. William Van Ness   } Presiding

Samuel S. Seward   }
Isaac Belknap   } Commissioners
Stephen Jackson   }

Martin Van Buren   }
Samuel R. Betts   } Prosecution
John Duer   }

Jonathan Fisk   }
William M. Price   } Defense
Edward Ely   }

Joseph Bostwick   }
William Brown   }
Cornelius Carman   }
Henry Cuddeback   }
Peter Gumaer   }
Benjamin Hulse   } Jurors
Peter Hulse   }
Daniel Ketchum   }
Joseph Ketchum   }
William Lockwood   }
Nathan H. Sayre   }
Jonathan H. Tuthill   }

February 26, 1819   } Trial Began
March 4, 1819   } Trial Ended

Verdict   } Guilty

The trial opened with witnesses such as Samuel Pitts and Noble Howell testifying to the discovery and condition of the deceased. Samuel Seward testified to the wounds and his opinion as to the cause of death. The prosecution then began calling witnesses who testified to the animosity which had existed between Teed and Jennings. This testimony would be particularly damning.[28]

The first witness produced by the prosecution to testify to the conflict was Abraham Stickney, who had been acquainted with both men (Teed and Jennings). Stickney testified that around 1816, he was at Teed's home when Teed said that Jennings had caused all of his problems and wished that "the old devil was dead." Stickney also recalled that Teed had said that he was "not too good to murder him." A conversation from the previous spring was then recalled, and Stickney told the jury that Teed had said to him, "he did not know that it would be any more harm to shoot him than it would be to shoot a squirrel," and credited his family as being the only reason he hadn't killed Jennings. He also testified that two weeks before the murder, Teed had expressed concern that he did not know how long it would be until Jennings took possession of the land and evicted him and his family, and he wished that he were dead.[30]

Apparently, Stickney had never considered that Teed would act upon any of his words and thought they were caused by the emotional strain of the circumstances. Under cross-examination, William M. Price, counsel for the defendant, asked him why he never warned Jennings about Teed's threats. Stickney answered that from what he knew of James Teed, he did not believe he was capable of performing such acts. He did admit, however, that upon reflection, he did harbor some concern that something could happen to Jennings.[31]

Additional witnesses would offer similar testimony. William McWhorter testified that he had heard Teed blame Jennings for all of his trouble, and that Teed had told him that if it were not for his family, he would kill Jennings. Teed also made a statement to McWhorter that would now come back to haunt him. He told McWhorter that he had offered a man one hundred pounds to kill Jennings, and that the man offered to do it for five hundred dollars. He did not follow through with this attempt out of fear of being caught. He also admitted to McWhorter that on three occasions he had held a gun up to Jennings, but never shot him out of concern for his own family.[32]

Another interesting piece of information that we learn from McWhorter's testimony is the existence of a proposed settlement: Jennings had offered to give the property to Teed if he would pay him the money back for it.[33] I can only imagine how this offer had enraged Teed, who felt cheated out of the property for which he had worked so hard.

Court had adjourned late on the first day of the trial – around midnight – and the jury kept overnight until 9:00 A.M. the following day (Saturday, February 27, 1819).[34] That morning, two additional witnesses would provide damning testimony. David Howell testified that he was present on an occasion when Teed held a gun to Jennings, and John Clark described to the jury a conversation which had occurred about two years earlier when Teed had said Jennings had ruined him, and that had he killed him years earlier, he would be more financially stable.[35] The prosecution had successfully portrayed Teed as bitter and angry over the land dispute, and had demonstrated Teed's desire to see Jennings dead, as well as his willingness to offer someone money to make that happen. Pretty damaging testimony considering that Teed was now accused of hiring Hodges to do just that! And the prosecution had now set the stage to introduce their star witness, Jack Hodges.

The prosecution called Jack Hodges, now a convicted murderer, to the stand, and he was sworn as a witness. Attorney General Van Buren began his direct examination by eliciting testimony that Jack had not expected a pardon in exchange for his cooperation as a witness, and that Jack expected to die (hanging was the sentence for murder). The testimony that followed was nearly seven hours long, and Jack described in detail the plot to murder Jennings, his own role in the crime, and the aftermath. The Attorney General produced the letter that Jack had been given when he was fleeing to New York, and in a moment that must have thrilled the gallery,

Jack identified it as the letter Conkling had given him.[36] Jack's testimony certainly was a major aspect of the prosecution's case, and the defense didn't do anything to try and shake his credibility. In looking over the testimony, I found some inconsistencies. Initially, under cross-examination by Price, Jack testified that Dunning had never discussed sharing the $1000 with him. Later, still under cross by Price, Jack said the Dunning was aware that he was to have part of the money.[37] Either Jack couldn't keep his story straight, his attorney didn't get the timeline right (perhaps one conversation was at an earlier date than the other), or the transcript did not reflect the testimony (which is possible – remember there were no stenographers or court reporters). Whatever the reason, it was a missed opportunity for the defense to try and raise doubt in the minds of the jury.

"The judge remained on the Bench, without adjourning the Court, for eighteen hours together – Who, that has attended this Court, will say, that a Judge does not earn his salary!"[41]

Jack was on the stand for nearly seven hours before Judge Van Ness stopped the cross-examination, explaining that such a lengthy time giving testimony was too much for any person, and that the defense would have an opportunity to cross-examine him at a later time. Van Ness directed that Jack be taken and provided with whatever refreshments he may need. The prosecution continued their case, producing witnesses who corroborated certain aspects of Jack's testimony and also testified about Jack's behavior while he was intoxicated (he could be quite violent).[38]

Hodges returned to the stand at 9:00 A.M. on Monday, March 1, 1819 (court had recessed late Saturday until then), and William Price, for the defense, continued his cross-examination. Hodges was asked again if Dunning had told him that he was to share $1000 for murdering Jennings, and this time, Jack said he did not recall if he had. Perhaps the defense had picked up on this inconsistency from their earlier cross-examination. However, there was no follow-up to shake his credibility. Rather, the defense questioned him about Dunning's actions on the day of the murder, and his temper.[39]

Defense counsel did try and create some doubt as to the veracity of Jack's testimony by asking him if anyone had told him he would be pardoned in exchange for his testimony. Jack replied that everyone had said he should be hung.[40]

THE VOLUNTARY EXAMINATION OF JAMES TEED

Magistrate Samuel J. Wilkin was called as a witness for the prosecution to testify about statements James Teed had made during his voluntary examination on December 30, 1818. He had been examined by the magistrates prior to his commitment. The examination was produced and read into the record:[42]

The voluntary examination of James Teed of the town of Goshen, taken in writing before us, the 30th day of December 1818; being charged on the oath of Samuel G. Hopkins Esq. with being accessory to the murder of Richard Jennings, about the 21st inst, and of aiding and assisting the murderer to escape.

Who saith he made no arrangement with Jack Hodges to stay at his house during his absence to New York, Jack Hodges had been at work with David Dunning, and boarded sometimes with Dunning and sometimes with him. The prisoner was called upon unexpectedly to go to New York on Saturday morning previous to the murder, and returned on the next Friday; did not hear that Jennings was missing until he returned home; prisoner's wife first mentioned it to him, and told him that it was supposed he was killed by Jack Hodges; he was not at home when the search was first made; he was told by others that Jennings the deceased was missing, and supposed to be murdered; that prisoner did not make search for the deceased; prisoner received a short letter from David Conkling, requesting him to call and see him; prisoner went to see Conkling on Saturday; saw Jack Hodges on Saturday morning; the prisoner, David Conkling, and Jack Hodges were together about five minutes in Conkling's barn, and does not know that any other person was present; they had some conversation at the back of the house, or in the barn, or at both places relative to the murder of Jennings; prisoner remarked that Jack Hodges was charged with the murder; prisoner remarked, if he was guilty of the murder, he would be off; Hodges made no reply, was intoxicated; prisoner left Conkling's in the afternoon, and went immediately home; on Sunday morning before the family eat breakfast, prisoner went to David Conkling's house; prisoner expected there would be a general search made that day for the deceased; the prisoner had no very urgent business to prevent him from joining in the search, no body called on him to assist; the prisoner, Conkling, and Jack Hodges were not together on Sunday; there might have been some conversation relative to the murder of Jennings; prisoner did not, at Conkling's express any alarm on occasion of the murder; prisoner went from Conkling's to Newburgh, for a thermometer, to assist him in distilling; that was his principal business.

Questions were put to the prisoner, relative to the account he had given before the jury of inquest, of his journey to Newburgh; he was asked why he had given such an unsatisfactory account of his journey, he replied that he did not consider himself bound to give an account of his journey.

When he got to Newburgh, was informed by capt. Griswold, that capt. Case was gone from Newburgh, he did not enquire for the thermometer, did not expect he could get it without seeing capt. Case; is pretty sure he did not see Jack Hodges from the time left home for Newburgh; when he left home on Sunday morning for Conkling's, he did not expect to see Jack Hodges;

The prisoner rode a horse of David Conkling's to Newburgh; after his return he went to the village of Sugar Loaf, he did not go to see the corpse, has not seen it. The journey to Newburgh was commenced on Sunday about noon, he took the East Division road and came out at Craig's; went from there to Moffatt's; and from there took the Little Britain road, and came out near the meeting house, on the road from Goshen to Newburgh, and from there immediately to Newburgh; on his return he came by the way of Montgomery, and John Seward's; was on board of one or two vessels at Newburgh; went on board of some to enquire for capt. Case; the reason of his going to Newburgh was to get the thermometer, he wanted to use it the beginning of the week; he cannot account for his going so early in the morning to Conkling's; he was on board of capt. Halsted's vessel; had some conversation with the captain; was on board of one vessel above and one below Halsted's; enquired for capt. Case's sloop, was on board of Case's sloop, enquired for capt. Case, did not enquire for his thermometer; he says Case's sloop is below Falls's store as he thinks; is positive he did not enquire for Jack Hodges; was not on board of the horse boat; made no enquiry for boats going across the river; staid all night at Terry's tavern in Newburgh, saw no person that he knew; made enquiry for no person there; it was on Monday he went on board of the sloops; he arrived in Newburgh about dark, and went immediately to Terry's; was out in the evening a short time, went to bed early; he did not suppose that capt. Case would take the thermometer back to New York with him; went on Monday to Stephen's distillery, to see the works, and enquire for one Ammerman; he was induced from curiosity to return by the way of Montgomery; had no business there; the prisoner did not see capt. Case in Newburgh.

After his return from Newburgh on Tuesday morning, he had no particular business to attend to. On Monday evening, before sun down, he returned from Newburgh to David Conkling's where he staid all night; he did not go to Sugar Loaf until he was called for to go on Tuesday morning. It was the request of Conkling's family that he should stay there all night.

Does not recollect ever to have said that he would give £100 to have Richard Jennings killed; never said he would kill him himself, were it not for his family.

Signed, S. J. WILKIN.[43]

Teed's statement was a blatant denial of any involvement in the murder of Jennings. To reinforce Teed's hatred and loathing of Jennings, the prosecution introduced four more witnesses who would give strong testimony which would show the jury Teed's state of mind. Sally Impson testified that she had lived in the Teed home for about four weeks back around 1815. She recalled an incident on July 2nd of that year wherein Teed had come home and observed someone burning brush in an adjacent field. When he learned that it was Jennings, he grabbed his musket, loaded it, and stormed out of the house, telling his wife that he intended to "clear the field." Benjamin Bradner, John Mahoney, and Stephen Hall would all give testimony which involved Teed making threats to kill Jennings or to hire someone else to do it for him.[44]

The prosecution recalled Samuel Wilkin as their final witness, who explained that he had spoken with Hodges numerous times and tried to detect any false statements, and he found that Jack's story had been consistent. After twenty-eight witnesses, the People rested.[45]

TEED'S DEFENSE

When attorney William Price began his opening statement, he knew that a man's life was at stake. A guilty verdict would lead his client to the gallows, and Price, with his co-counsel, intended to give Teed the best defense possible.

Price addressed the jury and essentially told them that the press was prejudiced and had already put forth Teed's guilt, and that he had also already been judged to be guilty by popular opinion. He then explained that while the law permits an accomplice to testify, that testimony should not be given any additional weight or strength without corroboration. Price then tore into Hodges's credibility, telling them that "the only evidence implicating the prisoner [Teed] was the testimony of Jack, a convicted felon and confessed murderer," and that he would prove that Jack's testimony was "fabricated and false in many important particulars." It was, according to Price, sufficient that one falsehood in the testimony be enough to dismiss the testimony in its entirety.[46]

When it came to the circumstantial evidence, namely the numerous witnesses who had heard Teed make threats against Jennings, he summed up that they were not anything that Teed would have acted upon. He cautioned the jury on the danger of convicting a man solely on circumstantial evidence and illustrated that there were instances where men had been tried and executed on circumstantial evidence only to have been proven innocent at a later time.[48]

"The Court House has been continually crowded . . . the concourse of people assembled in the village was truly astonishing. Not more than a third of them could get into the court-room, which will probably hold 600 persons."[47]

The defense would proceed to call a total of thirty-five witnesses over the next two days. Their first witnesses testified to Teed's character, and the fact that Teed and Dunning did not seem to get along too well. Apparently, Dunning was upset with Teed for taking rails from his fence and had contemplated suing him for the damage. Thomas Weaden testified that Teed had accompanied him on a business trip to New York (which was why Teed was absent at the time of the homicide), and that when he learned of the crime, he expressed to Teed that it was good that he was in New York at the time of the murder because he might otherwise have been a suspect.

William Van Ness, by John Wesley Jarvis, 1818. Oil on canvas, 33 x 26 ¾ in. Accession #1871.2. Collection of the New-York Historical Society.

Weaden stated that Teed's response to this was not one of relief, and he [Teed] said that had he been home, he may have had a chance to stop the crime.[49]

Around midnight, the court adjourned, and the jury sequestered for another evening. The court had been in session from 9:00 A.M. until around midnight, so the jury had listened to fifteen hours of testimony. Long days would be the norm for this and the remaining trials.[50]

Testimony resumed on the morning of March 2, 1819. The defense spent the day calling witnesses on behalf of the prisoner. The testimony, while helpful in portraying Teed as generally being of good character, was nothing of substance which may have helped to poke holes in the prosecution's case.

```
THE HONORABLE WILLIAM W. VAN NESS

    The man who presided over the
trials was William W. Van Ness.
He was from Columbia County, New
York, and was licensed as an
attorney at the age of 21. He was
an eloquent speaker and well-
regarded amongst his colleagues.
    His address at the sentencing
of the four men condemned to hang
was printed in 1851 in a
biography long after his death in
1823, at the age of 47.51
```

The defense elicited testimony which seemed intended to defer complicity in the crime to Conkling and Dunning. William McWhorter testified that he had seen Dunning on the day Jennings was found and asked him if was going to look for Jennings. Dunning said to him that Jennings had gone to the Delaware to obtain shingles. McWhorter then stated that he next saw Dunning near the spot where the body was around the time it was found. Dunning had been chopping wood. He stated that he later was telling someone that he found it odd that Dunning was near the body, but had not seen it, and suspected Dunning knew about the crime. Dunning had been listening and protested to him about seeing what may have been a hat and coat (where the body had been found), but he wasn't sure.[52]

Conkling was implicated by testimony such as that given by John Roe, who said that Conkling had told him before the court in the fall that Jennings was going to "ruin him" and "it was a pity that the old devil was not shot." Thomas G. Evans told the jury that he had spoken with Conkling when he was first in custody, and that Conkling was confident of his innocence and freely answered questions until he was asked about the letter that had been given to Jack. At this point, Evans said, Conkling refused to answer. Testimony such as this would occupy the court's business until around midnight, when court was adjourned until morning.[53]

Wednesday, March 3, 1819, was the last day of testimony in Teed's trial. The testimony presented on that day really didn't seem to do much to aid in the defense. In his opening, William Price had told the jury that he would prove Jack's story to have falsehoods; however, nothing particularly injurious to Jack's credibility was elicited during the trial. The last opportunity to give the jurors reasonable doubt fell to Jonathan Fisk who had served as one of Teed's attorneys.[53] Fisk was a brilliant attorney with an impressive resume. He had been certified to teach school and began to study law around the year 1776. During his career, he had served as United States District Attorney for the Southern District of New York, and he had been elected twice to Congress.[54] Teed's life hinged on the verdict, and it was a clever strategic choice by the defense to have Fisk deliver the closing argument to the jury. He would have been Teed's best – and last – chance at avoiding the gallows.

Fisk focused the beginning of his closing by reminding the jury that they must rely solely upon the weight of the evidence, and not to allow their own prejudices against the defendant to influence their decision:

> I am well aware, that it is almost impossible for any sett [sic.] of men to come here wholly divested of all preconceived opinions; for when an event of this kind takes place, every little circle in the community forms a tribunal, and decides on the merits of the case, on *ex parte*[55] evidence, wholly disregarding that benign principle of the law, which says, "that every man is to be considered innocent till he is proved guilty." I tell you again, if you have heard ought of this transaction out of doors, you must reject it; then your duty will not be a difficult one.[56]

The brilliant and talented lawyer, Jonathan Fisk,[55] delivered a spectacular closing statement to the jury, but it was not enough to spare his client, James Teed, from a guilty verdict and the gallows.[57]

If you are not ready to vote for an acquittal just wait. Fisk was only getting warmed up. He next turned his attention to the prosecution's star witness, Jack Hodges. This is definitely why he was chosen to deliver the closing. He needed to strike hard at Jack's credibility. If he could convince the jury that some or all of Jack's statements and testimony were false, then the jury would have to vote for an acquittal. I struggled with reproducing some of the direct quotes from this segment of the closing for two reasons. The first was, as I was writing this book, I found myself vacillating between summarizing and direct quotes. I didn't want the book to be too heavy in direct quotes, but, in many cases, the best way to convey the message or information was in the original words of the people who had spoken them. It also gives you a much greater level of access into the facts of the case which will enable you to draw your own conclusions. Regarding this particular section, it was also because Fisk really didn't pull any punches. The racial attitudes of the day are very apparent in his choice of language. Offensive as they may be, his words are best read as he delivered them. I did print a disclaimer in the preface of the book about the racial and offensive language, so the following section is not for the easily offended:

Let us enquire by what evidence the public prosecutor expects to convict the prisoner. The principle evidence is the murderer himself who stands before you convicted on his own confession, whose character is as black as the Ethiopean [Sic.] skin that covers him . . . he came here with confessions of his own guilt, and at the same breath incriminating others of a participation in the horrid transaction, with a hope of pardon, should they be condemned upon his evidence; and the prisoner is selected as a victim of his diabolical machinations. . . . I came here with strong prejudices against the prisoner, but I have endeavored to make up my mind from the evidence, and am fully convinced of his innocence, and that Jack's story is a malicious fabrication. . . . [Jack] is a bold headstrong desperado, of quick perception, and deep cunning.[58]

Fisk also summarized testimony of witnesses who had seen Jennings go alone into the field not far from where he was found murdered, and that Dunning had been seen around Teed's house the entire time that the murder was committed. Dunning's wife, Margaret, had even testified at the trial which, from the summation, we learn that she laughed hysterically while affirming that her husband had not left the Teed home. Apparently, her husband's arrest had a traumatic effect upon her. Fisk had used this information in an attempt to shatter Jack's story before the jury, and it would be great information for Dunning's defense, but it was Teed who Fisk needed to save. He concluded his summation by reminding the jury that their "deliberations will restore him [Teed] to his family, or cut him off in the prime of life, and in the vigor of manhood."[59]

The record of the trial states that Price followed Fisk in rounding out the closing argument for the defense. His statements were not reproduced in the available record because they were similar to the closing argument he made on behalf of his other client, David Conkling, and were printed with that trial.[60] If we rely upon the closing presented at the trial of David Conkling, then we can deduce that the sum and substance of the closing as it related to Teed focused on the credibility of Hodges, and the jury convicting based solely upon such evidence. In People v. Conkling, he used several vivid examples of convictions based upon circumstantial evidence which had later proven to be fatally wrong, and it is likely his closing in People v. James Teed also used such cases as a caution to the jury.[61]

Martin Van Buren summed up the case for the prosecution. Van Buren, a skilled politician, and the Attorney General of the State of New York, was no doubt quite an impressive site for the jury. I am sure that he induced a sense of awe in the jurors. After all, he was the Attorney General. He held a powerful office in the State Government and was standing before them, in Orange County, delivering the fate of another man into their hands. The weight of his office no doubt lent more weight to the strength of his words to the jury.

Van Buren addressed the jury on their duty to render a just verdict based upon the law and not their feelings towards the prisoner. He emphasized that as an accessory to murder, he was as guilty as the man who rendered the blows. He dismissed the defense's argument that Hodges acted alone by telling the jury that the indictment accused Teed as an accessory to Hodges (under the theory that Hodges had murdered Jennings alone), and another count as acting as an accessory to Hodges and Dunning (under the theory that Hodges and Dunning had acted together to murder Jennings).[62]

In his closing, Van Buren repeated what the District Attorney had said days earlier about the murder being the first recorded murder for hire, and this is most likely how it was ultimately attributed to Van Buren (and not Samuel R. Betts, the District Attorney):

> The law imposes upon him, who employs another to commit a murder, the same penalty as it does on him who inflicts the deadly blows. . . . This is the first time that such a crime has been committed in this state, the first time that the life of a fellow being has been taken away by the hands of hired assassins.[63]

Van Buren took his time summarizing the testimony against Teed (and Conkling) and even giving an interesting historical analogy to the jury. In discussing Conkling's reluctance to listen to Jack relate the intimate details of the murder, Van Buren compares it to Richard III who, wanting to maintain the crown, had ordered one Sir James Tyrrel to murder his two young nephews. Tyrrel did so by forcibly smothering them in their beds. After the murders, as Tyrrel began to relate the grisly details of the horrible crime to Richard, Richard interrupted him and told him no more, just as Conkling had interrupted Jack and told him no more.[64] Quite a grand analogy!

After Van Buren had delivered the remainder of his closing, Judge Van Ness charged the jury and, at 2:00 A.M. on Thursday morning (March 4, 1819 – 18 hours after court had begun at 9:00 A.M. on the third!), they retired to deliberate the fate of James Teed. More than sixty witnesses had testified over a time span which had exceeded four days of testimony with each day being twelve or more hours. But the jury took less than fifteen minutes to deliberate before reaching their verdict: guilty![65]

THE PEOPLE VS DAVID CONKLING

A late night court session was no reason to delay the start of the next trial. At 9:00 A.M., a mere six hours after James Teed had been convicted for his role as an accessory to the murder of Richard Jennings, David Conkling was placed at the bar to answer for his alleged role in the murder of Richard Jennings. District Attorney Betts opened the case for the prosecution by explaining the evidence that would be presented and the nature of circumstantial evidence. He also told the jury that they must not be influenced in their decision by the sentence associated with the offense (death by hanging), and to keep in mind that while the prisoner is in the prime of life and has children, so, too, did Richard Jennings have children and loved ones. He wrapped up his opening by reviewing any potential objections to the testimony which would be introduced by Jack Hodges.[66]

The witnesses introduced by the People included many who had previously testified at the trial of James Teed and offered similar testimony. As in Teed's trial, the star witness was Jack Hodges, and his testimony as elicited by the prosecution was consistent with that he had given against Teed and with his own statement. John Duer, for the prosecution, did elicit additional testimony from Jack which was damaging to Conkling. He recalled an occasion in the fall of 1818, prior to the court action over the land, when Conkling had been served with a notice of trial. It was Hodges's testimony that Conkling had said at that time that they should have killed Jennings and dumped his body in the brook. That same night, according to Hodges, Conkling had implored him to kill Jennings, because he had ruined Teed and would now ruin him

[Conkling]. He told Jack that he would pay him five hundred dollars if he was to murder Jennings.[67]

```
        THE PEOPLE                                    TRIAL QUICK FACTS[68]
           VS
      DAVID CONKLING


Hon. William Van Ness        } Presiding

Samuel S. Seward             }
Isaac Belknap                } Commissioners
Stephen Jackson              }

Martin Van Buren             }
Samuel R. Betts              } Prosecution
John Duer                    }

Jonathan Fisk                }
William M. Price             } Defense
Edward Ely                   }

Nicholas Bogart              }
Joseph Bostwick              }
John Brown                   }
Samuel Corwin                }
Jonathan Faulkner            }
Michael Halsted              } Jurors
Jephtha Lemareaux            }
Hezekiah Loring              }
George Phillips              }
Seely Weeks                  }
James Weller                 }
Daniel Wickham               }

March 4, 1819                } Trial Began
March 9, 1819                } Trial Ended

Verdict                      } Guilty
```

Hodges also testified to conversations that he had with Conkling during the fall court battle with Jennings. He recalled that one evening Conkling was concerned that Jennings was going to obtain possession of the land, and that he wanted to devise a way in which to get rid of him [Jennings]. Hodges also described a morning conversation with Conkling after Jennings had obtained possession of a house, but not yet the land. According to Hodges, Conkling was upset that his fellow residents would be talking about how Jennings was going to ruin him, and that if he was to lose the property, then they must do away with Jennings. A couple of days after this conversation, Jack said that Conkling told him that he and Teed had spoken, and they felt that it would be best to develop a plan to murder Jennings. He then stated that, on that same night, Conkling urged Jack to do the deed, and told him that Teed had alcohol and that if he was to go to Teed's to murder Jennings, then Conkling would have divided one thousand dollars between Hodges and Dunning. After his testimony, the court adjourned for the night.[69]

On the morning of Friday, March 5, 1819, court reconvened at 9:00 A.M., and Hodges was again placed on the stand for cross-examination by Jonathan Fisk. Fisk asked Jack if Durland (the man who had apprehended Jack in New York) had said to him, before he had confessed his role in the crime, that a witness on the day of the murder had observed him with a gun, and Jennings entering the buckwheat field alone. Jack said that he "believed he did." Fisk also asked if Durland had told him that there was enough evidence against him, and that if anyone else was involved in the crime, that he better admit it. Jack "believe[ed] he did say so." He also managed to illicit similar responses from Jack concerning other statements which Durland had made to him prior to the confession, particularly that Conkling had already told him about the broken pieces of the gun, that Dunning had sworn that Jack had admitted to shooting Jennings, then beating him with the gun, and that Teed and Dunning had provided all the evidence they could against Jack.[70]

Fisk's cross-examination was laying the framework for the defense's presentation and intended to raise the specter that Jack's entire story and confession had been fabricated out of revenge. He had, after all, learned that the others had already informed against him, and the punishment of death was certain. As the old saying goes, misery loves company. Was this motive for an intricately woven falsification?

The prosecution must have anticipated the defense strategy because after calling a few more witnesses, they closed their case by calling Reverend Ezra Fisk to the stand. Rev. Fisk had previously testified at Teed's trial and had offered similar testimony that he had been visiting Jack weekly and had impressed upon him the importance of telling the truth. He said that Jack had expected to hang for his crime and often appeared distressed and serious. Rev. Fisk (no relation to the attorney Jonathan Fisk) also testified that he didn't think Hodges was genuinely remorseful and had no "hope in Christ."[71]

Church was a very important part of the community at this time, and having Rev. Fisk testify about Jack's integrity would have been a bonus for the prosecution. Especially since after the Rev. Fisk had testified, Jack's confession was read into the record.[72] This was the impression that the jury would be left with as the defense began their case.

CONKLING'S DEFENSE

It was late in the evening on March 5 when Jonathan Fisk stood and addressed the jury on behalf of David Conkling. Always eloquent and dignified, Fisk began the attempt at dismissing Jack's credibility and, in the process, saving Conkling's life. He told the jury that Jack had known about the feud between Conkling and Jennings and heard their arguments. Fisk said that Jack's character had been poor his entire life and that his testimony should bear no weight. The jury was also told that Jack had acted alone to kill Jennings because of the controversy between Conkling and Jennings, but not with Conkling's knowledge. Jack's confession was, according to Fisk, crafted around the circumstances of the crime as had been related to him by Durland. Court adjourned for the night after Fisk concluded his opening statement.[73]

At nine the following morning (March 6, 1819), the jury was called back into the courtroom and the defense began their case. One of the early witnesses was Charles Teed, the nine year old son of James Teed.[74]

Charles had previously testified during his father's trial and had recalled that on the morning of the murder, Jack had said that "uncle Dick was going by," and he took the gun and said he was "going to shoot a partridge for his breakfast" and he went out.[75]

Under direct examination by Fisk, young Charles said that he had heard Lewis Dunning say that Jack had come to "kill old dick."[76] Lewis Dunning was David Dunning's son.[78]

AN UNUSUAL WAY
TO SETTLE A LAWSUIT

On February 3, 1819, Justice Elliot presided over an unusual civil trial at the door of the county jail. The matter was the case of David Dunning vs. David Conkling. The particulars of the suit are unknown other than that is involved money. The resolution of the litigation is not known.

It seems a bit trivial that two men, both facing upcoming trials for their lives, would be involved in such an action while confined in the "dungeons" of the jail.[77]

Charles also testified that his father had come back from New York on Friday and had gone to David Conkling's on Saturday. The Attorney General then said to young Charles that he previously said his father had returned on Saturday night. This caused the young boy to be confused and cry.[79]

Shocking testimony would then follow with the introduction of a witness named George A. Seaman. Seaman was, in slang terms, a *jailhouse snitch*. He had been confined for forgery and housed in the same room as Jack Hodges.[80] His testimony was clearly intended to cast doubt upon the statements of Jack Hodges. When asked by defense counsel William Price if he had ever spoken with Jack about the murder and David Dunning, Seaman answered, "I have had frequent conversations with him, in which he has told me, that Dunning had nothing to do with this murder, and wished he was at home with his family."[81]

John Duer, for the prosecution, then asked him if he had ever heard Jack make statements to David Dunning regarding Dunning's innocence. Seaman replied that on the night he entered the jail, he overheard Dunning say to Jack, "You know I am clear of it," to which Jack replied, "You are clear of it." He would also testify that Jack had stated Dunning was innocent of the crime, and that Dunning had often tried to convince Jack to state that he [Dunning] was innocent.[82]

Jailer John Penny took the stand and gave similar testimony as in Teed's trial. He testified to Jack's behavior in jail, which included the use of "rough language" and disorderly behavior.[83] He also testified that Jack had been moved to the "lower gaol" and had only been given a bed the evening before at the direction of the sheriff.[84] The function of the lower jail is unclear as prisoners were typically held on the third floor jail of the court house.[85] Perhaps the lower portion of the jail was used to house disorderly or problematic prisoners?

The County Clerk building in Goshen stands on the spot once occupied by the courthouse and jail where the dramatic trials unfolded[86]. In February and March of 1819, thousands of people gathered in this area to try and get a seat in the court room and catch the latest developments from inside the courtroom.

David Hendershot was also called as a witness for the defense. He testified that he had been at Conkling's on the day Jack had left for Sugar Loaf, and that he had seen Jack there and observed him take down the musket:

> I saw him take it down, and draw the ramrod, and put it into the gun, and I saw it bounce up, I said to him, your gun is not loaded, he replied, I see it is not. He then went and felt on the shelf, for ammunition I supposed, but I then went home, and did not see him get any, nor load the gun.[87]

This evidence was contrary to Jack's story that Conkling had taken the musket and given it to him. But was it enough to convince the jury that Jack was a liar who had fabricated the entire plot? The defense rested with this testimony and the confidence that they had shaken Jack's credibility.

In rebuttal, the prosecution called additional witnesses, including the Rev. Fisk, who advised that he had asked Jack if he had told Seaman that Dunning was innocent and was informed that he had not, and that Jack had related to him that he did tell Dunning he would be cleared, but only because Jack felt as if he would not be allowed to testify against him. Rev. Fisk told the jury that Jack had expressed a desire that all of the other defendants be cleared because they had families, and he was "a poor negro . . . [that] must be hung."[88]

Attorney Edward Ely then delivered the closing argument to the jury.[89] It was a magnificent piece of prose, and some of the statements that he made more than merit repetition in full. He first dismissed the prosecutions introduction of seemingly damning statements:

> This cause has been pressed on the part of the prosecution, in a most extraordinary manner, and the words, and actions, not only of James Teed, and David Conkling, but of David Dunning and Mrs. Teed, was well before, as after the transaction, and for their whole lives, have been pressed into the service of the prosecution, and a mysterious meaning given to the most innocent of them, and all brought to bear upon each individual separately, in the transaction.[90]

Ely proceeded to then dismiss Jack's testimony as being completely unsupported by any independent evidence, and stated that anything that is corroborated is simply because it has been based upon the circumstances. He continued that Jack only needed to remember two issues in order to maintain his story and the rest could be presented truthfully and thus viewed as supporting the whole story. The issues: did Teed and Conkling hire Jack to murder Jennings, and was Dunning present with Jack at the time of the homicide.[91]

As to the first issue, Ely pointed out that Jack claimed the conversation pertaining to the murder occurred at the hovel when no one else was around to be a witness. Thus, this aspect of Jack's testimony could be neither proved nor disproved. As for Dunning being present, Ely thought that the evidence at trial had shown he could not have been where Jack says he was at the time of the crime.[92]

Mr. Ely also questioned the authenticity of the letter Jack had purportedly received from Conkling, going as far as to accuse Jack of having it forged. He challenged the prosecution to introduce evidence that the handwriting on the letter was that of either Teed or Conkling. Of course, this is long before forensic handwriting analysis, so there was no expert testimony to be had on such an issue. He also told the jury that even if Conkling had written the letter, it would only support that he aided in the murder after the fact, which was not punishable by death.[93]

It was late in the evening when William Price stood to address the jury also on behalf of the defendant. Due to the time, he requested the court to adjourn for the remainder of the weekend, and Judge Van Ness agreed.[94]

Monday morning, March 8, 1819, court reconvened at 9:00 A.M. and Price had his opportunity to address the jury. He reiterated much of what he had said at the closing of Teed's trial. He warned the jury on the dangers of convicting on circumstantial evidence alone and especially that of a convicted felon [Jack Hodges]. Jack was, according to Price and the defense's theory, a manipulator and liar who had crafted his story around easily remembered facts to create the illusion of the truth.[95]

After Price had concluded, John Duer addressed the jury in summing up the People's case. He described Conkling as having come from a good family, and being an otherwise respectable, good man who was a husband and a father. He then told them very bluntly that the consequences of a guilty verdict would mean the death of Conkling:[96]

> The life of the prisoner will be forfeited. It is a sacrifice which public justice will exact. There is no reason to doubt, but that the sentence of the law *will* be executed, and his mortal course soon to be terminated, by an open and shameful death. Not only are his family to be plunged into that deepest, sorest distress, which always attends the sudden violation of the ties that binds the wife to the husband, the offspring to the parent, but an indelible blot is to be fixed on the name; a stigma that can never be effaced. The infamy of the father will descend to the children, and for generations to come, they will be condemned to weep over their bitter inheritance of public shame and reproach.[97]

Duer informed the jury that they needed to carefully deliberate on the evidence and facts, and to not allow their compassion or feelings for the defendant influence their decision. He reminded the jury that Richard Jennings had been murdered by Jack Hodges, and they needed to decide if he acted alone, or if he had been part of a plot to carry out the deed. The defense, Duer said, had tried to create the illusion that Jack had solely acted based upon his own motivation, yet they failed to offer any proof in support of that argument. He did remind the jury that the evidence supported that Jack had participated in the crime as part of a concerted plot.[98]

At mid-afternoon, Judge Van Ness addressed the jury and reviewed the key testimony. He charged them with their responsibility, and at 3:30 P.M., the jury retired to deliberate the case.[99] They had their work cut out for them. David Hendershot's testimony had presented a challenge to the jury: it contradicted Jack's testimony and account of the crime.[100] This issue certainly contributed to an overnight session of deliberations. A storm raged most of the night while the jury was considering Conkling's fate and, at 8:00 A.M. on Tuesday, March 9, 1819, the jury had reached a verdict, and court was convened at nine o'clock. The jury's verdict: guilty![101]

THE PEOPLE VS HANNAH TEED

An hour after David Conkling had been found guilty, his sister Hannah Teed was brought into the courtroom.[102] Her husband and brother had already been found guilty and were soon to face a gruesome death on the gallows. For Hannah, a conviction after trial was certain. The same evidence that had been used to convict James Teed and David Conkling would have been introduced against Hannah, and she would have joined the others on the scaffold.

The certainty of a conviction – and the prospect of hanging a woman – may have prompted the prosecution to arrange a deal with counsel for the defense and the court. As Hannah stood at the bar, her attorneys (she was represented by the same attorney's that had represented her husband and brother) withdrew her previous plea of *not guilty* and she entered a plea of *guilty* to the indictment.[103]

District Attorney Samuel Betts then informed the court that Hannah Teed had been indicted by the Grand Jury as being an accessory to the murder of Richard Jennings before the fact, and as an accessory after the fact. He told the court that, with their approval, he was entering a *nolle prosequi* on the count alleging accessory before the fact.[104]

Hannah Teed was described in court as being of a "feeble understanding" and that she had "acquiesced" and was a "passive" participant in the crime. Further, the District Attorney informed the court that Hannah was "in a delicate situation" which would have postponed her execution for some time. This was a nice way of saying that she was pregnant.[105]

The court consented to the proposed settlement and the District Attorney, with the full support of the Attorney General and John Duer, entered a *nolle prosequi* on the count of accessory to murder before the fact. Hannah Teed had been spared the gallows.[106]

THE PEOPLE
VS
DAVID DUNNING

The settlement of Hannah Teed's criminal case left David Dunning as the last to face a jury for his role in the crime. His trial began with an opening by the District Attorney which involved a review of the law and the evidence which would be introduced. The transcript of the opening was not printed in the available publications, so the exact wording has been long forgotten. But we can surmise that the opening echoed words from the other trials, as each relied upon relatively the same evidence and theory of the case.[108]

REPORT

OF

THE TRIALS

OF THE

MURDERERS

OF

RICHARD JENNINGS,

AT A SPECIAL COURT OF OYER AND TERMINER FOR THE COUNTY OF ORANGE; HELD AT THE COURT HOUSE IN THE VILLAGE OF GOSHEN, ON TUESDAY, FEBRUARY 23rd 1819.

WITH ARGUMENTS OF COUNSEL.

"Quem Deus vult perdere prius dementat."

NEWBURGH:

PRINTED BY BENJAMIN F. LEWIS, and Co. FOR THEMSELVES, and TIMOTHY B. CROWELL, Goshen,

Sold also by JUNIUS.'S LEWIS, Catskill, and Booksellers generally.

:::::::::::

APRIL. 1819.

This publication is the only known transcript of the trials. It was published and sold by the publishers of the Orange County Patriot, so much of the information in the pamphlet is similar to the newspaper articles from the Patriot.[107]

As in the previous trials against Teed and Conkling, Jack Hodges would once again take center stage as the principle witness for the prosecution. On the stand, District Attorney Betts admonished Jack to tell the truth, and told him that there was no hope for a pardon, and that if he were lying, the fate and punishment which awaited him after death was worse than the punishment he would receive in this life.[109]

```
          THE PEOPLE
              VS                              TRIAL QUICK FACTS¹¹⁰
          DAVID DUNNING
```

Hon. William Van Ness	} Presiding
Samuel S. Seward Isaac Belknap Stephen Jackson	} Commissioners
Samuel R. Betts John Duer	} Prosecution
Jonas Storey	} Defense
Cornelius Carman Stedman Chapman Horace Dibble Thomas W. Goble Peter Hulse James Jessup Joseph Ketcham William Lockwood Davis Strachan Job Tuthill Abel Wood Jacob Youngblood	} Jurors
March 9, 1819 March 10, 1819	} Trial Began } Trial Ended
Verdict	} Guilty

Jack testified that on Saturday, December 19, 1818, he and Dunning had agreed to murder Richard Jennings. According to Jack's testimony, Dunning was to act as a decoy and lure Jennings out to the lot where they had been taking wood, and that Jack would shoot him. He also testified that on the morning of the murder, he and Dunning were going to go chop wood at the lot in an attempt to draw Jennings and kill him, and, not long after, Jennings was observed walking past.[111]

As to motive, Jack testified that Dunning was not induced to participate in the murder by the offer of a reward. Rather, Dunning was concerned that he would be out of work in the summer if Jennings regained possession of the land.[112]

After only introducing a couple more witnesses, the prosecution rested their case. Jonas Storey now had the daunting task of defending Dunning, and it was an uphill battle. The prosecution had already gained two convictions based largely upon Jack's testimony. Efforts to undermine his credibility had obviously failed, and a successful defense was going to be nearly impossible.

One of the witnesses who testified for Dunning was a Richard Jackson, who previously testified at the trials of Teed and Conkling. Jackson told the jury that he had overheard a conversation in the jail when Dunning was challenging Jack on his story, and Dunning asked Jack if he recalled that on the day before the murder, he had warned him not to go through with it or Jennings "would appear to him."[113] Was Dunning trying to tell Jack that he would be haunted by the ghost of Richard Jennings?

David Hendershot was also called as a witness and gave testimony consistent with his earlier testimony at Teed's trial. In response, the prosecution called additional witnesses to discredit him and say that they had heard him [Hendershot] say that it was Conkling who loaded the gun.[114]

Testimony continued on Wednesday, March 10, 1819, with Jack Hodges back on the stand for additional cross-examination. Storey attempted to get Jack to admit that he had been promised a pardon in exchange for his cooperation and testimony against the others, but Jack did not budge from his testimony. He reaffirmed that he had not hoped for any pardon, and none had been promised.[115]

James Teed testified that it was his belief that Dunning had no interest or concern in the murder of Jennings. He also testified, under cross by John Duer, that Dunning was a man who could be violent and had a quick temper.[116]

David Conkling testified that on the Tuesday after the murder, Jack had come to his home and told him that he had shot Jennings and then beat him with the gun, because the shot did not kill Jennings. He said that he had not heard Jack include Dunning in the account of the crime until after Jack had been arrested. He also testified that Jack had said that he would not be discovered because he had acted alone, and he said he was not concerned about the spirit of Jennings appearing to him until nine days had passed.[117]

The defense summed up their case in a rather dramatic manner. Jonas Storey was a master of the English Language, and he began his closing statement with an address that could have been lifted from the pages of a gothic horror novel:

> This house which has been heretofore dedicated to the ordinary business of your county, has now alas, become the place of blood! Death is here! Already in her rapid course, within the compass of two weeks, had she added three victims to her empire. Within these walls she hovers over them with her black wings; you shall see them no more till that voice is hear, 'Arise ye dead and come to judgment!' Jack, Teed, Conkling, are among the slain, will you not now say to the destroying angel, 'Hitherto shalt thou go, but no farther; and here shall thy proud victories be staid [Sic.]?'[118]

Storey used the closing argument to describe to the jury what had made his case different from the others. He told the jury that Jack's description of Dunning's involvement in the crime was false. He dismissed the circumstantial evidence against Dunning, and reminded the jury of testimony which was inconsistent with Jack's account. He acknowledged that the defendant may have heard Teed and Conkling contrive to commit the crime, but he was unaware of any facts and free of any involvement.[119]

The District Attorney presented the case to the jury on behalf of the prosecution. He took time to boost Jack's credibility and dismiss any defense claims that Jack was untrustworthy. D.A. Betts methodically evaluated the various witnesses and their testimony, and how none of the testimony had discredited Hodges or proven the innocence of the prisoner. He also discredited the testimony of Teed and Conkling as having been given by two men facing death who would say anything to discredit Jack Hodges to save their own lives.[120]

Judge Van Ness explained to the jury that the prisoner had been tried as being involved in the actual murder, meaning that he was present at the time the murder was committed. This was, according to the Judge, the issue to decide. If the jury determined that Dunning was not present at the time Jennings had been killed, then they must return a verdict of *not guilty*.[121]

What I find interesting is how the Judge proceeded to review the testimony and evidence with the jury, essentially giving a succinct boost to the prosecution. He dismissed notions of Jack being dishonest by stating that anyone repeating a story day to day will make errors. He also reiterated to the jury Dunning's potential motive for killing Jennings, and essentially told the jury that Dunning had been in the field with Hodges at the time of the murder! He also admonished that the testimony of David Hendershot was so falsified as to have exposed him to be a perjurer.[122]

The jury retired to deliberate David Dunning's fate, and after deliberating about five hours, returned to the court to deliver the verdict of *guilty!*[123]

THE SENTENCING

After Dunning's conviction, the court had recessed for the night. On Thursday morning, March 11, 1819, court was called to order, and convicted criminals who had not yet been sentenced were brought before the court, including the four men condemned for the murder of Richard Jennings, as well as their more fortunate female conspirator, Hannah Teed.[123]

Three men were sentenced to state prison for the crime of grand larceny, another to prison for setting fire to a barn, and a fourth criminal was sentenced to the county jail for petit larceny. Also in court for sentencing was George A. Seaman, the jailhouse snitch who had testified at Conkling's trial. He was sentenced to seven years in state prison for the crime of forgery.[124]

Hannah Teed was the first of the conspirators to stand for sentencing. Judge Van Ness addressed her special circumstances- that she had been manipulated by her husband, and that her gender and her pregnancy (although that word is never specifically used!) warranted consideration. Her children, Van Ness noted, would soon be deprived of a father, and she would be their only source of care and protection.[126]

With the full agreement of the prosecution, Judge Van Ness handed down her sentence. He remarked that she deserved a more severe punishment, owing to the nature of the crime, however, under the circumstances, was entitled to mercy. The sentence of the court was that Hannah Teed be imprisoned in the county jail for thirty days.[127]

> " The mandates of a stern and inflexible husband might have influenced her conduct."[128]

The four men convicted of killing Richard Jennings were called up together to face their sentences. At this stage in the proceedings, their sentences were a given. The law only sanctioned death as the punishment for murder, so the judge had no discretion in passing this sentence. These mandates, which were not unique to New York, often earned judges the reputation as a *hanging judge*, although in reality the judges had generally no other alternative legally available to them.

The court room must have had a tense and foreboding atmosphere. The sentence of death was certain, yet no one standing before the court had heard the phrase, "[you are to] be hung by the neck until you are dead," since 1779.[129] The terror and fear that gripped the condemned men must have been palpable! They were described in the press as having been "an awful spectacle of human depravity."[130] Of the four, I envision David Dunning as being the most terrified and anxious among them, for he had protested his innocence and would keep doing so until his dying breath.

The sentencing phase of a capital trial was, in many ways, the first act of the drama of a public hanging. The judge was expected to deliver a powerful and moving speech to the condemned, which would serve also as a warning to those assembled to avoid being tempted by sin. There was no standard formula, and sentencing speeches varied depending upon the circumstances of the case and the personality and disposition of the judge.

Van Ness knew that his words would have weight and he chose them carefully in delivering the sentence. He was both the neutral arbiter of justice and a compassionate Christian as he addressed the weary murderers:

> The court are now called to close their labors. The end of trial is judgment. It is now my painful duty to pronounce the sentence of the law on four human beings, who have been tried by their country, and found guilty of the horrid crime of murder. In the whole course of my life, I have not witnessed a scene like the present. The collected history of human laws scarcely affords a parallel. You are convicted of the murder of an old man, on the brink of eternity, who in all human probability, if you had not sent his unsummoned spirit to his God, would have been called in the course of a few days, or at most within a few short years, to pay the debt of nature. By this act you have forfeited your lives to the offended laws of your country. You have meditated on this thing, you have brooded over it, till your feelings have become hardened, and its atrocity lost in the repetition and familiarity of thought. You have been convicted on testimony satisfactory to my mind. I have been overwhelmed with the weight of evidence, my judgment has been thoroughly convinced of your guilt. I cannot doubt but that the verdicts, in every case, have been such as the jurors will be enabled to reflect upon hereafter with satisfaction. You have had long and laborious trials, honest men have reflected long on your cases. You may be impressed with a belief that undue rigor has been exercised towards you by the public prosecutors, but I can assure you

·

that you have been heard with patience, and the most delicate dictates of humanity and fellow feeling, have been exercised towards you throughout the whole of their proceedings. It is true they have been industrious and unwearied in their endeavors to discover the hidden evidence of your guilt, and I must say, that it appears like the special interference of Providence, that they have been enabled to do so much; but they have done no more than their duty, and they deserve the thanks of the community; had they done less, they would justly have forfeited their claims to public confidence.

I came to this place a disinterested man upon this subject, I came with a determination to give it a thorough investigation, and if possible to find out the truth. During the progress of these trials, I have listened attentively; I have reflected, deeply reflected, both here and elsewhere; and I have devoutly prayed for light from him who is the fountain of all wisdom. Your trials have terminated, and you have been found guilty of murder; and I do believe that these verdicts are such as justice demanded. I am now to pronounce upon you the penalty which our laws have annexed to this crime. It is death. Almost all nations have punished the murderer with death, in ancient, as well as modern times; even the chosen people of God, by their laws struck the murderer from the face of the earth; 'whoso sheddeth man's blood, by man shall his blood be shed.' With these remarks nothing remains of my duty, but to pronounce the sentence of the law, which is,

That you be taken from hence, to the place from whence you came, and from thence to the place of public execution on Friday the sixteenth day of April next; that you there be hung by the neck, between the hours of two and three o'clock in the afternoon, until you are dead;

And here my duty, as an officer of this court ends; but as a man, and a Christian, I feel that I have other duties to perform. I wish to sympathize with you. I want to awaken you to a just sense of your situation. I wish to awake the nerve where agony is born. I wish to draw nigh to you in the agony of kindred souls, about to be separated forever. I wish to point you to an hereafter. Is death an eternal sleep? Oh no: a secret voice within assures us that we shall never die. I want to speak to you of life, and judgment, and immortality. I want to speak to you of the resurrection of the dead. I want to speak to you of God's redeeming love. I want to arouse you to a sense of your own lost and ruined state. I want to point you to the cross of Christ, that Christ who suffered an ignominious death for us. I want to speak to you of God and his Providence. I want to direct you to a saving knowledge of Jesus Christ. I want to assure you of his power and willingness to save, all who approach him through faith and repentance. 'Though your sins be like scarlet, they shall become white as snow; though they be red like crimson, they shall become as wool.'

Your crimes will be attended with the most dreadful consequences, humanity will weep over the scene. You have bought desolation into all your families. No less than three widows and how many little ones I know not, will in a single moment mourn their loss. You have cast a stain upon your posterity. Ignominy and shame will attend your helpless children through the whole course of their mortal existence. Can mortal man be in a more awful situation, than that in which you are now placed? Your anger has been cruel indeed.

My friends, if I can awaken in you one good sentiment, my labor will not be in vain; but if I can go one step further; if I can make you realize your awful situation, if I can induce you to think of eternity, my mind will be relieved of a heavy burden. Is it not so? You have but a day to live, the hour of your death is fixed. Is it not then your interest and your duty seriously to reflect, and earnestly to devote the remainder of your time on earth in solemn devotion to your God? It is but a little while. That Saviour who has died for you and me, will extend the arms of his merciful kindness; and remember that when the trump of God shall sound, the graves of the dead will be opened, and when *your* graves are opened, the grave of Richard Jennings will also be opened, and he will be your accuser before that Judge who cannot be deceived. Let me conjure you to prepare for that event, to improve the few remaining days you have to live, in striving to secure an .interest in Jesus, there is no other hope, his blood alone can cleanse you. Call to your assistance the pious ministers of our holy religion, pray with them, and let them pray for you, and endeavor to reconcile yourselves to your God.

In the course of your trials, Jack has been a principal witness against three of you, although you have not been convicted on his testimony alone, still you may harbor some resentment against him; but remember, you are to die, and if you expect forgiveness hereafter, you must not only extend forgiveness to *him*, but to all men; Strive to cultivate a forgiving disposition, extend forgiveness to all your fellow creatures, and especially to the unfortunate man who stands by your side.

Let me entreat you to procure faith. Let no earthly caress divert your attention from a future state. Let not despair seize upon you. Say not to evil, 'be thou my good,' for there is still hope in your case. Strive earnestly to attain an inheritance eternal and immortal.

With respect to you, Jack, you are an ignorant black man; you have not been favored with any of the advantages of education. You however possess a more than ordinary strength of mind. Providence has blessed you with a memory without a parallel in all my experience. You have been the means in the hands of Providence, to bring to light, this first instance in the state of New York, where a murder has been committed by a hired assassin. You have been the degraded and wicked instrument, and justice requires that you should be made an example to community.

To close. This is a scene which has cast a gloom over a large portion of the community, all are solemnized, and I hope all will profit by the lesson which it affords; although going to law is sometimes necessary and proper, still let all reflect on the consequences attendant on an indulgence of the bitter and malignant feelings excited by long protracted litigations, for unless curbed by the better feelings of our nature, they always eventuate in crime. Let every one reflect that it is one of the first duties we owe to society, to endeavor to detect crime, and unless examples are made, detection is useless.

This is the first time murder had been committed in this county since the revolution. It is remarkable that murder rarely, nay, never escapes detection. God's ways are not as our ways. There is a Providence in this thing. Various artifices have been resorted to in order to conceal this murder, false witnesses have been enlisted, and no stone left unturned; but he who rides in the whirlwind, and directs the storm, has in a wonderful manner brought it to light; and ofttimes the very means used to conceal the fact, leads to detection.

I speak not to reproach you with your crimes, I feel for you. I point you to immortality. God is merciful as well as just. By repentance and faith you may gain a seat at his right hand; and if you can obtain a hope in Christ, your few remaining days, so far from being the gloomiest, may yet be the happiest of your lives; and when you mount the gallows, be enabled triumphantly to exclaim, '0 death, where is thy sting: 0 grave, where is thy victory!' May God Almighty have mercy on your souls.[132]

"That you be taken from whence you came, and from thence to the place of public execution on Friday the sixteenth day of April next; that you there be hung by the neck until you are dead."[131]

These were the words of a firm, yet compassionate Judge who, consistent with the beliefs of the time, was compelled to address more than their earthly punishment. The Judge, through the tone and context of the speech, certainly didn't "harangue them for hours" as Barrell described the sentencing in his 1975 account of the crime.[133]

Judge Van Ness then addressed Jack and said that it was the determination of the court that "after the execution, [his body] should be delivered to the President of the Medical Society of Orange county for dissection." Jack apparently "bowed" as if he had acknowledged this additional sanction of the court.[134] But he may not have understood the exact meaning. It was later reported that when he had been told his body was to be dissected, Jack thought that he was to be "lacerated and cut to pieces before his execution," and was apparently in an anxious state until the actual meaning had been explained to him.[135]

In further addressing Jack, Van Ness sought to assure himself and the court, as well as the public at large, of the veracity of Jack's testimony in the crime. He said to Jack:

Jack, you stand here a convicted and acknowledged *murderer*, as such your doom is fixed. You have also been a principle witness against those three unfortunate men sitting near you.

Your situation is awful indeed. Innocent blood is upon your hand. But tenfold more horrible, must be your state, if in addition to the murder of one man, you become the guilty and diabolical instrument of taking away, by falsehood, the lives of three more innocent men. Remember what I tell you. There is another bar, before which you must shortly stand. There is a Judge whom you cannot deceive. Before that bar and before that Judge, you and I must both appear. If you have said ought but the truth, against these men, take the earliest opportunity to correct it. It is not too late. Speak now and let it be known, before the fatal moment arrives. If you have sworn falsely, to take the lives of these men, you are the greatest monster I ever beheld. I know not how to express the *baseness* and *wickedness* of your character and conduct. If you carry that falsehood with you to the judgment, most horrible will be your destruction. I have not language to express the indescribable torments you must endure in the unquenchable flames of hell: I therefore conjure you, if you have said ought but the truth, persist in it no longer. Speak out and relieve your conscience. Declare it before it be too late, and your guilty soul be plunged into the awful fire of inconceivable ruin.[136]

Prompted by the Judge's admonition and compelled to reaffirm, not only his own guilt, but that of his co-defendants, Jack informed the court that he had "spoken the truth, and had no more to say."[137]

The legal drama had began with a Grand Jury hearing evidence on February 23, 1819, and had concluded by March 11, 1819; a remarkable amount of time considering their were five separate trials with court days often lasting twelve or more hours! The wheels of justice didn't grind as slow then as they often seem to today! For the four men under sentence of death, all they could do was sit and wait for their fatal moment on the gallows.

POETIC BEAUTY AMONGST SORROW

I have enjoyed finding very unique, fascinating, and long forgotten pieces of this story. Particularly interesting was this poem that appeared in *The Orange County Patriot*. The poem had been found on the ground near the courthouse on the evening of March 8, 1819. That night, a storm raged outside while a jury deliberated the fate of David Conkling. The poem is the words of a sorrowful mother to her son. The author of the poem was Bethia Conkling, David Conkling's mother:[138]

Dark howls the tempest round yon place of sorrow,
But darker is the cloud that veils to-morrow!
Deluded man, thine aching temples bind
And calm the transports of thy tortured mind.

Where now's the smile that oft has lent its ray,
When home-born pleasures crown'd the closing day!
Friends, wife and children, round thy table bent,
Rich with the blessing heaven in mercy sent.

How chang'd the scene! no gleam of pleasure plays
Within thy bosom as in former days:
Thy children sireless, and thy widow'd mate
Left to lament alone thy wretched fate.

The breeze that murmurs, and they winds that blow,
The leaves that rustle and the brooks that flow
Convey no pleasure – ev'ry ear's unstrung
All, all, were dissonance tho' scarphs sung.

Had feverish dream disturb'd thy restless head
And this sad scene around thy pillow spread,
How had the sanguine phantom made thee start
Tho' the embryo crime lurk'd in thy heart?

The dawn of day had be'er appeared so bright:
"Ans O how welcome was the morning light!"
Each friend was dearer and each foe forgot –
Peace and contentment smiled around thy cot.

Peace, once the inmate of thy breast is gone;
And sweet contentment, child of heav'n had flown.
O where's the blood, this scene does not congeal?
"Horrid to think – how horrible to feel!"

Who now shall smooth thy brow that's knit with care?
Or cool the tearless eye, fierce with despair?
No cheering hope dispels the thick'ning gloom,
Guilt and remorse stand pointing to the tomb.[139]

These are the painful words of a mother who is grieving the anticipated loss of her son. It is our only glimpse into the feelings of those directly influenced by the trials. There is nothing written that can place any of the family members in the courtroom at the time of sentencing. It is easily imagined, though, that it would have been a heart-wrenching scene with sobbing family members listening to the words of Judge Van Ness echoing in the courtroom, with the grim reality of their deaths now fixed. The final grip of justice would reach a climax soon enough on a scaffold.

Cover of a pamphlet published after the trials and executions.[140]

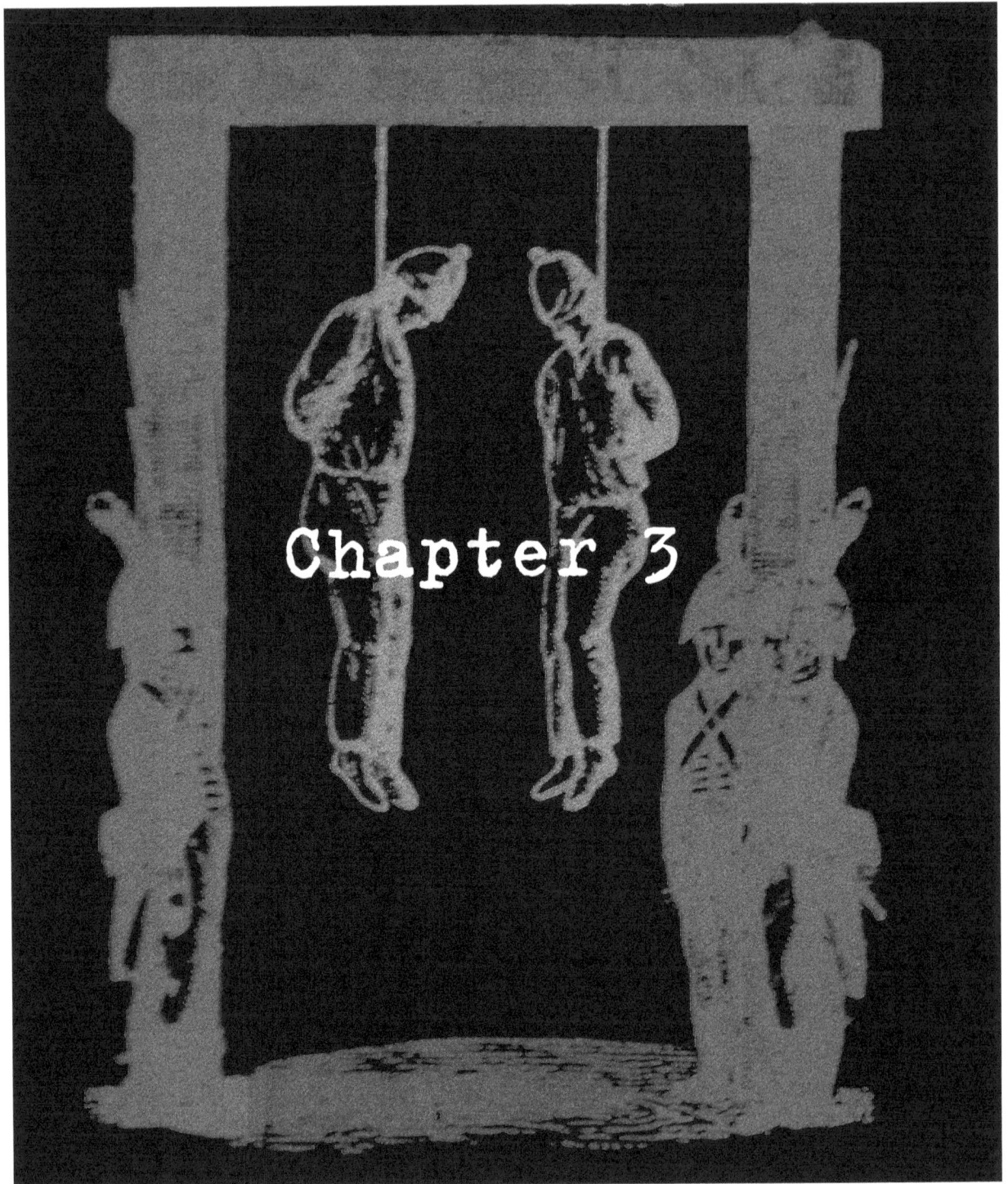

Chapter 3

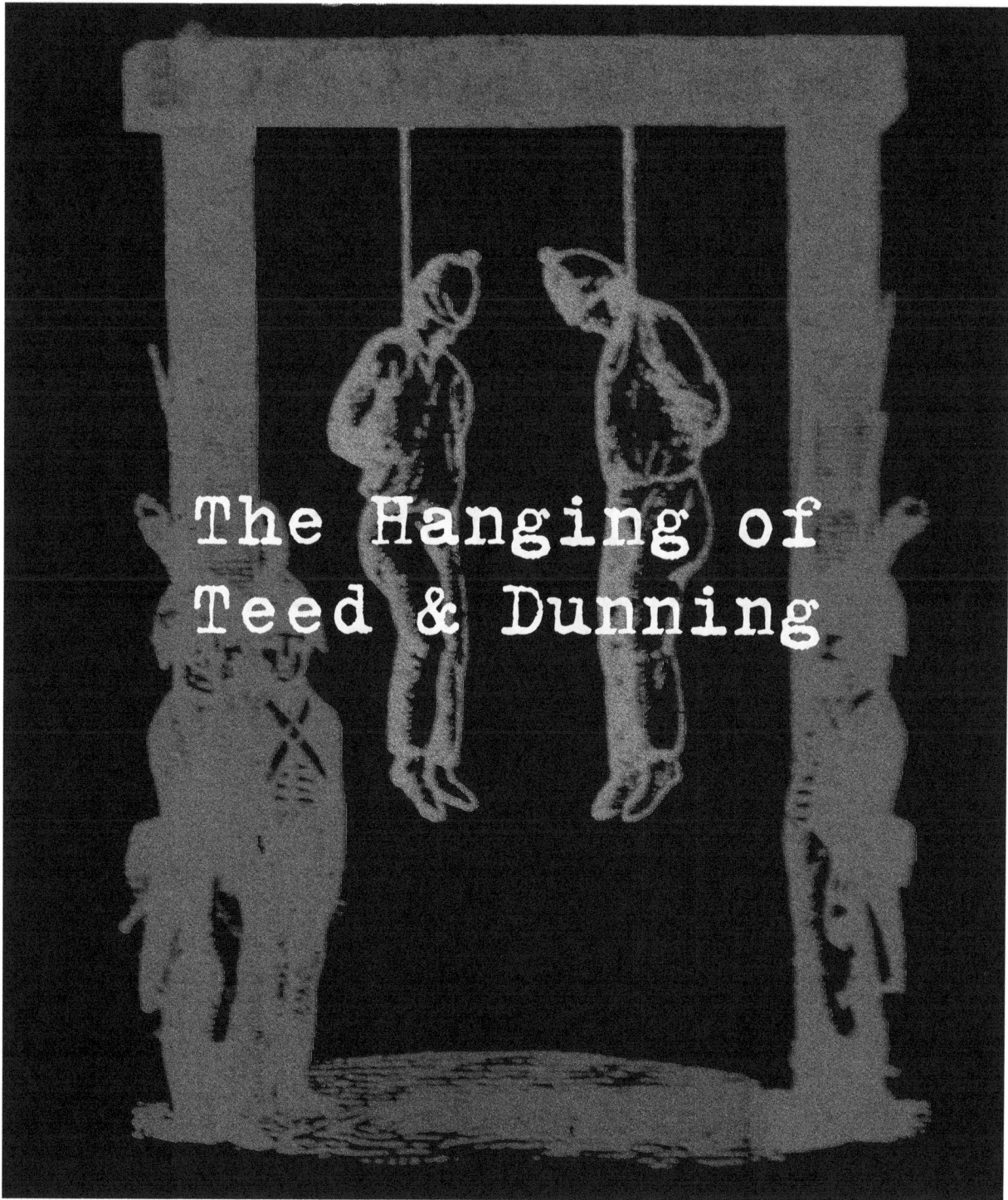

The Hanging of
Teed & Dunning

HANGED BY THE NECK UNTIL DEAD

In the nineteenth century, a condemned prisoner did not have to wait long for his or her appointment with the hangman. For Teed, Dunning, Conkling, and Hodges, this wait would be just over a month. Having been sentenced to death on March 11, 1819, their public hanging had been set for the early afternoon hours of April 16, 1819.

Public executions were big events and would draw large crowds of spectators wanting to see the macabre details of the hanging played out. It was almost a form of public theater, with processions, speeches from the gallows, religious ceremonies, and, of course, the stars of the show – the condemned – who were expected to face the gallows bravely and even perhaps make a last minute confession. Confessions were big news, being often printed and sold (even at the hanging!) and pamphlets, broadsides, and newspaper articles would have memorialized the execution for those who were unable to attend in person. (The printed confessions of James Teed and David Dunning are on pages 89-93 of this chapter.) In 1819 Orange County, there had not been a hanging since the 1770s, so county officials would have known that this was going to be a well-attended spectacle and needed to plan accordingly.[1] To add to the pressure, this was to have been a quadruple hanging and the public would not have tolerated disappointment.

NOTICE.

THE 16th of April inst. being the day appointed for the Execution of *James Teed, David Conkling, David Dunning & Jack Hodges:* The Under Sheriff, Deputy Sheriffs and all Constables within my Bailiwick, will appear at the Court-House in Goshen, on said 16th of April, at 9 o'clock A. M. to act as occasion may require.

M. D. BURNET, Sheriff. Goshen, April 3d, 1819. -

Notice printed in the Orange County Patriot by Sheriff Moses D. Burnet.[2]

PARDONS

Moses DeWitt Burnet, Sheriff of Orange County, had the responsibility of executing the condemned men. As such, he, along with other county officials, would have had to begin planning the executions almost immediately after the verdicts had been delivered. And while Burnet was planning a public hanging, others had been planning on saving one – if not more – of the condemned men from the noose.

On March 31, 1819, New York State Governor DeWitt Clinton sent a letter to the State Assembly from Judge Van Ness recommending Hodges for a pardon.[3] This is the full text of that letter:

Albany, 31ˢᵗ March, 1819.

Sir.- The following persons were tried and convicted at the special oyer and terminer, lately held in the county of Orange, for the murder of Richard Jennings, vis: Jack Hodges, (a black man) and David Dunning as principles, and James Teed and David Conklin, as accessories, before the fact, and they are sentenced to be executed on Friday the sixteenth of April next.

As the accessories could not by law be tried, until after one of the principles had been convicted, Hodges was first brought to trial, and being found guilty, the public prosecutor next proceeded against the accessories, who were separately indicted, and made use of Hodges as a witness against them, as he also did against Dunning. The verdicts in all the cases were perfectly satisfactory, as well to myself as to all the judges of the common please, who were associated with me in the trials. The manner in which Hodges gave his testimony; the promptness with which he answered all the questions that were put to him; his great consistency and apparent candor and frankness throughout the whole investigation, inspired both the court and jury with entire confidence in his credit and integrity as a witness.

Since the trials, I have carefully and maturely examined and considered how far, under all the circumstances, Hodges, being an accomplice, and having been used as a witness on behalf of the government, is entitled to mercy; and I find it to be a settled rule in the criminal law, that an accomplice who is received and used as a witness; who fully and truly discloses the joint guilt of himself and his companions; who answers honestly to all questions that are put to him, and appears to have acted a fair and ingenuous part, by giving a faithful relation of all the facts within his knowledge, is equitably entitled to the favor and mercy of the government. On this point, I considered it my duty, to consult the chief justice and the other judges of the supreme court, and I am authorized by them to state, that they concur in the opinion I have expressed, and I accordingly recommend Hodges as a fit object of pardon. Whether the pardon, however, ought to be absolute or conditional, is worthy of serious consideration. Sound policy, and a due regard to the public safety, would seem to require, that so dangerous a man should not, at lease for some time to come, be set at liberty.

I am very respectfully,

Your obedient servant,

W.W. VAN NESS.[4]

Van Ness had written to Governor Clinton asking for a pardon for Jack Hodges, a black man. This, for me, speaks to Van Ness's character and integrity. We need to keep in mind that in 1819, slavery was still legal in many parts of the United States, and, where it was illegal, African Americans were not treated as equals to their white counterparts. So for a well-esteemed judge, in 1819, to take the initiative to write to the Governor of the State of New York asking for a pardon for an African American is quite remarkable. Van Ness had put his name – and, with it, his reputation – on this request. He backed it up with the full support of the other judges of the court. These are not the actions of a man who did not have firm convictions for fairness and equality under the law. He could have done nothing. He could have allowed Hodges to face the hangman pursuant to the sentence of the court. There was no statutory duty that I can find that would have compelled him to ask for a pardon. Van Ness was convinced of Jack's honesty (and guilt) and recognized that without Jack, convictions would not have been secured against the other defendants.[5]

I also look to the specific language Van Ness used when he described the manner in which Jack conducted himself during the trials. Again, these are words which must be placed into the context of 1819. Van Ness must have been a man of character and compassion, and his actions at the sentencing of the defendants, as well as those in requesting a pardon for Hodges, are a testament to this.

J ack Hodges was certainly the main focus of the pardon that would be discussed in the legislature. On April 6, 1819, the House of Assembly considered a bill to pardon Hodges.[7] The "use of [Jack Hodges] by the court ... as a witness on behalf of the people" was essential to the case against Teed, Dunning, and Conkling. The House of Assembly, presented with the fact that "without Hodges's testimony they [Teed, Dunning, and Conkling] could not have been convicted," voted

> "The manner in which Hodges gave his testimony; the promptness with which he answered all the questions ... his great consistency and apparent candor and frankness ... inspired both the court and jury with entire confidence in his credit and integrity as a witness."[6]

"unanimously" to grant a pardon to Jack Hodges. I do not believe this was an unexpected outcome. However, what happens next is, for me, a bit odd. There is discussion on the pardoning of David Conkling, but no mention on how – or why – this had come about. According to the contemporary news accounts, after "some debate, a division was taken on pardoning David Conkling, and carried in the affirmative, 54 to 43."[7]

James Teed did not fare as well with the Legislature. His name was added to the pardon by way of a motion, but it was voted down by a vote of 52 to 46. During this same session, after he had been added to the bill, and after Teed's exclusion, another motion was brought to the House to remove David Conkling from the bill "which, after some debate, was carried." The bill, in this form, was agreed to and approved.[8]

LAWS OF NEW-YORK.

CHAP. CLI.

AN ACT *to pardon Jack Hodges and David Conkling.*

Passed April 10, 1819.

I. *BE it enacted by the People of the State of New-York, represented in Senate and Assembly,* **That Jack Hodges, a colored man, and David Conkling, be and they are hereby pardoned of the murder of Richard Jennings, whereof they were convicted at a court of oyer and terminer and general gaol delivery, held in and for the county of Orange, in the months of February and March last, and for which they were sentenced by the said court to be executed.**

II. *And be it further enacted,* **That instead of the punishment of death, the said Jack Hodges be and hereby is directed to be imprisoned in the state-prison at New-York, at hard labor, for and during the period of twenty-one years ; and that instead of the punishment of death, the said David Conkling be and he is hereby directed to be confined in the said prison, at hard labor, for and during the term of his natural life ; and that it shall be the duty of the sheriff of Orange county forthwith to remove the said Jack Hodges and David Conkling from the gaol in the said county, and them safely deliver to the keeper of the said state-prison ; and that it shall be the duty of the said keeper to receive the said Jack Hodges and David Conkling into the said prison, and them to keep there in the manner aforesaid for and during the several periods above mentioned.**

The law passed which granted pardons to Jack Hodges and David Conkling.[12]

If you are getting confused, hold on, because it is just starting to get interesting! The State Senate did not agree with the bill granting a pardon only to Hodges, so it added Conkling back into the bill and sent it back to the Assembly.[9]

On April 10, 1819, the House of Assembly again considered the bill and approved an amended bill which pardoned both Hodges and Conkling.[10] Another vote was then taken on adding James Teed to the bill, which passed by a vote of 54 to 51, with the entire bill [now pardoning Hodges, Conkling, and Teed] approved by a vote of 53 to 46.[11] But as we know, there was no saving James Teed from his date with the noose. The Senate, upon review of the amended bill, did not approve of the amendment and it was returned again for consideration. This time, the name of James Teed was stricken, and only Jack Hodges and David Conkling ended up in the final bill approved by both houses of the Legislature.[13] I am certain that James Teed never knew how close he had come to avoiding the gallows, which is probably for the better. For had he known that he had been in the bill then removed, it may have made his last days on earth that much more torturous. As for David Dunning, I find it very interesting that he was never considered for a pardon. His fate was sealed the day he was sentenced to death.

EXECUTION LEGENDS

James Teed and David Dunning had been scheduled to die on April 16, 1819. The executions and aftermath are surrounded with local legend and lore. I have spent a great deal of time researching these various legends, trying to determine if they are based upon fact and, if not, then where did they originate? Locating facts and tracking down sources is easy compared to sifting truth from legend. Early on in my research, I obtained a copy of Donald Barrell's *Along the Wawayanda Path. From Old Greycourt To Chester To Sugar Loaf.* Published in 1975, his account of the Richard Jennings murder, trials, and aftermath, including executions, had been viewed by

DeWitt Clinton, Governor of New York State.[14]

many as a historically accurate account of the events. However, as I have stated elsewhere in this book, Barrell's work is not sourced. The murder of Richard Jennings is just one chapter in the book, and there are no footnotes or endnotes to cite sources of information. I urge readers to keep in mind that Barrell's research was done at a time long before computers and the Internet made such endeavors easier. So I am sure that he was limited in identifying, locating, and obtaining primary source materials. Without knowing where he obtained some of his information, I can only make assumptions that he may have had access to oral histories and some limited printed materials, and I can trace most of the legends back to Barrell's account. I believe that his work is what other writers used as a source of information on the case, so the stories and legends surrounding the case were spread on. More on these legends as we progress through the events of April 16, 1819.

APRIL 16, 1819

Riday, the 16th day of April, 1819, became indelibly burned into the history of Orange County and the State of New York. The double hanging of James Teed and David Dunning for the first murder for hire in New York had been big news. Papers throughout the young United States had shared the details of the crime, trials, and pardons, and now would share the gruesome details of the ultimate punishment for these two felons. The best accounts of the executions come from those news stories which were published in the days after the executions. Many of the accounts are nearly identical (albeit with the occasional slight variation or mistake) and most likely originated with the same source article, which I suspect may have been the highly detailed account published in the *Orange County Patriot,* which, in my opinion, is the most reliable primary source document for the details of the executions.

Crowds had begun to gather on the morning of Friday, April 16, in what was described as a "solid mass of men, women and children." Sheriff Burnet must have anticipated the influx as the site of the execution was to be held about a mile south of Goshen rather than the center of town.[16] This is an area today which may be west of Hatfield Lane between 17A and Police Drive. I have come to this conclusion after several years of research and am confident that this is the correct location.[17]

The events of the day began around 10:45 A.M., with "the sound of the bugle" and "a procession . . . formed in front of the court-house" at 11:00 A.M.[18] The procession was an important aspect of a public execution, a big part of the theater and drama that witnesses would have expected. It was

THE PATRIOT.

GOSHEN, APRIL 20, 1819.

The Execution.—On Friday last, agreeably to the sentence of the court, the Execution of *James Teed* and *David Dunning* took place about a mile from the village, a little south of the Goshen and Minisink Turnpike road.

The April 20, 1819, edition of the Orange County Patriot has a detailed accounting of the executions and served as the basis for my research in reconstructing the events of that day.[15]

also a way in which local authorities demonstrated the seriousness of the events, while reminding people of the fatal consequences of criminal actions. At a time before there were organized police forces as we know them, this was seen as a vital aspect of the public execution.

At 11:10 A.M., the condemned men were escorted from the courthouse, "dressed in white, prepared for the grave," their heads reclined (which was expected given the shame that would have come along with a public death.)[19] An eyewitness to the spectacle wrote that they "appeared quite calm and undaunted until they saw their coffins, when they were both appalled, and wept bitterly."[20] A wagon had been backed up to the courthouse door, and both men ascended onto the wagon along with two members of the clergy. "At the sound of the bell the musick [sic.] struck up to the solemn death march" and the procession towards the gallows began. It was, according to the *Orange County Patriot*, "a slow, solemn, and regular pace."[21]

A. L. Ball, Esq., is identified as having been the officer of the day. Military units "consisted of Capt. Watkins' troop of horse, Capt. Belknap's uniform company of infantry[22], and Captains Ball, Barker, and Jackson's companies of infantry."[23] Upon arrival at the gallows, the military units formed a circle around the gallows, with the soldiers on foot forming the ring closest to the gallows, and the cavalry behind them. The citizens arriving to view the spectacle had to stand behind this ring of military guards.[24] Even now, nearly 195 years removed, it is easy to imagine the drama which had unfolded that day.

The day
before the
executions,
Teed and
Dunning
were
baptized by
Rev.
Richard F.
Cadle, from
the St.
James
Protestant
Episcopal
Church in
Goshen.[25]

THE PROCESSION:[26]

A L Ball, Esq
Officer of the Day

Cavalry

Moses D. Burnet
Sheriff

Under Sheriff and Deputies

Musick [sic.]

Infantry

Constables

Prisoners and Clergy
(flanked by guards)

Coffins

Constables

Infantry

Civil Magistrates and Members of the Bar

Cavalry

Citizens

Once at the scaffold, the prisoners stepped down from the wagon and climbed the steps of the gallows. Dunning is described as having walked alone while Teed required the assistance of the Sheriff. Once on the scaffold, the condemned men sat while Sheriff Burnet read the death warrants for all four of the condemned men, after which he read the pardons of Jack Hodges and David Conkling, and their respective punishments as commuted by the legislature.[28] Sheriff Burnet then addressed the crowd. His words were eloquent, thoughtful, and demonstrated the integrity and compassion of a man called upon to perform a difficult task. His speech from the gallows was so moving that in the days following the execution, it would be memorialized and commented upon in the press:

It is more than thirty years since any person in this County has suffered the last pain of the law for the crime of murder.

I am now however called to the performance of a necessary, but painful duty, appertaining to my Office: I hope I shall discharge it with the feelings that become me. – Let me request your attention a few moments, before the commencement of that awful spectacle, which will engross every power, and bind up every faculty in terror and commiseration.

The cause which stirred up the vindictive passions of the unfortunate men you now behold was in itself trifling– In its consequences, how tremendous! An aged and infirm man, in an unsuspecting moment was the first victim of violence, and they, the authors and contrivers of this death, are now about to become the necessary sacrifice offered by the law for the example and for the safety of all– Doomed to death, in the midst of health, in the prime of life– taken in a moment from the most endearing connections; from wives and children– In agony and shame they go to those dark and mysterious abodes where penitence is unavailing, reformation impossible, and their destiny eternal. By your serious and orderly conduct, let the lesson of their punishment have its full effect– give to them your pity– let them have your prayers: By the inexorable decree of that law they have dreadfully violated, it is all they can ask – it is all you can grant.

And God have mercy on their souls![27]

Divine services were then conducted. The "Rev. Mr. Cummings read from the platform the 88th Hymn, 1st book, which was sung. Mr. Cummings then addressed the Throne of Grace in a fervent prayer – [and] the 26th Hymn of the 2nd book was sung." But it was the sermon delivered by the Rev. Ezra Fisk that would be long remembered and even memorialized in a pamphlet. Based upon the

EXECUTION SERMON.

On Wednesday next, will be published, at the Office of the *Orange County Patriot*, in Goshen, the Sermon delivered at the Execution of James Teed and David Dunning, By the Rev. Ezra Fisk, A. M.
Goshen. Oct. 18, 1819.

Advertisement in the Orange County Patriot announcing the publication of Ezra Fisk's execution sermon.[28]

"23rd verse of the 32nd chapter of Numbers," the discourse was titled *Sin Finds Out the Criminal*.[29] It has been written that the divine services took two to three hours which may not be that far off; the men were hanged somewhere between 2:00 – 2:30 P.M., which would put the length of the entire ceremony at the scaffold at around 2 ½ hours.[30]

Divine services concluded with a prayer by Rev. Mr. Wilson, and the "51st Psalm long meter was sung" and "Benediction pronounced by Mr. Fisk." The prisoners were observed to have been united in "great fervor" during the services, "particularly Teed" who people hoped had "died at peace with his God." The condemned men both knelt in prayer, with Teed described as having prayed quite audibly. This praying may have lasted as long as fifteen minutes.[31]

This undated photograph from the collection of the Chester Historical Society purports to depict the location where Teed & Dunning had been executed. The caption supplied with the photograph stated, "A hollow near the center of the picture marks the spot in the Stewart woods where Teed and Dunning were hung on Friday the 16ᵗʰ of April 1819." Photo courtesy the Chester Historical Society.

Sheriff Burnet, having a hanging to officiate, stopped the prayers and informed the two men that "his duty compelled him to interrupt them" to which both men stood up and were pinioned. Teed required the assistance of the Sheriff to walk under the gallows, and I can't begin to imagine how terrified he must have been. He was visibly distressed and was heard to say "warning – warning!" Dunning is recorded as having said, "Gentlemen, I am guilty, and I deserve to die, but I did not take the gun out of that black man's hands, and beat Mr. Jennings's brains out." He then walked alone under the gallows and stood firmly and waited while Sheriff Burnet adjusted the noose around Teed's neck. When the sheriff pulled a cap down over his face Teed said, "O, there is a reality in religion." These would be James Teed's last words.[32]

Dunning's last words were made while standing under the gallows. He said, "I hope this will be a warning to all never to keep company with black people." Dunning would go to his death denying his role in the murder.[33]

Image depicting the double hanging of James Teed and David Dunning from an 1819 pamphlet.[34]

After he had finished adjusting the noose around Dunning's neck, Sheriff Burnet pulled a cap over the condemned man's face, after which he descended the steps of the scaffold, and then Teed and Dunning were dropped through the trap door and "launched into eternity." "An involuntary groan seemed to issue from every part of the field" when the men fell through the trap to their deaths. Teed barely moved while Dunning struggled for a "few moments."[35] Hanging at this period would have involved a short drop, meaning that Teed and Dunning would have fallen through the trap only as far as the slack in the rope between their necks and the beam to which the rope was attached, which in reality, was probably only a few inches. Death by this manner of hanging is usually caused by blocking blood flow to and from the brain.[36]

What happened to the mortal remains of Teed and Dunning will be explored in the next chapter.

A DRAMATIC REPRIEVE ON THE SCAFFOLD?

According to Donald Barrell's 1975 account of the hanging, the condemned (his account includes Teed, Dunning, Conkling, and Hodges, in addition to Hannah Teed) were "required to mount the platform and kneel on the trap door as the ropes were adjusted by the Sheriff."[39] It is now known that only Teed and Dunning were brought to the gallows. Hannah Teed had already been sentenced to 30 days in jail and had never been sentenced to death, and Hodges and Conkling were not produced and brought to the scaffold.[40] Barrell also wrote how Sheriff Burnet "deliberately pulled from his pocket a long official paper," and then read "his authority for holding the executions" then read the last minute pardons for Hannah Teed, David Conkling, and Jack Hodges."[41] Although it seems plausible, this dramatic, last minute reprieve didn't happen. Where, then, did this aspect of Barrell's account originate? I believe that I have this piece of lore explained. I have encountered many historical cases where facts have become intermingled, and, in this case alone, there is intermingling of details with the hanging of

THE GREAT ESCAPE?

The April 22, 1819, edition of the *Berkshire Star* ran a brief article stating that the "persons convicted for the murder of Jennings" had escaped from the county jail. The article alleges that all four of the men had managed to escape, and that it was "supposed" that a "turnkey" had assisted them in this effort. We know that the four men never escaped from the jail, and that by April 22, two of them had already been executed. While the information may be erroneous, the article does note that the information was "as we receive it, without vouching for its authenticity."[37]

Interestingly, the rumor of an escape must have been widely shared, for several newspaper accounts of the executions began with a brief line clarifying that the escape reports had been unfounded.[38]

Claudius Smith in 1779. I believe that certain aspects of an 1805 public execution in Cooperstown, New York, may also have been mistakenly interwoven with the executions of Teed and Dunning:

```
The ropes
used to
hang Teed
and Dunning
were made
by Luke
Farley, an
Irish
immigrant
who had
been a rope
maker in
Ireland.⁴⁴
```

On Friday, July 19, 1805, Stephen Arnold was to face the hangman after having been convicted of a brutal murder. Without getting into too much detail, Arnold had been convicted of a particularly heinous crime: he had beaten his six year old niece, Betsey Van Amburgh, numerous times and exposed her to the elements until she died. His actions had been instigated by the child's failure to properly pronounce the word *gig*. On the date of the scheduled execution, a last minute reprieve had arrived in the morning, and the sheriff decided to keep the reprieve a secret. As such, the entire execution ceremony was conducted as scheduled, including the procession to the gallows and divine services. When the execution drama had reached the point where Arnold was to be hanged, the sheriff adjusted the noose around Arnold's neck but did not fix the rope to the scaffold. Dramatically, the sheriff produced from his pocket the reprieve and read it aloud.[42] This had to have been a spectacular scene. A man seconds away from death spared in a dramatic, last-minute reprieve that seems more fitting for a movie than a real life incident. Arnold's crime, trial, and near-hanging was big news at the time and would have been remembered for decades to come. Is it possible then, that this reprieve became blended into the events of April 16, 1819? I think it is highly likely, but without knowing what sources Barrell relied upon, I can not say for certain that the two events became intermingled. I leave that up to you to decide.[43]

HOW MANY PEOPLE ATTENDED THE EXECUTIONS?

One of the fascinating aspects of this entire case is the sheer number of people who witnessed the executions. Accounts vary depending upon the source, with the highest estimates putting the number in attendance at 20,000, although historian Donald Barrell believed the number to be "nearer two thousand."[45] During my research, I wanted to determine just how many people may have witnessed the executions. Unable to travel back in time and take a head count, I, instead, relied upon the news accounts of the day. This did not make the task any easier because as I located sources, I started to find contradictory estimates.

The estimates seemed to fall into two groupings: one placing the crowd at 15,000 to 20,000 people, and the other at "upward of twelve thousand persons" as being present.[46] One article, however, deviated from these two basic estimates, and this provides our best clue as to an accurate estimate: "The number of spectators has been variously estimated, from twelve thousand to thirty thousand – probably there were not more than fifteen thousand."[47]

The source of the estimate above is the primary source document which I have relied heavily upon to provide the most accurate depiction of the hanging: The April 20, 1819, article "The Execution" in the *Orange County Patriot*. Based upon the information available, I believe that the estimate of around 15,000 people is likely to be the most accurate and is not unreasonable given the fact that the hangings had been big news and a rare event in Orange County. Morbid curiosity and the chance to witness a public execution would certainly have drawn people in from all over the county and surrounding counties. It was written at the time that on the morning of the execution, by 10:00 A.M. people were arriving from "every direction," and this would certainly have been consistent with a large turnout of people.[48] If this estimate is accurate – as I believe it is – then that is an incredible amount of people to have gathered in rural 1819 Goshen. To place the crowd size into context, we can look to the 1820 census. According to the census, the Township of Goshen in 1820 had a population of 3,441 persons, with a total county population of 41,213 persons.[49] If we accept that the estimate of 15,000 persons is accurate, then nearly 36% of the population of Orange County would have been in attendance at the executions! That's pretty impressive.

THE MAN WHO HANGED TEED & DUNNING

Sheriff Moses DeWitt Burnet was 27 years old when the duties of his office required him to carry out the public executions of James Teed and David Dunning. As a law enforcement officer, I have wondered how Sheriff Burnet reacted when he first learned he was going to need to preside over a quadruple hanging. It was certainly his responsibility and I am sure that, when he first took office, it was a responsibility of which he was aware. However, there had not been a hanging in Orange County since 1779, so putting myself in his shoes, I wonder if he viewed a potential hanging as something that may happen, but was unlikely. Just as most police officers know that they may be called upon to use deadly force and take the life of another in the line of duty, most will go their entire careers without ever being placed in such a situation. But it is a potential that is always there, and most police officers train and prepare for that day and hope that it will not come. So I tend to think that way of Sheriff Burnet. He probably knew it could happen, just never really expected that it would. So what was he thinking when he initially had to organize and preside over a quadruple hanging? I have been unable to find anything written by Burnet which may shed light upon his feelings towards the hanging, so we may never know.

What is known is that he viewed this as a serious and solemn event. He clearly wanted the execution to be as dignified as possible, making sure that the sentence of the court was carried out with dignity, and the public given the necessary warning against crime that would come with it. I am sure that he felt little relief when Hodges and Conkling were pardoned: for he still had to end the lives of two men, albeit under the auspices of a judicial hanging.

Sheriff Burnet was commended by the press for his behavior and coordination of the executions. His address to the large mass of people who had gathered to witness the hangings was printed throughout the United States. In one letter to a newspaper, local attorney Jonas Storey complimented the actions of Sheriff Burnet by saying, "... from the commencement of the preparations at the prison, till Teed and Dunning had taken their flight to 'worlds unknown.' [sic.] your whole conduct so distinctly marked the dignity of the officer, and the man of feeling, that one spontaneous burst of the most unequivocal admiration must have issued from the bosom

Moses DeWitt Burnet (1792-1876). By Charles Loring Elliott c. 1835. Oil on Canvas, 30⅛ x 24¾ in. Accession #1953.34. Collection of the New-York Historical Society.

of every beholder."[50] I find Storey's remarks interesting – especially in light of the fact that he had represented David Dunning during the trial.

So what became of the man who hanged Teed and Dunning? Burnet, a War of 1812 veteran, moved to Syracuse, New York, in the mid 1820s where he became a prominent member of the community and a respected businessman. He died December 29, 1876, at the age of 84. He was survived by his only son, John Burnet, who, in 1886, donated 115 acres of land to the City of Syracuse, New York, for a park in honor of his late father.[51] Moses D. Burnet Park is still there in Syracuse. Few people probably know who the park is named after, and fewer people know that in 1819, he presided over a double hanging in Orange County, New York.

DUNNING'S DISTURBING DENIAL

David Dunning had, in his final moments, insisted that he had not used the gun to beat Jennings to the head. He took his denial to the grave with him. This must have been distressing to some of the witnesses of the execution, and they may have legitimately wondered if Jack had lied about Dunning's involvement in the crime. This would have been a frightening revelation: if Jack had lied, then Dunning may have been hung unjustly.

Immediately after the executions, an unidentified man visited Hodges at the jail. The conversation which followed left no doubts to the public as to Jack's integrity and honesty. I view the discrepancy between Jack's and Dunning's stories as a major, unanswered question. Who was telling the truth? I have included a transcript of the post-execution conversation to assist you in drawing your own conclusions:

> 'Well Jack – Dunning has gone out of the world, and his last words were, *that he did not take the gun out of your hands, and beat the old man over the head.* If he has spoken the truth, *you,* of all beings, are the most execrable monster, that ever existed in the shape of man, and it would hardly surprise me, if the just vengeance of Heaven, should issue in a flame of wrath, and consume *your* body to ashes, before *his* corpse is cold in the grave!'
>
> Jack replied with calmness and composure:–
>
> '*If I had been guilty of swearing false, to take away the life of an innocent fellow being, then I must expect the severest judgment of God: I am sorry Dunning has gone out of the world with a lie in his mouth; but I have spoken the truth, and Dunning knew that I spoke the truth: my conscience is at ease on the subject.*'[52]

There was also a last moment attempt at shaking Jack's story and credibility. The day before the hangings, David Conkling arranged with the sheriff to meet with Jack. By this time, Conkling knew that he had been pardoned, but this information had been kept secret from Hodges, who expected to hang the following day. A debtor imprisoned in the jail reported the conversation which was later printed by the local press after the executions.[53] The excerpt below illustrates that Conkling was attempting to get Jack to make a pre-hanging declaration that he had lied, under the pretense that he [Conkling] was looking out for Jack's soul:

> *Conkling.* We have but a short time to live, and I hope before we die we shall reconcile ourselves to each other and to our God, that we may die in peace.

Jack. Ah, God knows this in the earnest desire of my heart.

Conkling. But Jack, can you expect to die in peace if you persist in lies until death shall seal your lips?

Jack. If I conceal a lie, or harbor an evil heart I can expect no mercy from God: What lies have I told, Mr. Conkling?

Conkling. The conversation you swore to in the oat-field?

Jack. . . . you well know that such a conversation as I swore to did take place in the oatfield.

Conkling. I have no recollection of it. The conversation at the *hovel* too, was not that false?

Jack. . . . you certainly know we had such a conversation, and that every word I swore to was true.

Conkling. I have no recollection of any such conversation there. Well, did you not tell a falsehood about my loading the gun? You know what Hendershot swore to?

Jack. Hendershot swore to what was not true. You know that you loaded the gun for me . . . [and] another fact, which I forgot to mention on the trial: Do you not remember when you loaded the gun, that you told me I had better take with me the *large butcher knife?*

Conkling. (after a pause) I have no recollection of loading the gun, or saying anything about the butcher knife.

Jack. . . . you deny everything and remember nothing . . . it is useless for us to talk. I have spoken the truth, and my conscience is at rest on that subject.[54]

If Conkling sought to clear himself, Teed, and Dunning from any guilt, it didn't work. The conversation between Hodges and Conkling was certainly aimed at getting Jack to make an inconsistent statement or at least admit to one falsehood. Had Jack admitted to making false statements at the trial, would Teed and Dunning have received a reprieve or pardon? That is a question rendered moot by Jack's steadfast answers.

Any doubts about the truth of Jack's story had been dismissed and, with Dunning's guilt affirmed, the community could rest comfortably and without concern that the wrong man had been executed. In the coming decades, Jack Hodges would never waver from his account of the crime, leaving no doubts that he had told the truth.

HISTORICAL LEGACY

Life in Orange County gradually returned to normal. But the sensational murder, trials, and public execution were far from forgotten. Three pamphlets were published in 1819 and sold to the public. They survive today to offer us a connection with our past and sources of information which have proven invaluable in developing an accurate and factually reliable account of this historical event. These big three sources are suggested reading for anyone who wants to delve deeper into the details of the case:

Report of the Trials of the Murderers of Richard Jennings. At a Special Court of Oyer and Terminer for the County of Orange, Held at the Court House in the Village of Goshen on Tuesday, February 23rd, 1819: With Arguments of Counsel. This is the only transcript of the trials available and offers insight into the case, as well as nineteenth century legal proceedings. It is not an official court record or transcript, and it is unclear what, if any, official court records were created. If there was an official transcript, is has been long been lost to time. It has been suggested that the Sewards and the Conklings made a concerted effort to conceal records and obliterate all references of the trial and incident.[55]

An Account of the Murder of Richard Jennings; Together with the Confessions of Teed & Dunning. As the title suggests, this is an account of the crime, trials, and punishments of the criminals. The pamphlet also contains the confessions of both James Teed and David Dunning, and the cover page has an engraving which depicts the double hanging. This pamphlet was plagiarized and repackaged in several books on sensational and famous crimes which were published in the 1830s and 1840s.[56]

THE REV. EZRA FISK, D.D.

Rev. Ezra Fisk, D.D., pastor of the First Presbyterian Church, Goshen, New York.[57]

Sin Finds Out the Criminal. A Sermon Delivered at the Execution of James Teed and David Dunning, for the Murder of Richard Jennings, April 16, 1819. When I first read that the execution sermon delivered by Rev. Fisk took over two hours, I had an image of a fire and brimstone preacher admonishing the crowds on the dangers of sin, while telling the condemned they were about to suffer eternal damnation! Being the stubborn person that I am, I spent two years tracking down a copy of the sermon, anxious to learn what the Rev. Fisk had preached from the scaffold. The text that I would ultimately receive was far from fire and brimstone. *Sin Finds Out the Criminal* is a well-written, thoughtful, inspirational sermon, which served to admonish those gathered against sin and to remind the men about to suffer death that they may be saved in the next world.

I also don't believe that the sermon took two long hours to deliver, and from the accounts of the executions, the men appeared to be greatly affected by the words of the divine services. I am sure that in their last terrifying minutes on earth, Teed and Dunning drew some comfort from Rev. Fisk's discourse and in particular, his conclusion:

> Now, O compassionate Savior, who didst pardon and accept the thief on the cross, stoop down and lead these dying men through that gloomy vale– Conduct their spirits to the bosom of glory, sheltered and washed by thy blood– That they may live and reign with thee forever. Amen.[58]

In the mid-1890s, Goshen First Presbyterian Church Pastor Robert Bruce Clark would write of the sermon: "in the application and appeal to the condemned men at the close, both justice and mercy are interwrought like mingled lightning and rainbow, and the judicial phrase, 'May God have mercy on your souls' is worked out in detail . . . "[59]

I wonder if Rev. Fisk ever thought his words would be reflected upon so many years in the future. Or, for that matter, Judge Van Ness, Sheriff Burnet, or any number of other people connected to this case. The actions on April 16, 1819, of so many people would forever become part of our history, even if many in the century to follow would know little, if anything, of the details of the crime and trials which led up to that awful moment on the gallows, and the ultimate fates of those who were spared the noose.

CONFESSION OF JAMES TEED

The night before his death, James Teed made an oral confession to members of the clergy. The confession was later printed in the newspapers, as well as in the pamphlet published after the hangings, *An Account of the Murder of Richard Jennings; Together with the Confessions of Teed & Dunning,* as follows:

TEED'S CONFESSION

On the evening before the execution, the Rev. Mr. Johnson, and the Rev. Mr. Wilson had a conversation with Teed by himself. By request, he was separated from Conkling and Dunning, with a view to this conversation.

> SIN FINDS OUT THE CRIMINAL.
>
> # A SERMON,
>
> DELIVERED
>
> AT
>
> ## THE EXECUTION
>
> OF
>
> JAMES TEED AND DAVID DUNNING,
>
> FOR THE MURDER OF
>
> RICHARD JENNINGS,
>
> APRIL 16, 1819 :
>
> BY REV. EZRA FISK, A. M.
>
> " *Whoso sheddeth man's blood by man shall his blood be shed.*"
>
> JEHOVAH.
>
> GOSHEN :
>
> PRINTED BY T. B. CROWELL.
>
> 1819.

Rev. Ezra Fisk's words must of made an impression to have been published as a pamphlet in the fall of 1819.[60]

It was stated to him, that his duty to society, and to God, rendered it proper for him to state the whole truth relative to the part which he had taken in the murder of Jennings, and that his concern with this world was near an end.

He said, he wished to state the truth candidly, and would endeavor to do so, though he could not recollect all that he had said on the subject. Jennings, he said, had provoked him greatly, and that he had had very bad feelings towards him; that he had often spoken very loosely respecting Jennings; that he and Conkling had often talked before Jack, about putting the old man out of the way; but that he could not recollect all. He was asked, if the manner in which he had talked to Jack had been the means of instigating him to commit the murder? He replied, he thought it had. He was then asked, if he remembered whether he intended it to have that effect? His answer was, "I cannot well remember what I wished. I did not think that Jack would kill Jennings, but I might have intended to excite Jack to

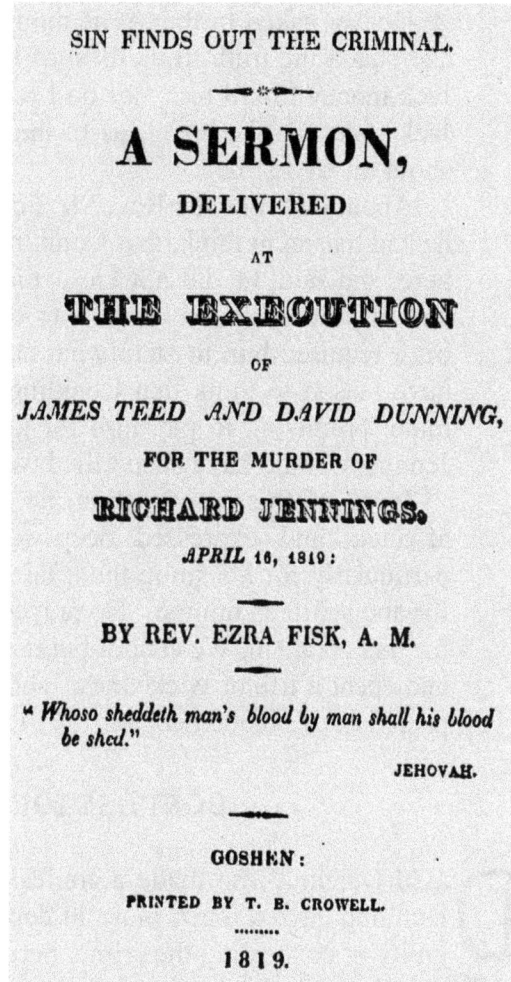

kill him. Jack told me he would kill Jennings, but he was afraid I would not like it, as he *(Jennings)* was my relation. I told Jack I did not regard that."

He was asked further, if he thought that Jack, in his testimony before the court, had stated the truth to the best of his knowledge? He answered, "I never offered Jack money to kill him, nor do I remember that I had any talk on that subject. As Jack states, in the hovel; as to the rest, I think he may have thought all he said about me to be true."

About this time the Rev. Mr. Fonda came into room. Teed was asked, whether he had reason to think, that Conkling had hired Jack to kill Jennings? He hesitated here, and said, he did not know that he should state any thing but what he knew himself. He appeared to wish to evade; but when he was told, that candor and truth required him to state what he thought he had reason to believe, he said, "I have reason to think that Conkling did bargain with Jack, in his own name and mine, promising to pay him for killing Jennings. I have reason to believe, that Jennings would have been killed two years ago, if it had not been for me."

In all of this conversation, he appeared to be in great distress, very greatly affected, and expressed deep sorrow for the wickedness of his life, and particularly for his sin in the affair of Jennings. On the scaffold, he prayed aloud for about fifteen minutes. He prayed for the pardon of all his sins, and particularly for this great sin. We cannot but remark, how impressive the fact, that a man, who had spent a life of wickedness, should be heard, when near death, praying in the presence, of 20,000 people![61]

CONFESSION OF DAVID DUNNING

David Dunning also made a confession on the eve of his execution. Unlike James Teed, Dunning gave a much more in depth and lengthy confession, and reasserted that he was guilty of concealing the crime, but not being directly a part of it. His confession was, like Teed's, widely printed, whetting the public's appetite for all of the salacious details of the crime:

DUNNING'S CONFESSION

Made April 15, 1819, in the presence of Mrs. Dunning and John Dunning.
                                                        Richard F. Cadle.

Previously to the making the following confession, Mr. Dunning was addressed in these words:

"A sense of duty and a regard to your interest compel me now to intreat you to think of your awful situation, and, in the confession you are about to make, to adhere to the truth. You are a dying man; in a few moments you will be in the eternal world; you will stand before the judgment seat of God – and if you now wilfully mistake and utter any falsehood, I verily believe there is no mercy in store for you. All liars will have their part in the lake which burneth with fire and brimstone – the smoke of their torment will ascend up forever – they will suffer the pains of the worm that never dies, and of the fire which never is quenched. God is now present with us, he sees your heart, be knows and will hear what you are about to utter; and if you deceive us you cannot deceive him, but he will swear in his wrath that you shall not enter into his rest! If you are guilty of the murder of Mr. Jennings, you must, as you hope for salvation, confess it; nothing else will answer – private and secret sorrow is not sufficient – God requires you to disclose your guilt. It is no matter what the world thinks – your soul is of more value than ten thousand worlds – you will shortly be removed from the earth, and you will find it to have been your true wisdom to have secured the favor of God."

DAVID DUNNING states that "he went to live at Mr. Teed's in the month of April, 1818. He says there never was any dispute between him and Richard Jennings. He had a conversation with Mr. Jennings last fall, who was going to serve a notice on David Conkling to attend the Circuit Court, when he gave him encouragement that he should not lose his labor, when possession should be obtained of the property that had been so long in dispute. Mr. Jennings asked him if Mr. Conkling had promised to indemnify him, and if he had security? He answered that he had a promise, but no security for its fulfilment. Mr. Jennings further told him that he would not wish to do to him (Dunning) as Mr. Conkling had done to him – shut him up in prison and reap his grain.

The next time Mr. Jennings and he met, was at Mr. Coe Teed's, soon after the circuit court, and they were friendly to each other. He asked Mr. Jennings if he expected to regain the land, he replied that he did. He then asked if, when he came in possession of it, he would refrain from prosecuting Mr. Conkling, and live on friendly terms? Mr. Jennings answered, he would not, for Mr. Conkling had locked him up in jail, and kept him twenty four hours without meat or drink. Returning Mr. Jennings mentioned that he would not allow Mr. Teed to remain in the house, but that he, Dunning might. This was the last time they conversed together; and they parted, he believes, with mutual good will.

Soon after the circuit court, Mr. Conkling and Mr. Teed drank tea in his room. The conversation turning, while they were in Mr. Teed's room, on Mr. Jennings, Dunning said in a jocose manner, they had better get Hubbard and put him out of the way. Mr. Conkling observed, that Hubbard would not do, as he belonged to the same church that his mother did; adding, as Dunning thinks, that there could be dependence placed in Jack. After tea Conkling and Teed went out of doors, and he heard them conversing by the side of the house next to the road. Mr. Conkling did not come into the house again, nor, as far as he recollects, did he see him before Jennings' body was found. He does not remember hearing Mr. Jennings' name mentioned afterwards, until Jack Hodges came to Sugarloaf, the Saturday night before the murder. His son Lewis came out from Teed's room into his, and said Jack had the old musket; he asked what he was going to do with it, his son replied that Charles Teed had said he was going to kill old Dick. Jack came then into his room, where were Hila Conkling and Mrs. Dunning; Jack asked him to go out, and told him that he intended to take the life of Mr. Jennings; he thought him in earnest, but did not dissuade him from the purpose, not supposing it his business or duty, and Jack at the same time being considerably intoxicated. He did not ask Jack if he was come to assist him, nor tell him that he himself was ready.

On Sunday, while they were at the haystack, Jack said he would like to see Mr. Jennings; Dunning asked him if he had been hired by Mr. Conkling to kill Jennings? to which he replied, no, he did not want any pay – Conkling is too good a man to be used as Jennings had used him. Mr. Dunning told him he would never have any peace if he did this act, as his spirit would appear to him; Jack said he had killed, as far as he can recollect his expressions, many a better man; and told him the particulars of his murdering a white man in New York. Jack stated that there was a mulatto girl in New York, to whom he was much attached, and that while he was gone to sea, she was kept by a white man. Being informed of this after his return, and having become acquainted with his rival and drank with him on a Sabbath day, they went at evening on board some vessel, where he shot him with a pistol belonging to the mate, and threw him overboard. Mr. Dunning told Jack he had better not commit the murder, and Jack then concluded to drive Teed's cow to Mr. Weaden's the next day, and as Teed was not at home as he had promised, he would go home, and return another day. On Monday morning, Mr. Dunning was told either by Jack or Teed's children, that Mr. Jennings was passing; and Jack then went into Teed's room, brought out the gun, and as he went through his room said he was going to shoot a partridge. Dunning acknowleges he thought the intention of Jack was to destroy Mr. Jennings, but most foolishly and wickedly, as he now laments, did not interfere to prevent the murder, supposing it was not his business, also thinking that Mr. Jennings would be in sight of Coe Teed's house before Jack could come up with him, and that probably he would not commit the murder in so public a place; and further, that Conkling and Teed and Mrs. Teed were so anxious for the death of Mr. Jennings, that he did not exert himself to oppose their wishes. He states he was chopping wood at the door, when he heard a gun fired, and believes he said, "I guess he is dead." Mrs. Teed, he thinks, then observed, she feared there was no such good news. He was at the stable when Jack returned, who told him he had killed Jennings, and then took the broken pieces of the gun into the house, through the door commonly used by the family of Mr. Teed. Jack soon came into Dunning's room, who thinks he told him he ought to inform him of what was done, fearing lest he himself should be blamed; when Jack said – oh no, Dunning, you would not want to have me hung – and earnestly begged him not to reveal the murder, and also threatened his life and his family's if he did. He told Dunning he found Mr. Jennings in the woods, who made some enquiries respecting the timber, and asked him if the gun was loaded, he answered it was not. He then fired; but Mr. Jennings not being killed, he struck him violently on the head, and at every stroke he groaned. Soon after this account was given, Mr. Dunning promised Jack he would not disclose his crime unless he should be examined under oath. Mr. Dunning states he was not employed to decoy Mr. Jennings into the woods, that he might be murdered by Jack. He further states that on the night after the murder, he asked Mrs. Dunning if he had not better go to Sugarloaf to inform against Jack, and that he did not go, as she was afraid to be left in the house with Jack; and not sufficiently considering that this was his duty, nor aware of the consequences of its neglect, he afterwards concealed his knowledge of the murder.

He confesses that he was not at East Division on the day Mr. Jennings was missing, and that he was guilty of falsehood in his declaration to Mr. Vanduzer.

He states that on the day Mr. Jennings' body was found, he was loading wood at a short distance from it, that he saw what appeared like a hat, but not the body;

that he however thought it probable the body was near there. He believes he did mention Mr. Jennings was gone to the Delaware to procure shingles for a barn. He further states that when he and Mrs. Teed and Mrs. Dunning were at Sugarloaf about to appear before the coroner's jury, he begged of them to tell the truth as Jack had stated.

He wishes to warn all not to become interested in any property, which is the subject of dispute, from the awful condition to which he is reduced. He believes he is punished for his general sins, and more especially for an impious wish expressed by him the last summer, after the loss of a horse he much valued, when "he hoped God would take him away next, as he met with nothing but misfortunes on earth." He acknowleges that he is guilty of the crime of concealing the murder, but not of actual agency in it. He looks back with sorrow on his past life, and hopes his miserable death will prove a useful lesson to all who live carelessly. He confesses the justice of God in his sufferings, and if he exchanges this for a happier world, does not much lament that he is to be cut off by an ignominious and sudden death, He professes his forgiveness of all mankind, and particularly of him on whose testimony he was convicted, and begs of God to forgive him all his trespasses, before he goes hence and is no more seen."[62]

THE EXECUTION SITE TODAY

The location of the gallows, as mentioned earlier in the chapter, was an area between present day 17A and Police Drive in Goshen, New York. It can be viewed from the area of 30 Hatfield Lane, looking out towards the hills which make up a natural amphitheater.

When looking at these modern-day photos, transport yourself 194 years (or more depending upon when you read this!) into the past. Envision 15,000 people crowded around the gallows, trying to push their way closer for a better view; the militia and cavalry encircling the scaffold; and the site of the condemned men kneeling in prayer and minutes away from death.

This may be the area where Teed & Dunning were executed in 1819.

Area between present day 17A and Police Drive where the gallows may have been erected.

Looking towards the area where the scaffold may have been erected.

Chapter 4

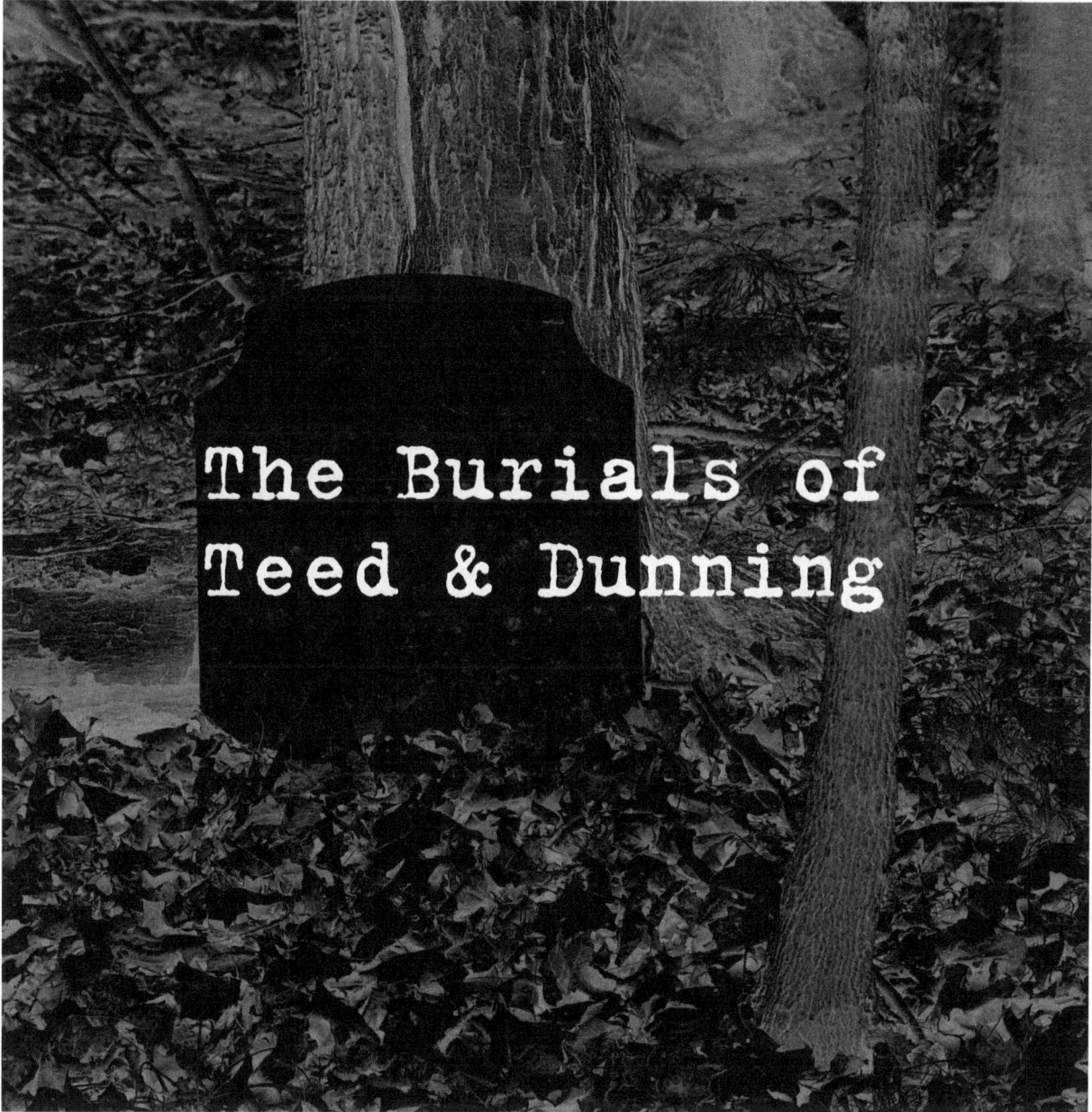

The Burials of
Teed & Dunning

STAKED TO THE GROUND:
WHAT REALLY HAPPENED TO THE BODIES
OF TEED AND DUNNING?

The burials of Teed and Dunning are, by far, the most bizarre and intriguing aspects of this entire case. When I first began researching the incident, I was fascinated by the lore surrounding the disposal of their bodies. It certainly helped contribute to my obsession to uncover as many facts and details as possible and, in a way, became a focal point of research. In this chapter, I solve the mystery surrounding the burials of the condemned men, and definitely answer the question of what really happened to the bodies of Teed and Dunning. The facts as I have uncovered them may not be as sinister, but they are still intriguing and lend even more fascination to this event.

On the hill behind the large tree is the location of the Sugar Loaf Cemetery where, according to tradition, the bodies of Teed and Dunning were buried. [1]

According to the lore, after Teed and Dunning had been cut down from the gallows, there was a major problem: where to bury the bodies. It was said that no local cemetery would allow the men to be buried within their walls, and the owners of a small private cemetery (identified in one source as a Mr. James Hallock and his wife) finally agreed to permit the men to be buried there on the condition that the murderers be buried outside of the cemetery gates. Perhaps driven by superstition that an executed criminal could return from the grave, a group of men visited the cemetery that night and drove locust posts into the ground above each grave and, presumably, into the coffins and bodies. The locust stakes were said to be visible for many years after.[2]

What may have fueled this macabre act? It was not uncommon for the body of an executed criminal to be buried in unconsecrated ground, so this aspect of the lore tends to lend credibility to the claim. Some superstitions held that a body buried in unconsecrated soil may not rest and could potentially return from the grave and terrorize the living. Thus, driving a stake into a body (think of a vampire having a stake driven through the heart!) would keep the corpse in the grave. Did the party of men go there to *keep* James Teed and David Dunning in their graves? While this late night staking party would make a great scene for a horror film, it never happened.

I realize that I may just have committed historical heresy by dismissing a timeworn legend. The facts and evidence, however, tell the real story of what happened to Teed and Dunning's mortal remains. And the truth, in this matter, is almost as strange as the fiction.

EVALUATING THE EVIDENCE

A bold statement dismissing a local legend requires a preponderance of evidence

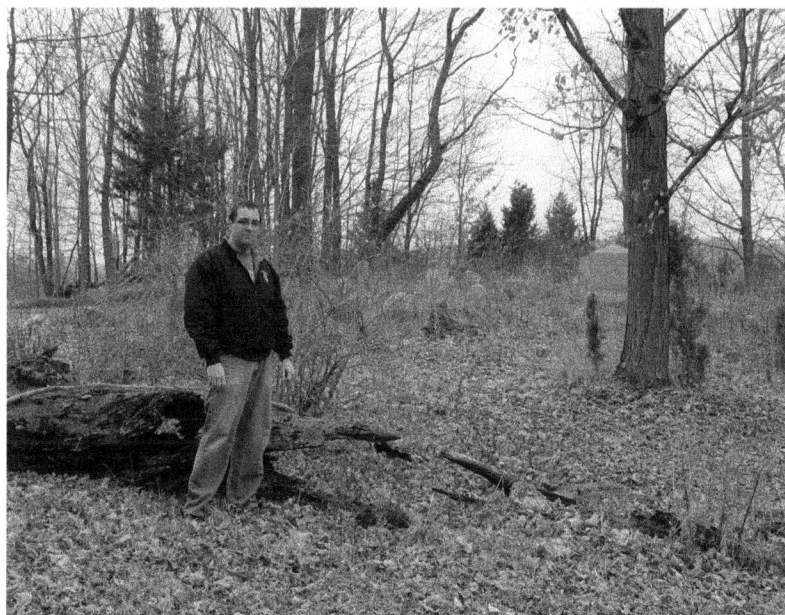

Photo of me taken at the Sugar Loaf Cemetery in the fall of 2009. This was early on in my research into the case.

and information which tend to support the claim. Since beginning the research into this and other historical crimes, I have learned the importance of critically evaluating sources. Sources closest to the events being studied are generally more reliable than sources written at a later time. Thus, my first step was to try and locate primary source documents which would support the burial story and the staking of the graves. As of the time that this book went to press, I have not been able to find any. In fact, the primary source documents I did locate provided evidence to the contrary and aided in making my final determination on this issue. The only sources I could locate which mention the burial legend all seem to be from the 1970s to the present.

Even in the main published histories of Orange County, New York, there are no mentions of the burials or stakings. The lack of printed accounts in these sources does not automatically dismiss the lore, but it certainly doesn't help support it. In fact, in one account, the only mention of the hanging has to do with the man who made the rope (see Chapter 2, page 83), and another has the wrong dates. One volume of Orange County history omits any reference to the murder whatsoever.[3]

The newspaper accounts of the executions, including the detailed article from the April 20, 1819, *Orange County Patriot*, make no mention of the burials. If the lore is correct – if both men had to be buried outside the walls of a cemetery and had stakes driven into their graves – then this would most certainly have been included in the first printed articles about the hangings.

Photos taken at the Sugar Loaf Cemetery during my 2009 visit. The cemetery is not maintained, and I suggest going in the fall if you wish to visit yourself.

I did not locate any evidence of locust stakes, and trying to determine where the fence or walls of the old cemetery may have been was rendered nearly impossible by the passage of time.

The press had happily published every other detail of the executions, so why would this not have been included? Even if the full details of the burials were not known when the first articles had gone to press, they would have certainly shown up in the subsequent articles in the weeks that followed. But there is nothing in any of the newspapers that hint at the hasty burials and stakings.

The evidence which dismisses the lore, however, is overwhelming and tells the story of what really happened to the bodies, and also hints at what may have generated the story of the clandestine staking of the graves.

THE ULTIMATE FATE OF TEED'S BODY

Evidence suggesting that James Teed received a more normal burial can be found in the April 27, 1819, edition of the *Orange County Patriot*, as well as in letters written after the execution by members of his family. According to the newspaper account, after the hanging, James Teed was brought to David Conkling's home and buried on Sunday with "funeral solemnities."[4] This brief description of Teed's burial is not consistent with a hurried burial at the only cemetery willing to accept the body, and, again, there is no mention of a locust stake having been driven into the grave sometime after burial. Based upon the newspaper account, it seems that the circumstances surrounding Teed's burial were not out of the ordinary.

More compelling evidence was found in a collection of Teed family letters held at the Delaware County Historical Association, Delhi, NY. A letter written to a John Teed from Nathanial and Deborah Knapp dated August 16, 1819, references James Teed's unfortunate fate.[5] John Teed was married to Phanny Teed, James' sister, and was also their cousin. I have transcribed the relevant portions of the first page of the letter:

> . . . I reseved your letter that requested me to send one of them little books to you but I have not sen one nor I dont care to see any For I think that so unfare a thing shuld happn it grieves me some and all of his agants to think that after the trial was over judgement against fore of them condemd to dy that thay should then releas the principle in the Murder and Principe in the Acessory and have hung the two least guilty in my opinon that I dont care See or hare of such triel in my Life agane I have Don all that I could Doe to get a repreve But all in vaine hang James thay Wold and after I found that thare was Know Parden for him I Went to the Sherif and reqested the Body of James Teed and had him laid out on my own table and Buried him with his Children he had gon & left us to morn his hard faight But not Without Having a hope that he has gon happy and know vists with his Saver Who was hang on a tree . . .[6]

Four months to the day after the hanging, a reliable source is writing about having claimed the body of James Teed and that he "buried him with his children."[7] Did James Teed's sister and her husband claim his body and arrange for him to be buried?

August the 16th 1819

Dare Brother and Sister I one more set own to wright
to you with plesure Consarning our willfare We are all
well at Present hopping that these fu Lions may find
you all in goying the sam Blesing as thay leve us
I resevd your letter that requsted me to send one of
them little books to you but I have not sen one nor
I dont care to see any For I think that so unfare
a thing shule hppe it grieves me sore all of his agants
to think that after the triel wafs over juegment agnst
fore of them condemd to dy that thay should then Releas
the princple in the Murder and Principle in the tresserry
and have hung the two the least guilty in my opinon
that I dont care see nor have of such triel in my
Life agane I have don all that I could Doe to get
a repeve But all in vane hang James thay wild
and after I found that thare was know parden
for him I went to the Sherif and requsted the
Body of James Teed and had him laid out on
my own troble and Buried him with his
Children he has gon & left us to mern his hard
faight But not without Leving a hope that
he has gon happy and know rests with his
Saver who was hong on a tree Coe and
Benjamin Teed are know at home on the
old farm and are know Wanting to sell the
farm very much to go to ohio Benjamin
Iaryr and fanaly are well at Present

2010.22.21

First page of the August 16, 1819 letter to John and Fanny Teed from Nathaniel and Deborah Knapp. From the Teed Family Letters, Delaware County Historical Association, Delhi, NY.

I believe that this is the most likely scenario. The letter writer also references that he [James Teed] was "buried with his children" which seems to refer to the Teed children being present at the burial, as opposed to him being buried with previously deceased children of which I was unable to find any evidence.[8] All of this is contradictory to the lore that no cemetery would accept Teed's body. There is one minor discrepancy between this letter and the *Orange County Patriot* account: the newspaper article stated that Teed had been taken to David Conkling's home after the hanging, whereas, in the letter, it appears as if the Knapps claimed the body and brought it to their home. This does not in any way detract from the validity of the circumstances surrounding Teed's burial which have been uncovered.[9]

On a side note, in the letter, there is mention about sending a little book. This is a reference, I believe, to one of the pamphlets published about the crime and seems to have been requested by John Teed, who may have been interested in learning more about what had led his cousin to the gallows. The Knapps, it seems, were not too keen on sending it.[10]

Other letters in the Teed Family Letters Collection shed light on how the family felt about the executions, believing that James Teed had been wronged. A letter, which appears to be dated January 8, 1820, from Julia Ann Teed (James's sister) to John Teed contains a statement in which she writes that "they had condemned the innocent and clerd the gilty." Julia must have been particularly affected by the trial and execution of her brother. In a letter dated March 1820, Julia expresses her hope to John Teed that ". . . they [other family members] will knot look on us with contempt because of our Brother I think he was a clear of consenting to the murder as any of us. . . ." His family clearly believed in his innocence and mourned the unjust loss of a brother.[11]

I also believe that, if Teed had been buried according to the lore (and a locust stake driven into the grave), that this is something that would most likely have been mentioned in one of the Teed letters. If the family felt that the sentence was unjust, then they certainly would have felt that the disposition of his earthly remains (as described in the lore) was another injustice heaped onto the deceased Teed.

So where is James Teed buried? Here is where fact and fiction may actually merge into something credible. I kept going back to the cemetery – why Sugar Loaf Cemetery? How was this selected as the location of the bodies? I could find nothing to suggest that this was the right cemetery; in fact, the owner of the cemetery in which Teed and Dunning were allegedly buried, was identified in one source as being a Mr. James Hallock.[12] There are no existing records which show any Hallocks buried in the Sugar Loaf Cemetery; however, there is a James Hallock buried in a "Howell – Hallock Burying Ground" on the west side of Sugar Loaf Mountain.[13]

The link which connects James Teed to the Sugar Loaf Cemetery is a rather simple one: his sister, Deborah Knapp, and several of her children are buried there. So this would explain how Sugar Loaf Cemetery became interwoven with the lore. Is James Teed buried there? I don't know. One dead end in my research has been identifying a specific burial site for Teed. I know he was buried, but I don't know where. If his sister, Deborah Knapp, and her husband had claimed the body and buried him, it just may be that he is buried in that little cemetery on the hill where legend says he had been buried. There was no burial outside of the walls and there was no stake driven into the grave. If he had been buried there – which I think is very likely – then he would have been buried within the confines of the cemetery. However, the exact location and plot, if it existed, are now lost to time.

DAVID DUNNING'S POSTMORTEM WANDERINGS

David Dunning did not rest in peace after his gruesome death on the gallows. Dunning is an enigma: there is little known about him, and piecing together anything about his life was difficult. So piecing together what happened to him after death posed an even greater challenge.

What is known about Dunning's burial is that his body was claimed by his friends after the execution and he was buried later in the day.[14] As with Teed, there is no reference or mention of a problem with finding a cemetery willing to accept Dunning's body, nor to staking the grave with a locust pole. Those events I have proven didn't happen. But what did happen to David Dunning after his burial may explain some of the lore and are, in my opinion, even more bizarre and fascinating.

David Dunning, it seemed, did not want to stay dead. There were reports that he had been seen and, even more troubling, had been spoken with after the executions. There were reports that he had been restored to life and headed west to a new life. And then there was the rumor that the anatomists had dug up his body and dissected it, and yet another which stated he was dead but had never been buried.[16]

Those were a lot of rumors to swirl around the death of one man! The rumors generated enough interest – and even fear – as to require further investigation. On the evening of April 27, 1819,

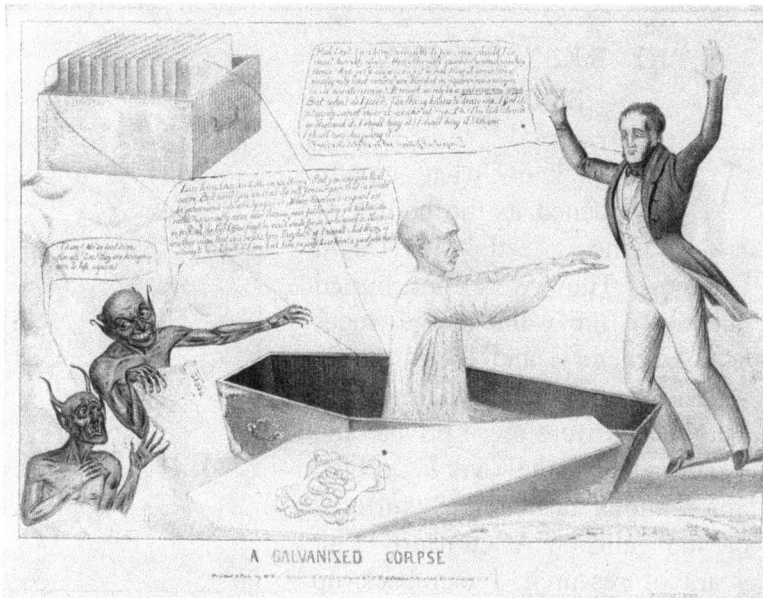

An 1836 cartoon depicting a corpse resurrected from the grave through galvanic experimentation.[15]

nearly a week and a half after his death, a group of residents set out for Dunning's gravesite. Are you picturing a mob armed with torches and pitchforks? Well, it probably wasn't that chaotic, but their intent was clear: to determine whether or not David Dunning's body was still in the grave. Once the group had arrived at the place of burial (which was never identified in any of the newspaper accounts), the coffin was unearthed and, in what must have been a terrifying and anxious few moments, opened. To the relief of all, the body of David Dunning was still laying there in the coffin in the same position it had been in when he had been interred. David Dunning wasn't roaming the countryside as a reanimated corpse, nor was he happily on his way west after having been secretly resuscitated. He was quite dead and in his grave where he belonged.[17]

But the rumors surrounding his death (or rather *after* death) were not entirely unfounded. Apparently, there had been attempts to restore Dunning to life. "Some simple experiments" had been tried on Dunning, but were unsuccessful.[18] What exactly were these experiments? Most likely galvanic experiments aimed at using electricity to reanimate Dunning's dead body. The bodies of executed criminals were usually sought after for such experiments, and it is not the only case where I have come across a reference to experiments being attempted on a recently executed criminal. (The hanging of Jesse Strang in Albany, 1827, is one example – Strang's case is the subject of another book in the *Crime Scene* series.) Galvanism was quite popular during this time period, and perhaps those experiments contributed to the rumors of Dunnings post-mortem wanderings. It certainly provided some inspiration to author Mary Shelley, who would write Frankenstein in 1818.

The postmortem interest in David Dunning passed from the pages of the newspapers and memory. But did these rumors help fuel the local lore that would later be written about in the 1970s? I think they may have. Dunning was alleged to have been seen after his death, as well as having never had been buried, and that he had been restored to life and headed out west. Then there was the very real late night exhumation to verify that Dunning was still in the grave. It is speculation, but this may have all become interwoven to give us the story that Barrell wrote about in the 1970s. Without knowing his sources on this lore, this remains as speculation.

THE REST OF THE STORY

We now know what actually happened to the bodies of James Teed and David Dunning. They were not buried outside of the walls of the Sugar Loaf Cemetery, and locust stakes were never driven into their graves. The burials were more private and sedate than the very public, ignominious deaths they suffered on the gallows. After nearly four years of research, I can back up those facts with credible sources. What I can't provide is an actual final resting place for either Teed

Another view of the Sugar Loaf Cemetery. The cemetery occupies the top of the small hill.

or Dunning. I have speculated that it is likely Teed may have been buried in the Sugar Loaf Cemetery, but I can't prove that. And David Dunning's final resting place is still elusive as of the time that this book went to press. Perhaps someday their graves will be located, but for now Teed and Dunning are holding on to one last mystery: their final resting places.

A view from the edge of the cemetery looking towards the road. Is this the edge of the cemetery where lore has it that Teed & Dunning were buried?

Is the body of James Teed buried somewhere in the Sugar Loaf Cemetery? Perhaps in an unmarked and long forgotten grave, James Teed clings to one last mystery.

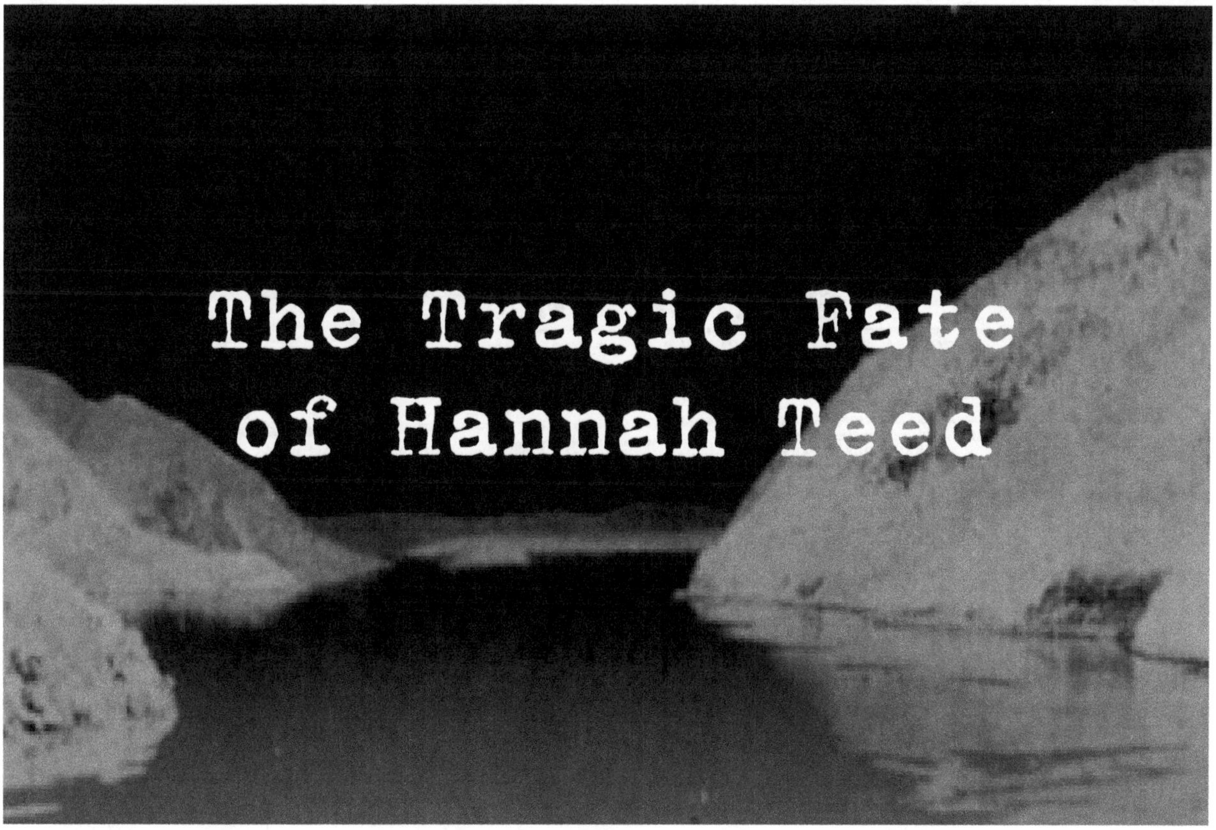
The Tragic Fate
of Hannah Teed

THE ULTIMATE JUDGEMENT OF HANNAH TEED

T he story of Hannah Teed after her conviction is the shortest chapter in this book. I had entertained thoughts of meshing her story in with another chapter, but I devoted a chapter to the burials of James Teed and David Dunning, and a chapter each on David Conkling and Jack Hodges on their lives after the trials. So to be fair, I decided to go with a brief, but important look at her life after April of 1819.

It may be brief, but then again, so was her life after she faded from the spotlight. I was unable to find any information about her for the time period between 1819 and the summer of 1823, when her lifeless body was found floating in the Hudson River four years after the death of her husband.[1]

For some time in the early 1820s, Hannah Teed had lived in a home along the Hudson River (then referred to as the North River) in Newburgh, NY. In the summer of 1823, she had begun showing signs of being deranged, "discontented and unsettled." In the midday hours of July 30, 1823, she was seen heading "in haste" towards the river.[2] Her body was found a few days later in the water below New Windsor, NY. She had apparently killed herself, leaving behind four children as orphans.[3]

Front page of the August 11, 1823, edition of the Orange County Patriot.[4]

What drove Hannah Teed to throw herself into the river and her own death is a mystery. There can be no doubt, however, that the events of her life beginning with the fateful decision in December of 1818 to kill Richard Jennings played a role. Since the trials, life must have been difficult, and the events of 1818-1819 and double execution would have been fresh in people's minds. Her brother was serving a life sentence in state prison for his role in the crime. Her own husband had died on the gallows before a crowd of nearly 15,000 people. She, herself, narrowly escaped a death sentence. Whatever demons she faced, they must have become too much to bear. She took her secrets with her to her grave. Where she is buried remains unknown.

The fate of her children is unknown as well and can only be speculated upon. According to Donald Barrell, the children were raised by good Orange County families and grew up to become respectable citizens.[5] Teed descendants probably still reside in Orange County, New York, today, and may even have read this book without knowing about this dark chapter in their family history.

I stated a whole page earlier that this was going to be a short chapter. Richard Jennings had lost his life on December 21, 1818, and countless more lives were changed forever. Hannah Teed was one of those lives. Hannah's story is sad and tragic, and perhaps she finally found a peace that had eluded her for many years.

Death of Mrs. Teed.—Mrs. Hannah Teed, widow of the late James Teed, who was executed as one of the accomplices in the murder of Richard Jennings, and also the sister of David Conklin, who is now in the state prison for life, for the same crime, put an end to her life on Wednesday, the 30th ult. as is supposed, by drowning herself in the North river, at Newburgh. For a short time previous to this dreadful result, Mrs. Teed appeared to be discontented and unsettled in her mind, and at times, would even discover symptoms of partial derangement. In surveying the North river, which she could do from her own residence, she would sometimes express surprise and alarm: and a kind of fearfulness seemed to possess her when she looked at the water, as it was dashing along the shore at the bottom of the garden, attached to the house where she lived. On the Wednesday above mentioned, about the middle of the day, she was seen to go in haste through the garden, towards the river. No particular notice was taken of this at the time: but soon after, she was missing, and was not found until the Saturday following, when her lifeless corpse was picked up below New-Windsor.

Article about Hannah Teed's death from the August 11, 1823, edition of the Orange County Patriot.[6]

Chapter 6

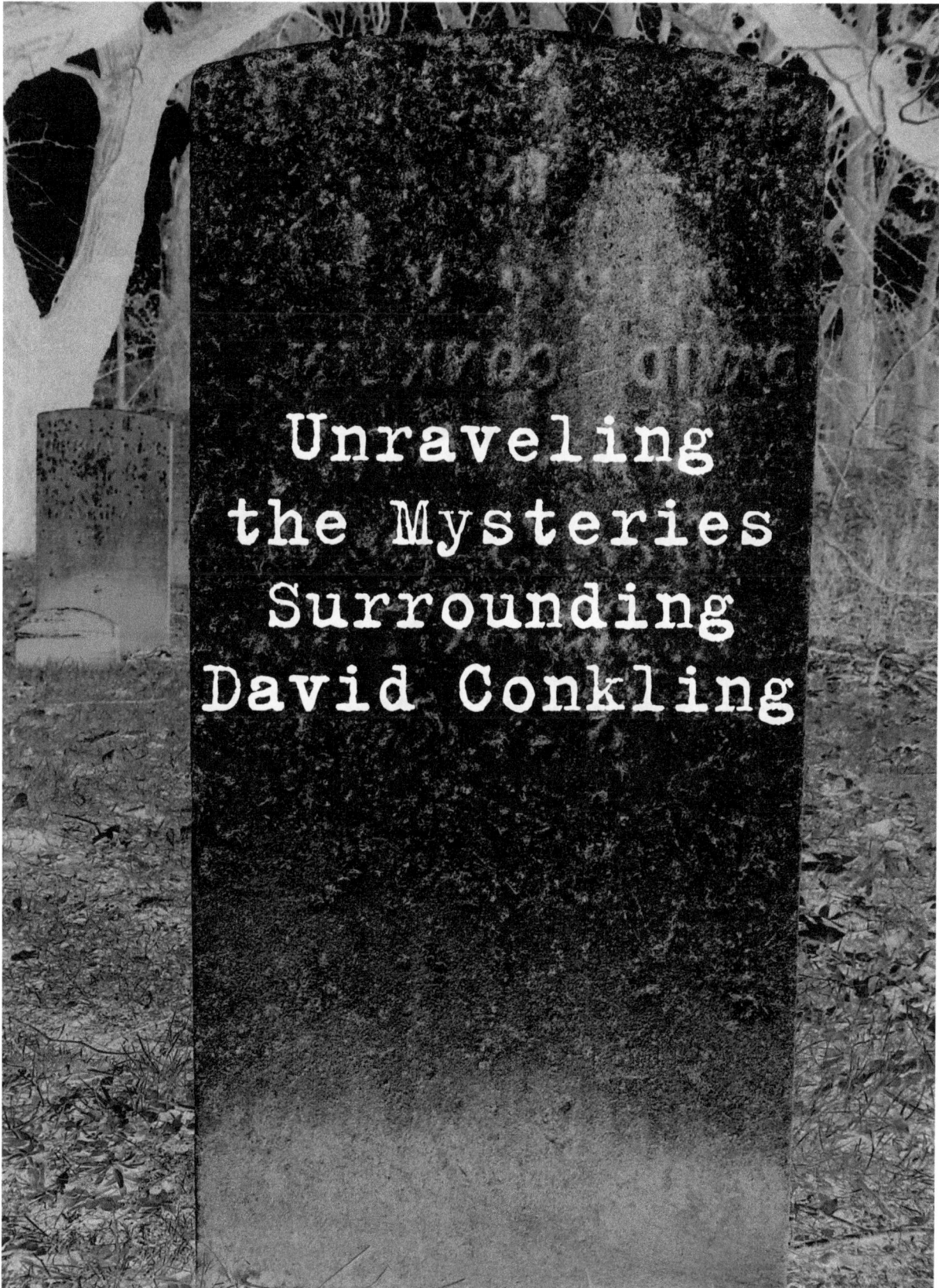

Unraveling the Mysteries Surrounding David Conkling

FACT VERSUS LEGEND: DAVID CONKLING AFTER THE TRIALS

After the hangings, David Conkling faded silently into history. Piecing together Conkling's life after 1819 has been difficult. Most of the information available was from twentieth century accounts of the case, and most of it surrounding David Conkling was local legend or lore. Not much to go on, but it was a start. So in trying to figure out what really became of David Conkling, I started with the popular myths and lore.

According to the lore, David Conkling served around thirteen years or more of his prison sentence, but suffered from rheumatism, and he was pardoned by Governor William Marcy and died shortly after being released from prison.[1] He had been married to Fannie Knight, who was from a fine Orange County family.[2] She stood by him, lived to be over 90 years of age, and is buried in Monroe, New York.[3] And hinting at a cover up, it is said that Conkling changed his name to Daniel Conklin, and "the date of his death was recorded on his gravestone as 1810, instead of 1832-1835 as his actual death."[4]

New York's first state prison, Newgate, circa 1814.[5]

The lore surrounding David Conkling had been a big focus of my research. The legends didn't seem to make sense to me. Why would he change his name to Daniel (his middle name) when his wife was from such a prominent family, and it was likely that people would know who he was anyway? And why record 1810 as the death date if the correct date of death was much later? Again, if he were buried by his wife, it would be clear who he was, and, secondly, what would be the point? I did not see how these pieces of lore showed a methodical attempt to hide Conkling's true identity.

I wanted to know what *really* became of David Conkling, and if the legends surrounding him, like those surrounding Teed and Dunning (and, indeed, the case itself), were true. If they proved to be legend and nothing more, could I explain how those legends may have developed? The research and investigation were difficult. There are just not a lot of documents available from the time period, and those that are available are piecemeal at best. Tracking down documents, sources, and information added months of research and delayed this book, but, in the end, the rest of the story of David Conkling is told, and more local legends are explained (rather than shattered).

On April 20, David Conkling, spared from the noose, was taken from Orange County Jail and brought to the state prison, located in what is now New York City's present day Greenwich Village.[6] Known as Newgate, the prison, by 1819, was a filthy, overcrowded, and hellish place to be confined. Discipline for even the most petty of infractions was not uncommon, and the discipline meted out bordered upon torture. These punishments

Sing Sing Prison twenty years after David Conkling's pardon (circa 1855)[7]

included the now clichéd diet of bread and water, whipping, and being secured in chains and placed in a cell so small that a man could neither fully stand up, nor lie down… often with multiple prisoners at one time![8] While there is nothing in the available records to suggest that David Conkling suffered any of these punishments, the atmosphere of Newgate was such as to intimidate, degrade, and inspire fear in the convicts. This is no doubt how David Conkling lived at Newgate. How long he was held there is uncertain. Newgate was gradually phased out by the addition of two new prisons: one at Auburn and another at Mt. Pleasant.

In the mid-1820s, Mt. Pleasant began receiving inmates, and David Conkling was among those that were transferred there from Newgate. A trip *up the river* from New York City would have been Conkling's journey to the new prison, which was situated along the banks of the Hudson River. Today, that prison is known as the Ossining Correctional Facility, but most still refer to it as Sing Sing. The original cell house, now just a shell of stone walls, is still visible on the grounds of the facility today.

The first fact I wanted to determine was Conkling's exact pardon date. The legend has Conkling serving somewhere in the time range of thirteen years or more of his sentence before being pardoned due to rheumatism.[9] And here is where legend meets some fact. After hitting quite a few dead ends and following up fruitless leads, I found what I was looking for in old government records. On January 16, 1834, David Conklin (no *g* at the end of his name in the source documents) was pardoned from Mt. Pleasant Prison, having served nearly fifteen years of his sentence.[10] The Governor of New York at the time was indeed William L. Marcy, so it is likely that Governor Marcy did pardon him.

NAMES.	Ages	Their occupation while in Prison.	REMARKS.
Hiram Parmerter, ...	25	Stone-cutter.	
Israel C. Martin, ...	37	Shoemaker....................	Was a shoemaker when rec'd.
John Lace, alias Emmott, ...	23	Tailor..........................	" tailor when rec'd.
William Provost, ...	25	Stone-cutter.	" stone-cutter when rec'd.
Michael Craig, ...	24	Shoemaker....................	" shoemaker when rec'd.
Joseph Moore, ...	28	do	" do do
Squire Day, ...	35	Blacksmith...................	" blacksmith when rec'd.
John Wilson, ...	27	Stone-cutter..................	" carpenter when rec'd.
Francis O. Lano, ...	22	Quarryman.	
John Van Tassell, ...	18	do	
David Conklin, ...	50	Spooler........................	Invalid when rec'd.
Alfred Simpson, ...	27	Barber, tailor and stone-cutter.	
Henry Garrison, ...	26	Quarryman.	
Jim Clason, ...	18	Waiter.	
William Donagan, ...	30	Blacksmith, painter and hatter. .	Painter when received.
Samuel Rice, ...	24	Tailor.	
Richard M. Ellison, ...	36	Cooper.	
Amasa Startivell, ...	25	Stone-cutter.	
Zingo Stout, ...	32	Laborer.	
William Foster, ...	34	Quarryman.	
Almon Aylsworth, ...	25	Cooper........................	Invalid nearly the whole term of his imprisonm't.
James Hays, ...	25	Stone-cutter and cooper.	
Barnard Trainer, ...	39	Laborer.	
George Robinson, alias Handy, .	24	do	
James Mulgreve, ...	20	Stone-cutter.	

Table listing inmates discharged from Mt. Pleasant State Prison listing David Conklin as an invalid when received at the prison.[11]

Was Conkling crippled from rheumatism at the time of his release? I can document that he did suffer from *something* – something debilitating because in a list of convicts discharged from the State Prison at Mt. Pleasant (from September 1, 1833, to March 1, 1834), it is noted that Conkling was an invalid when he was received at the prison.[12] The only historical source which states that Conkling suffered from rheumatism is found in Eager's *An Outline History of Orange County*. According to Eager, "Conklin behaved well in prison, and being sick and afflicted with rheumatism, was pardoned."[13] There is no documentation to support this statement, and it is important to note that Eager's account of the entire incident begins with the wrong dates (month and year), and appears to be derived directly from newspaper accounts from 1818 and 1819.[14]

David Conkling, or Conklin as it now appears, was a free man in early 1834. How long does he live after this? Did he die "soon after" his release?[15] To answer this question, I had to get out of the office and into the field... or rather the cemetery. But before I could go searching for a grave (and to ensure that I was locating the correct grave), I had to learn more about the man. During Conkling's trial, a witness for the defense, John Hallock, testified that he [Hallock] had been a Captain in the militia during the War of 1812, and that David Conkling had been an Ensign in his company.[16] In historical research, this is a *eureka* moment! David Conkling was a war veteran, which opened up a potential wealth of information available from pension and service files.

I requested the Combined Service File and Pension File for David *Conklin* from the National Archives (I had previously learned this process researching another historical crime involving a Civil War veteran), and about a month later (and daily trips to the Post Office, sometimes two!), the documents arrived on CDs. The pension file alone provided the clues necessary to piece together not only Conkling's correct date of death, but, ultimately, find his grave and determine if the year of death was really recorded as 1810.

According to the pension file, Fanny Conklin (again, no *g* at the end of the last name) applied for a pension as the widow of David Conklin, who had been an Ensign in Captain Hallock's Company, N.Y. Militia.[17] The application notes the couple was married on February 15, 1807 in Goshen, NY, and that the soldier (David Conklin) had died December 13, 1840, in Monroe, NY.[19] 1840! 1840 is certainly many years more than *shortly* after getting out of prison. But having the date of death documented in government records is not the subject of the local lore. I needed to find out what date [and name] was memorialized on David Conkling's gravestone.

Governor William L. Marcy, the man who pardoned David Conkling.[18]

SEARCHING FOR A GRAVE

It was a cold and windy afternoon in November of 2012 when my wife, Renee, and I set out to find David Conkling's final resting place in the Community Cemetery located in Monroe, New York.[20] Although not the largest cemetery I've ever had to explore, it was still large enough to pose a challenge. The cold air was bordering on painful when the wind would blow, so neither of us was looking forward to a long afternoon of wandering. Fortunately, we would not need to search too hard to find the grave. The cemetery is situated so that an older section is set off to one side. Bordered by an old stonewall, it was easy to discern the typical older looking stones which gave us a starting point.

Searching for gravestones is the kind of research activity that is fun, yet frustrating. You generally don't know where the stone is located, what it looks like, and, when dealing with old burials, if the stone is even legible or still there. There is also the possibility that there never was a stone to begin with. So there is always a large element of the unknown. As with most gravestone hunting trips I have been on, there is an added aspect of competition: who can find it first! So Renee and I split up and began walking amongst the rows of weathered stones. I scanned the names as quickly as possible and had to even get down and remove dirt on some stones which had fallen and were being reclaimed by the earth.

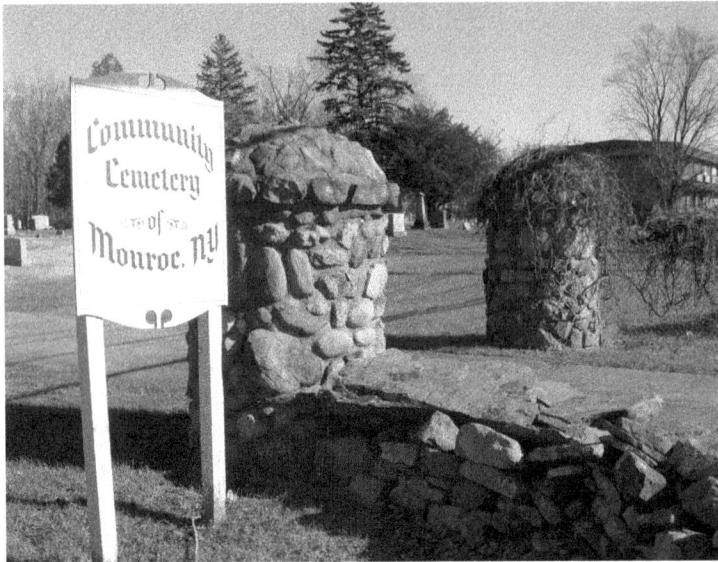

Community Cemetery, Monroe, New York.

I figured I had the edge in this game because I knew the names (Renee kept forgetting them) and, more importantly, that it was likely that Conkling's widow would have her maiden name (Knight) on her gravestone. My plan was to scan not only for the name Conklin (or Conkling), but Knight as well. However, it didn't take long to figure out that there were a lot of Knights buried in this old cemetery, so there went my perceived advantage. The old section of the cemetery is not very big and our search did not take long. At nearly the same moment, Renee and I stumbled upon the graves of Fanny Knight and David Conklin! To be fair, Renee did point them out first, but by my estimation, only by a few milliseconds! But she did win this one.

When I first saw the graves, I had a moment of exhilaration. This was, for me, the culmination of years of research. Here he is – David Conklin – a convicted murderer, spared the noose, with a weathered old stone like so many others around him. Hundreds of people drive by this section of the cemetery each day, and none realize that they are passing by the grave of a man who was a big part of a major historical event in Orange County. At that moment, Renee and I were probably the first visitors in decades, if not longer, to the grave – and probably the only

Posing next to the grave of David Conklin just minutes after Renee had found it.

two who even knew the significance of this otherwise ordinary man. I felt a familiarity with the man who was buried here – I had come to learn so much about him and his life. It was almost as if I were visiting the grave of an acquaintance or someone I had known while they were alive.

We had located the gravestone and now needed to determine what was engraved on it. Fanny's stone was in remarkable condition and easy to read. David's, on the other hand, had not held up as well. 172 years of weather and pollution had taken its toll. His name was easy to read, but not much else. I took a series of photos and studied the faded letters and numbers on the stone. It was clear from the gravestone that Conkling had been buried as *David Conklin*, and not as *Daniel Conklin*. If he, David Conkling, had changed his name to Daniel Conklin, he should have been buried with that name. He wasn't. His widow also has his name as *David Conklin* on her stone. I felt comfortable in determining that one aspect of the lore had been dismissed. But David Conklin (since he was buried as David Conklin, I will now refer to him using the last name of Conklin for the rest of the chapter) wasn't ready to give up all of his secrets. The date of death, faded and difficult to read, looked as if it could be 1810! I tried to trace the worn numbers with my finger and even tried looking at it from different angles. Yes, it could have been 1840, but the date just looked too much like 1810. I said to Renee that maybe this was one of the myths that was actually going to be proven true. Even if he had not changed his name in order to distance himself from the crime, maybe his family did change the date of death. I was unable to make a conclusion either way, and the cold wind cut our visit short. I planned on a second visit to clarify the date.

Final resting places of David Conklin (right) and his wife, Fanny Knight Conklin (left).

Four days later, I returned to David Conklin's grave armed with a secret weapon: Linda Zimmermann, and some powdered charcoal and a brush. Linda has accompanied me on quite a few grave hunting adventures, and I knew that her keen eye would help pick up the fine details on the stone. I used the powdered charcoal to provide some contrast between the engraved letters and numbers on the stone, and it worked pretty well. The lore surrounding the date of death engraved on David Conklin's gravestone was about to be either substantiated or dismissed.

The author using powdered charcoal on Conklin's gravestone.

After some diligent work we were able to ascertain the complete inscription on Conklin's stone:

IN
MEMORY OF
DAVID CONKLIN
WHO DIED
DEC. 13, 1840
A. 56 YR'S 7 MO
& 22 D

The evidence was clear: Conklin's date of death had been accurately recorded on his headstone. There was no deceit involved in the burial. How then did the lore surrounding him begin? The answer was right there in the cemetery. As I had been working on Conklin's stone, Linda had examined nearby graves and found one that seemed to be made from the same type of stone, had similar engraving, and was from the same time period.[21] She pointed out that the engraved numeral '4' on this stone looked very much like the numeral '1' due to the way the numeral had faded over time.

There was the simple answer. Weathering over time had rendered much of the detail in the numeral '4' indiscernible, causing the date to look like '1810' instead of '1840.' The angled portion of the numeral on both gravestones was shallower and not as deeply carved. There was less to begin and thus, as the years progressed, it weathered until, on Conklin's gravestone, it was nearly indiscernible as the number '4'. Did this weathering lead to the lore? It's a plausible explanation. Perhaps historian and author Donald Barrell visited this gravesite as part of his research into the Jennings case, expected to see a date of death between 1832 and 1835, and upon seeing the weathered date, thought it was 1810? His account of the case is really where the lore is first documented in writing. But without written evidence of such a visit, I can not be sure. The one thing that I can be sure of is what the gravestone reads. It is there in Monroe Community Cemetery to judge for yourself.[22]

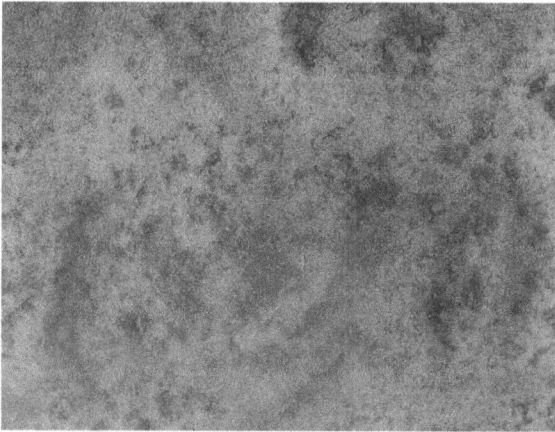
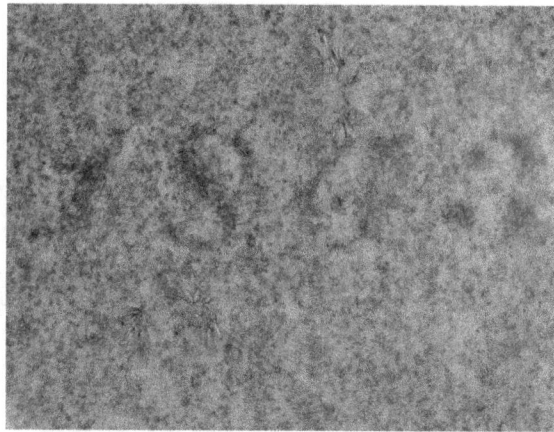

Above left is a section of David Conklin's gravestone showing the faded date. On the right is a stone of similar style and engraving with a faded date of 1843 which, at first glance, appeared as if it were 1810 due to the weathering.[23]

Whatever life David Conklin had after his release from prison is lost to time. His widow, Fanny Knight, was granted a Widow's Pension on February 4, 1874, of eight dollars per month.[24] She survived him by nearly four decades, dying March 26, 1879, less than two weeks shy of her 94th birthday. She must have truly loved her husband and stood by him, as evinced by her final resting place.

A MASONIC CONSPIRACY?

During my research, I found a rather interesting notice in the advertising and legal notices section of the *Orange County Patriot*. Running on several dates, local Masonic Lodges took out a sizeable notice to dispel any rumors that David Conklin had been a member of the Society of Freemasons.[25]

From the text of the notice, it can be deduced that there must have been a rumor that David Conklin was a member of the Masons and that his Masonic connections must have helped land him legislative favor – sparing him from the shame that would come with a death on the gallows. Even in 1819, there were Masonic-related conspiracy theories! While the only references I found regarding this are from the printed notice, there is evidence that Conklin's pardon may not have been well-received by the public.

Fanny Conklin's gravestone in Monroe Community Cemetery.

David Conklin's weathered gravestone. Photo taken on my first visit to the gravesite.

David Conklin's gravestone photographed during my second visit after applying powdered charcoal.

MASONIC.

WHEREAS a report is in circulation that *David Conklin*, one of the men convicted of the murder of Richard Jennings, is a member of the Society of Freemasons; and that that was the reason of the extraordinary exertions to procure his pardon, and of the extention of that pardon by the Legislature.

We the undersigned therefore certify, that at a numerous meeting of the members of St. John's Lodge No. 19, and of neighboring lodges, at Florida, in the county of Orange, on the last anniversary of St. John the Baptist, were appointed a committee to ascertain the truth of said report, and that after deligent inquiry, in which we were assisted by the Grand Visitor, and on the best information, we do not hesitate to say, that the said David Conklin is not nor ever has been a member of any regularly constituted lodge in this county, and that he is not nor ever has been a Mason.   September 15, 1819.

   Nath'l Bailey, of Olive Branch Lodge, No. 102.

   Sam'l G. Hopkins, of St. Johns Lodge, No. 19.

   Isaac Otis, of Hoffman Lodge, No. 300.

   Holly Seely, of Mount Moriah Lodge, No. 189.

N. B. All Printers friendly to the Craft and desirous of checking unfounded and injurious reports, are requested to give the above an insertion in their respective Journals.   3w

Masonic notice printed in The Orange County Patriot, disavowing any relationship with David Conklin.[26]

In *An Account of the Murder of Richard Jennings; Together with the Confession of Teed & Dunning*, published in April of 1819, there is mention that public sentiment regarding the selection of Conklin [and Hodges] for pardon was "made from partial and incorrect representations" to the Legislature.[27] There is no real documentation to support what those representations may have been or who they may have been made by. But it is unlikely public sentiment motivated the Legislature to pardon Conklin, as public perception was, according to the April 1819 source, that Conklin was "the original contriver, instigator, and promoter of the murder."[28]

Perhaps the public, under the belief that Conklin was the true instigator of the crime, thought that Conklin should have been hanged, maybe even more so than Teed, who was out of town during the murder, and they looked for answers as to what was seen as an unjustified pardon. After all, the reasons for Conklin's pardon is unclear: as we know he was not the initial subject of the bill before the Legislature.[29] In fact, his name was added to the bill, and also once removed from the bill, prior to passage so it is easy to see how local residents may have tried to explain the situation by alleging Masonic connections spared him the noose.[30]

THE LAST WORD

David Conklin was not buried under a different name (other than dropping the letter g off of the last name), and the year of his death was not recorded as 1810 in an effort to hide his true identity. He lived about six years after his release from prison, leaving behind a devoted widow, Fanny Knight, who would go on to survive him by nearly four decades. The lore surrounding him may have been explained away, but there is one secret that David Conklin took with him to his grave: his real involvement in the crime. Was he, as Jack Hodges claimed, the instigator? Was he the man who loaded the musket and gave it to Jack Hodges? Did he instigate the first murder for hire in New York by contracting with Hodges to kill Richard Jennings? The jury certainly felt that he did: they found him guilty.

But was he guilty? Or was he the victim of false testimony given by a convicted murderer? It was largely Jack's testimony that convicted Conkling, as well as James Teed and David Dunning. The implications are startling. If Jack Hodges lied in his testimony, then David Conkling, James Teed, and David Dunning were wrongly convicted. And that means that Teed and Dunning suffered on the gallows as innocent men. The truth is now buried in time. It is up to you – the reader – to determine whether David Conklin was the man who contrived a terrible murder or a man who was wrongly convicted of a crime he did not commit.[32]

"if a distinction were proper, Conkling was the first of the four that ought to have been set apart for execution."[31]

Linda Zimmermann unraveling the last secret of David Conklin.

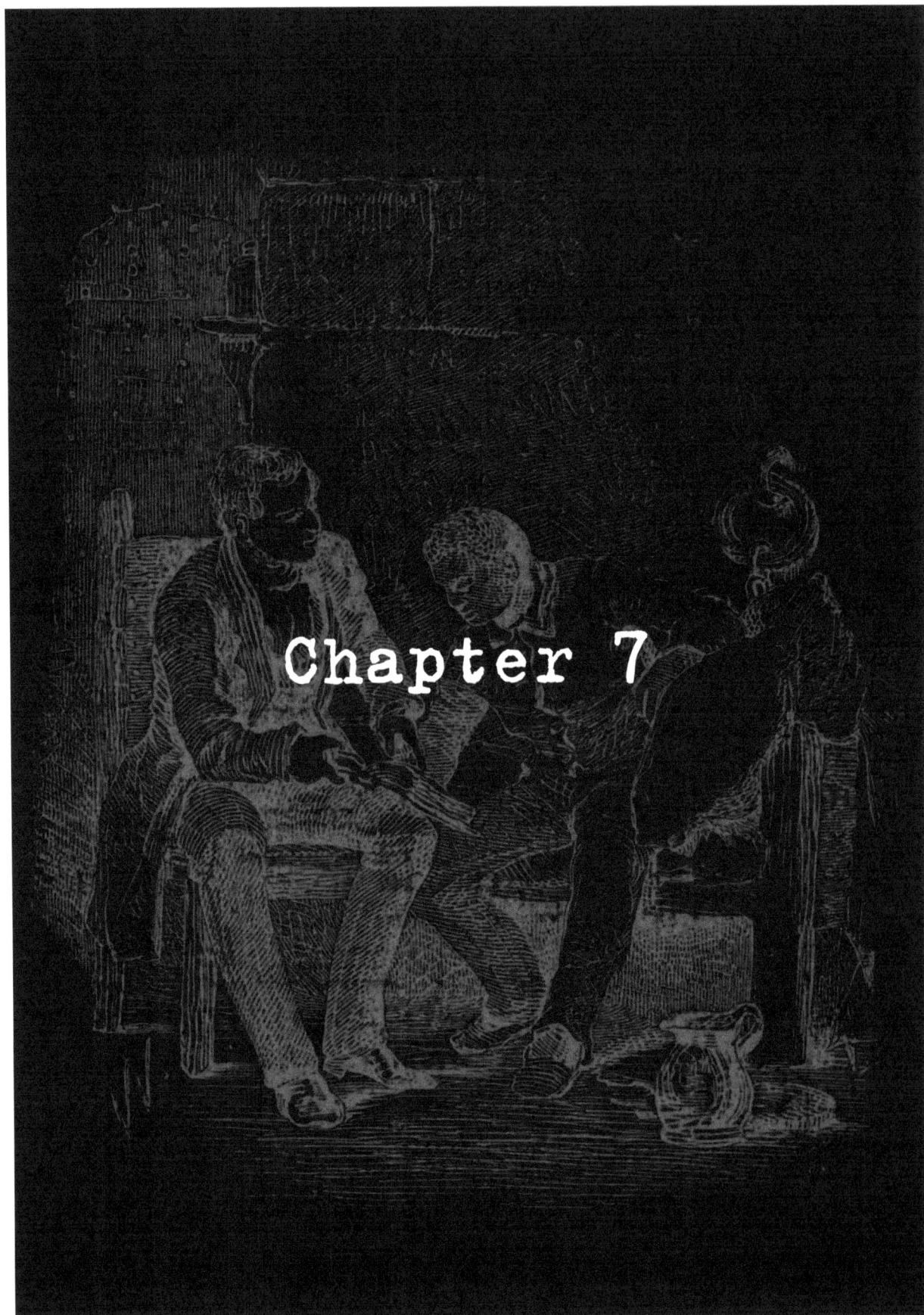

Chapter 7

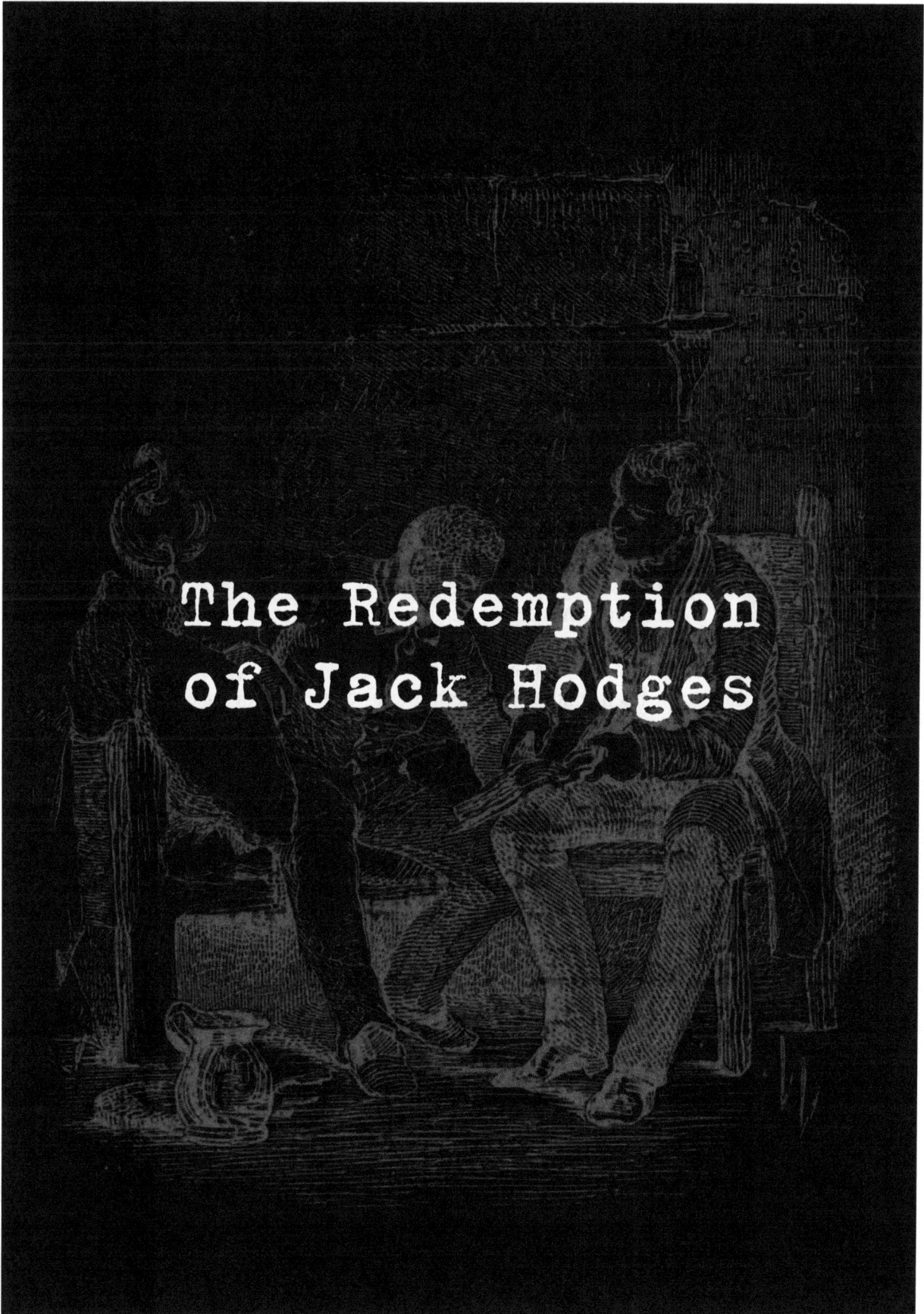

The Redemption of Jack Hodges

THE REDEMPTION OF JACK HODGES

Jack Hodges became a celebrity in his own time. More information is known about his life after the murders than any of his co-conspirators. He is one of the most dynamic and intriguing persons involved in this case, and his story is compelling: the wicked convict who finds redemption and salvation in prison.

It was primarily the testimony of Jack Hodges that convicted the other men in this case; testimony that was found credible both during the trials and later after the executions, when there was some doubt raised by Dunning's denial on the gallows. Was Hodges an honest man with sincere remorse or a malicious perjurer who wrongly convicted three men? To answer that question, I first had to determine just who Jack Hodges was. That would not be as simple as I first thought. With so much written about him, this should have been the easiest chapter to write. It wasn't! Hodges' story, it seemed, could fill an entire book, and that had already been done in 1842, so I needed to really distill the information to get to the heart of the story.

HIS LIFE STORY

According to the various accounts of his life, Hodges did not know his exact age.[1] During the trial, he had testified that he was around the age of 35 years old[2], yet a newspaper article about him put his age at around 40 during that same time period.[3] He is recorded as being 50 years of age in 1825 when he was received as an inmate at the State Prison at Auburn,[4] and another government source puts his age around 70 in 1829.[5] The 1842 book about his life puts him as having been born around 1763[6], and on his monument in the Old Pioneer Cemetery, Canandaigua, New York, it is recorded that he died around 80 years of age (he died in early 1842).[7] While I have been unable to determine an exact age or year of birth, I tend to believe that he was born sometime around 1763.[8]

"...who is more reckless and abandoned than a homeless, friendless African sailor!"[13]

Hodges' place of birth was also unknown, and different sources place it as either Lancaster or Philadelphia, Pennsylvania. Most sources identify him as having been born in Lancaster, PA, of free parents,[9] although Hodges testified at trial that he had been born in Philadelphia.[10] One source deviates from the Pennsylvania location and identifies Norfolk, Virginia, as his birthplace, although no information is provided on how this was determined.[11]

At the age of ten, Hodges had been sent to work "on board the schooner Lydia, of Philadelphia, in the West India trade, in the capacity of waiting boy."[12] He continued in this capacity on board different vessels, eventually becoming a sailor where he is described as having "visited almost every port in Europe, as well as other countries, mingling in scenes of degradation and vice abroad, till he acquired the hardness, enterprise and viciousness of the most dissolute seaman."[14]

His life as a sailor was one of intemperance, and he was "always profane and always bad."[15] During Teed's trial, when asked had he always been in the habit of becoming intoxicated, Jack replied, "I have now and then like other sailors."[16]

He continued as a sailor until after the War of 1812, when he ended up in New York and found himself unable to find any work, owing to his

The State Prison of New York, known as Newgate, circa 1797.[17]

lack of sobriety and integrity. Eventually he settled in Orange County, New York, living without moral restraint and indulging in all of the vices of a sailor, only now he was on dry land.[18] Hodges had lived in Orange County since around 1814 and, at the time of the murder, had been living with David Conkling for about two and a half years.[19]

AFTER THE TRIALS

Hodges had been transferred on April 20, 1819, to the first State Prison, Newgate, located in New York City, along with co-defendant David Conkling.[20] Newgate was a place of punishment, not reform. It was a place to contain and punish the lawless, rather than educate or rehabilitate them. The time Hodges would have spent there would have been focused on hard labor, although Jack would later say that he had been provided with adequate food and drink and had not been overworked.[21]

His time at Newgate is best summed up by Ansel Eddy, who wrote about Jack's life in *Black Jacob, A Monument of Grace*:

> Towards Jacob Hodges, a miserable African, a murderer, there may have been some severity, owing either to his own refectory temper, or the character of his keepers. . . . He was treated as an ignorant, abandoned, wretched murderer, who, though he had escaped the gallows, was undeserving of the ordinary kindness and sympathy usually extended to the less flagrantly guilty. We can easily imagine, too, that Jacob's prison-dress; the necessary associations with his past history; his strongly marked, dark African features, together with his stately, resolute carriage, may all have served to turn away all sympathy, and to excite far other than charitable feelings towards him.[22]

View of Auburn Prison in the 1850s. The prison building is towards the left with the cupola visible.[23]

Had Jacob Hodges served the complete term of imprisonment there at Newgate, his story may have ended very differently. Fortunately for Hodges, he would be among the first inmates transferred to a new prison in upstate Auburn, New York, and, unlike David Conkling, Jack's journey within the penal system is much better documented. In April 1825, Jack was transferred to Auburn.[24] It's there at Auburn that Hodges would begin his powerful transformation.

The new State Prison at Auburn was much more than a warehouse for convicts. It was a new system for their education and reform. Prisoners, although still felons, were seen as being capable of change and reform, and prayer and religion were viewed as integral to that process. Hodges thus began his new life in a new prison and under a new system with the guidance of the prison chaplain, the Rev. Jared Curtis.

One of the few items of property inmates were permitted to own was a Holy Bible. Hodges had one in his cell; however, he could not read. He had never received any form of education and had, up until this point in his life, lived with neither morals nor religion. The Rev. Curtis sought to correct this. He took it upon himself to teach Jack Hodges to read, beginning with the first word printed in the Bible, 'in':

> The first lesson he gave him was the first word in the Bible, I-n. The chaplain said to him, That word is in. Can you see how many letters there are in it? Jacob replied, Two. He was then directed to look for the same letters on other pages of the Bible, and soon learned to understand the difference between letters which resembled each other, til he comprehended their force when combined in words.[25]

This first lesson would have a profound impact upon the rest of Jacob's life. He slowly began to teach himself to read, working his way up to understanding short sentences which the chaplain would later discuss with him. And in learning to read, Jacob came to reflect upon his life and his sins, and opened the door to what can only be described as a spiritual revelation.[26]

Image from the Auburn Prison Register of Male Convicts showing Jack's entry. One piece of information gleaned from this source is Jack's height: the register has him listed as being five feet and six and one-half inches tall.[27]

Jacob Hodges would later recount his great spiritual awakening in a well-documented conversation with the Rev. Louis Dwight, Secretary of the Prison Discipline Society. Rev. Dwight had become acquainted with Jack in the fall of 1826 at Auburn Prison, where the two men formed a lifelong bond. In March of 1828, during his second visit with Jack, Rev. Dwight learned of Jack's near mystical religious experience. Jack explained that, one evening, Rev. Curtis had come to his cell and explained to Jack that his sins were more than just sins against man, but were sins against God. This had a deep impact upon Jack and it affected him greatly. A week later, still troubled, he prayed, after which he recalled that Mr. Fisk, [Ezra Fisk, the minister who had tended to him while incarcerated in the Orange County Jail], had instructed him that anytime he had a chapter of the Bible read to him, he should have the 51st Psalm read to him. Hodges described how there was no one to read it to him, so he prayed to God, asked God to "show me that chapter, that I may read it with understanding."[28]

"Jack Hodges was the only man that ever reminded me, by his air, his gravity, his native dignity, his step and tread, of Washington."[30]

Hodges then described to Rev. Dwight how he was able to find and read the 51st Psalm: "Now . . . when I came to the words, 'Deliver me from blood-guiltiness' I was struck dumb. I could not say any more at that time. I fell upon my knees, and prayed to God to have mercy upon me. . . ."[29]

Jack continued to explain how he had prayed and struggled for some time after, until one day he fell to his knees and prayed for mercy, seeing all of his past transgressions and sins flash before his eyes, and losing himself in despair and hopelessness. Hodges said to Rev. Dwight that all he could do was pray the 51st Psalm, over and over again, until, in Jack's own words:

And in my prayers, my sins were moved from me, and I was lightened, and I thought I could fly. I felt as though I could fly. I looked around me, and my cell appeared to be as big as two such cells, and all appeared to be as light as noon; just the same as if I was in a palace. I looked around me, and it appeared to me that I could see my Savior upon his cross, bleeding for poor sinners. I could see the blood gushing out from his side. I rose up, and I began to bless his holy name. My sins, my load of sins, moved away from me, and I felt light, as though I could fly. I stood upon my knees, and all I could say was, 'Glory to God! Glory to God!'[31]

This is a striking scene and a pivotal moment in Jack's life. He had begun his genuine and earnest religious life, and, for Jack, prison had become a place of freedom. He had earned the admiration of the prison staff and visitors to the prison. Hodges would also relate the intimate details of his December 1818 crime, and never once did he waiver from the testimony he had delivered at the trials in 1819.

FREEDOM FOR JACK HODGES

Hodges may have considered himself as having found freedom in prison through religion, but he was still an inmate within the walls of a penal institution. His transformation, however, certainly played a role in securing him his freedom. The new Jack Hodges, remorseful and immersed in religion, was pardoned on February 26, 1829.[32] Although he was apprehensive about being released from prison, the nearly seventy year old Jack began his new life as a free man. He left the prison with his Bible and dressed in a nice set of clothes. The farewell had been emotional, with the prison chaplain and keeper moved by Jack's departure, and the superintendent himself wished Jack success. Jack had been seen as the first "fruit" of the newer methods of prison management.[33]

Hodges' first meeting with the Rev. Jared Curtis, Chaplain at Auburn Prison. This is the only known depiction of the actual face of any of the five conspirators involved in the murder of Richard Jennings.[34] (On page 81 in the illustration of Teed and Dunning on the gallows the men are depicted with hoods covering part of their faces, so we never actually see what they may have looked like.)

An old photograph of the original building of the Auburn Theological Seminary. Jack may have walked these grounds in the early 1830s.[38]

Hodges spent his first two years of freedom in Auburn, where he secured employment at the Auburn Theological Seminary in the home of the steward.[35] An intriguing story connected with Hodges' time in Auburn is that he resided in the home of future Secretary of State William H. Seward, a nephew of Richard Jennings.[36] However, like many of the other legends and lore attached to this story, that was not the case and there is no evidence to support that claim. Perhaps over the years, the word 'steward' was misread or misprinted as 'Seward' (William H. Seward did have a home in Auburn), and the misconception that Jack resided with the nephew of the murder victim was born.

After about two years, Hodges moved to Canandaigua, New York, where he became a member of the First Congregational Church and resided in the home of a widower, Harriet Martin.[39] The Rev. Ansel Eddy, who penned the story of Jack's life and conversion to Christianity, was the pastor at the church, and Jack became a well-respected member of the church and community. Residing in Auburn, Jack continued to maintain his account of the murder. In an interesting conversation, which the Rev. Eddy would later write about, Jack explained that the character of Jennings was not a justification for his [Jack's] involvement, and he maintained that his role in the crime would not have proven fatal [the gunshot to the side of the head]; however, he still felt as if he were a murderer and that his original sentence of death had been justified.[40] Keep in mind that David Dunning went to his death on the gallows maintaining that he had not beaten Jennings to the head, as Jack had testified. Nearly two hundred years later, the question still lingers: who was telling the truth? Do we believe the words of David Dunning, a man about to go to his death, with no hope of a reprieve and nothing to gain by lying? Or do we believe the testimony of Jack Hodges who, once he had told his story, never wavered, but certainly had much to gain by lying (i.e. his life)? This is a question left for you to decide.

LIFE IN CANANDAIGUA

Around Canandaigua, Jack became known as Black Jacob. He was given great trust and responsibility in the home of Mrs. Martin, and developed a close bond with the Rev. Eddy. It is documented that he did not associate "with the people of his own colour" because "their ordinary habits of feeling and life did not at all correspond with his [Jack's] devotional desires, and the current of his every-day thoughts and pursuits."[41] He never reverted to his earlier vices and remained a reformed man.

In late 1839, Jack would meet up with Rev. Dwight for a visit to the jail where Jack had once been incarcerated. According to an account of this meeting by Rev. Dwight, Jack had said to him, "O, Mr. Doit, little did I think, when I saw you at my cell in the Auburn prison, that I should ever walk by your side in the streets of Canandaigua."[42]

An old photograph of the First Congregational Church, Canandaigua, N.Y.[45]

As I mentioned at the beginning of this chapter, there was a lot of information available about Hodges. To sum up his life after prison in a chapter such as this hardly begins to do justice to the story of his life and redemption that could be written. He was a well-respected member of the congregation and the community, described as being an example of good conduct, and that he had a "piety of a very high order" and was "a striking illustration of the mighty power of Christianity."[43]

He remained in the home of Mrs. Martin, and when she sold the home to Myron Clark in late 1841, Jack remained in the home working for the new owners. Myron Clark, it is important to note, would later go on to serve as Governor of New York in 1855-1856.[44]

Sometime in late January or early February, 1842, Jack took ill, and towards the middle of February, it was clear that he was on his death bed.[46] On the last morning of his life, he was asked if there was anything that he needed, to which Jack replied, "O, I want more grace in my heart!"[47]

At 6:00 P.M., on February 16, 1842, Jack Hodges passed into eternity.[47] He was around eighty years of age. The last of the co-conspirators in the murder of Richard Jennings had faded into history. His loss was heavily mourned in the community, and the day he was laid to rest is best described in the words of Rev. Eddy: "The day he was buried was intensely cold and stormy. Some of the most respectable gentlemen of the village bore him to his grave, while others felt it a privilege and honour to attend him to his resting-place among the dead."[48] He was buried in the Old Pioneer Cemetery in Canandaigua. A silver plate was affixed to Jack's coffin, and engraved upon it were these words:

Jacob Hodges, A Respectable coloured man, aged eighty. He rests from his labours, and his works do follow him.[49]

The former home of Mrs. Harriet Martin on East Gibson Street, Canandaigua, N.Y., where Jack Hodges resided. Photo courtesy the Ontario County Historical Society, Canandaigua, N.Y.

AFTER JACK'S DEATH

T he Rev. Thompson, Pastor of the First Congregational Church, gave an eloquent sermon on the Sabbath after Jack's death which was published in the New York Observer, as well as other publications of the time. Jack was remembered as a pious man of prayer, who was a humble and useful Christian.[50] Jack's most prized possession was his Bible. He had refused to part with it while alive, having a special connection with the book which he felt had delivered him from his life of sin. This prison Bible – the book so cherished by Jack – was left to Rev. Dwight.[51] I wonder whatever became of this Bible which Jack had so cherished. Perhaps it is sitting on a shelf in an historical society or packed away in a box in an archive. Or it may simply be lost to time. It would certainly be a fascinating artifact of the case to uncover, but as of the publication date, I have been unable to determine what became of the Bible.

David Dunning and Jack Hodges had two very different accounts of what had happened in the wood lot in 1818, but there was one thing both would have in common after death. A rumor had circulated amongst the "coloured people" of Canandaigua that Jack's body had been stolen from his grave and sent off for dissection.[52] The rumor was so strong that around two weeks after his death, the body of Jack Hodges was exhumed from the grave. His coffin was found to be intact and his body was in the coffin and undisturbed. Jack Hodges was reburied and left to his final rest.[53]

In death, Jack Hodges also shares something in common with David Conkling: you can visit his grave. In the Old Pioneer Cemetery, Canandaigua, N.Y., there stands a large monument in his memory, donated by the Prison Discipline Society. There, inscribed on the monument, are worn letters which stand as a final testament to the life of Jack Hodges. The inscription was at some point replaced with a bronze plaque bearing the same words, preserving Jack's memorial for future generations (see inscription on page 139). The plaque was donated by Charlotte Clark, who occupied the home with her father, Myron Clark, where Jacob had resided until his death.[54] If you want to visit Jack's grave, the Old Pioneer Cemetery is located on West Avenue in the City of Canandaigua, N.Y.

The large monument on the left is the memorial marking the final resting place of Jack "Jacob" Hodges. Photo courtesy of the Ontario County Historical Society, Canandaigua, N.Y.

*Jack's monument. Photo courtesy of the Ontario
County Historical Society, Canandaigua, N.Y.*

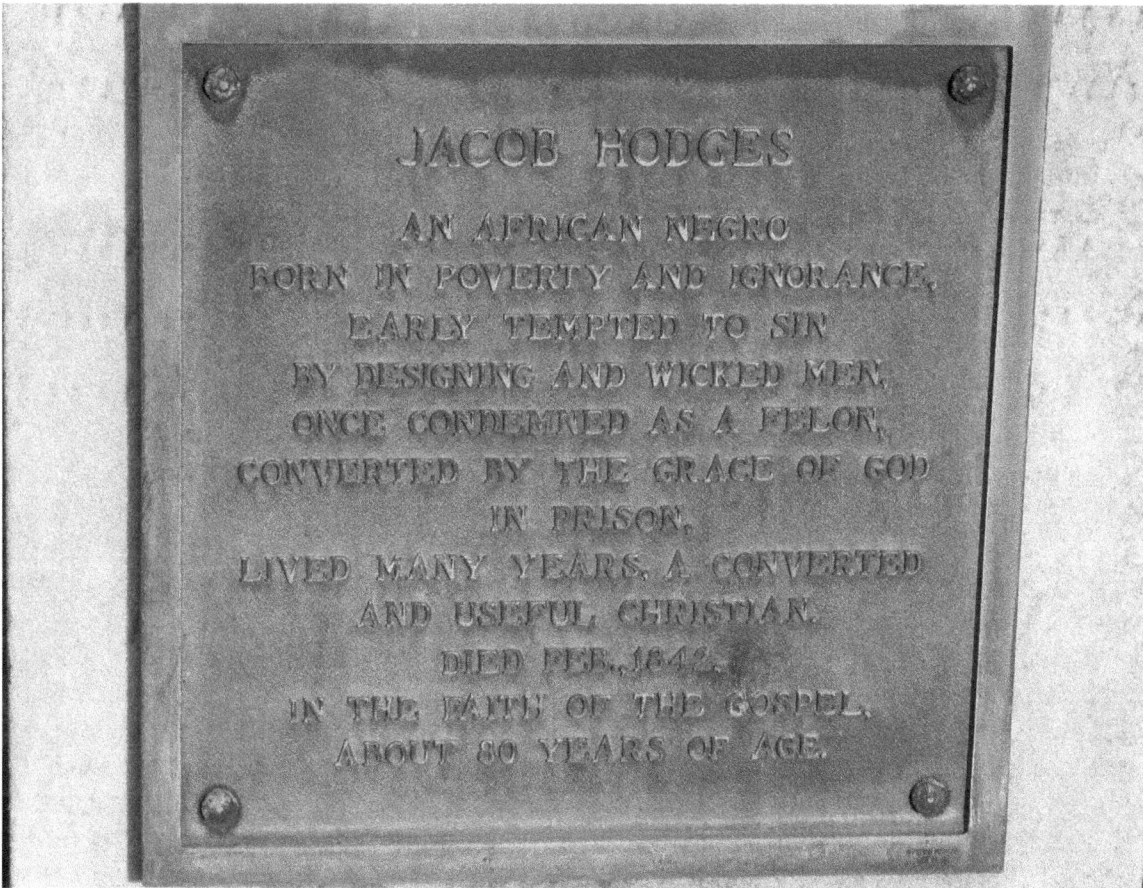

Close up of the plaque affixed to Jack's monument in the Old Pioneer Cemetery. Photo courtesy of the Ontario County Historical Society, Canandaigua, N.Y.

JACOB HODGES

AN AFRICAN NEGRO
BORN IN POVERTY AND IGNORANCE,
EARLY TEMPTED TO SIN
BY DESIGNING AND WICKED MEN,
ONCE CONDEMNED AS A FELON,
CONVERTED BY THE GRACE OF GOD
IN PRISON,
LIVED MANY YEARS, A CONVERTED
AND USEFUL CHRISTIAN.
DIED FEB., 1842,
IN THE FAITH OF THE GOSPEL,
ABOUT 80 YEARS OF AGE.

LEGACY AND CONTROVERSY

Not everyone seemed to share in the enthusiasm that Rev. Eddy, Rev. Dwight, and others had for the reformed Jack Hodges, and there was even criticism aimed at some of those who touted Jack as a symbol of reform. In an 1845 book supporting the abolition of the death penalty, author Charles C. Burleigh references the story of Jacob Hodges and uses his life and redemption to support his anti-capital punishment stance. He writes of Jack [quoting in some instances directly from Ansel Eddy's *Black Jacob*]:

> He [Hodges] was highly esteemed, both in his social and religious connections, led often in the devotional exercise of the church of which he was a member, and "by his modesty, consistency, and religious fervor, the practical excellence and beneficence of his life, and the trusting tranquility of his death," proved that it is not impossible to reclaim even "the most atrocious" in crime.[55]

Burleigh's use of Hodges to support abolishing the death penalty drew harsh criticism, particularly in 1846 from a Rev. George B. Cheever, D.D., who wrote in *A Defence of Capital Punishment* that while he has "always read the account of Jack's *experience* with deep interest," it should have not been a case used in support of abolition. Rev. Cheever argued that Hodges, by his own admissions, would have continued with his past intemperate habits and vices had he not been sentenced to death and ultimately sent to prison. Additionally, Jack had accepted the justness of his sentence, and had never condemned the penalty of death for the crime of murder. Thus, Hodges was, in the opinion of Rev. Cheever, a bad example to have used.[56]

IRONY?

The Governor of New York in early 1829 was Martin VanBuren – the same Martin VanBuren who, as Attorney General, aided in the prosecution of the murderers of Richard Jennings. One has to appreciate the irony that it is very probable that the man who helped condemn Hodges ultimately freed him.[58]

Rev. Dwight also received some criticism for his inclusion of Jack's story in the *Seventeenth Annual Report* of the Prison Discipline Society. The Massachusetts State Legislature expressed its disapproval of the report by withholding their annual grant to the Prison Discipline Society (about $125.00),[57] and a review of the report in *The Monthly Miscellany of Religion and Letters* chastised the report – or more specifically Rev. Dwight – for, among other things, "distasteful phraseology," and for promoting the views of "one class" of Christians while the society is supported financially by a different "class" of Christians.[59] If we read between the lines, the use of the word *class*

may help put the criticism into context. *The Monthly Miscellany of Religion and Letters* was a Unitarian publication, so was it seeking to criticize the report for promoting Protestant religious beliefs which may have been expressed through the account of Jacob Hodges? Or was it a reflection of 1843 American racial views: white Christians being one class, and non-white (specifically African American) Christians the other? Either way, there was a clear bias in the criticism.

Bias can be a problem with any source, including historical ones, and looking at the many positive writings about Jack Hodges did raise the question of whether or not his redemption was mildly inflated. Inflating Jack's story would certainly have aided the Prison Discipline Society by illustrating that reform and rehabilitation were viable alternatives to punishment and harsh discipline. But a New York State government document independently verifies what Rev. Eddy and Rev. Dwight have described about Hodges.

A biographical abstract of inmates released from Auburn Prison in February 1829, includes Jack Hodges and concluded that Jack was "a remarkable convict, and there can be little hazard in calling his a case of clear and decided reformation."[60] This independent source helped verify that the stories of Jack's life and redemption had not been exaggerated.

For me, Jack Hodges is an enigmatic, fascinating, and complex person. He affirmed his role in the crime, as well as that of the others (including David Dunning)

"**Black Jacob**,"
A MONUMENT OF GRACE.

THE LIFE

OF

JACOB HODGES,

AN AFRICAN NEGRO,

WHO DIED IN CANANDAIGUA, N. Y., FEBRUARY, 1842.

BY A. D. EDDY,
Newark, N. J.

REVISED BY THE COMMITTEE OF PUBLICATION

AMERICAN SUNDAY-SCHOOL UNION.
PHILADELPHIA:
No. 146 CHESTNUT STREET

Rev. Ansel Eddy published the authoritative work on Jack's life. It is suggested reading for anyone interested in learning more about Jack Hodges.[61]

until his death. But discrepancies remain, leaving a lingering mystery for future generations to consider. What is your conclusion? Was Jack Hodges honest in his testimony? And was he a genuinely reformed man, or was he a master manipulator who escaped the gallows? Here is where you get to play judge and render your own verdict.

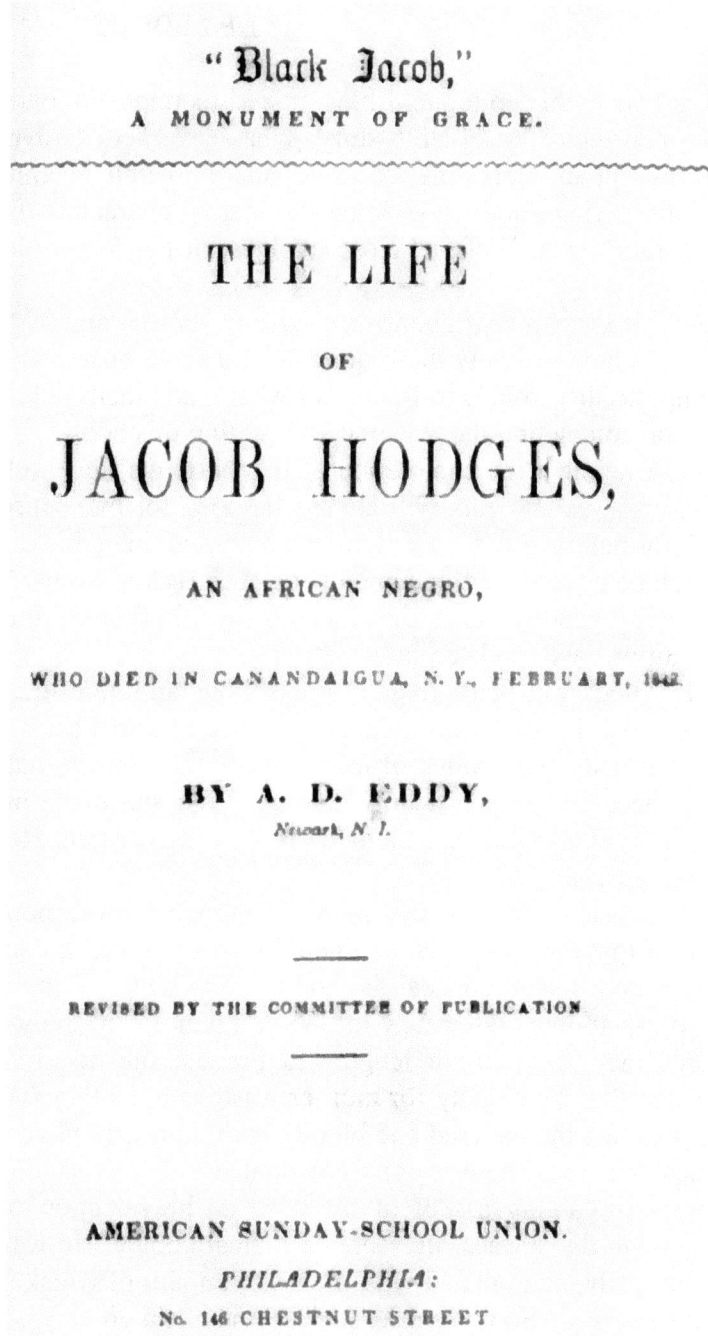

EPILOGUE

As I write this epilogue, I have mixed feelings. On one hand, I am excited to have had the opportunity to tell this story. I have worked hard to verify facts, obtain sources, and present an interesting, accurate, and enjoyable account of this tragic event. On the other hand, I am saying goodbye to some fascinating characters that I have grown quite close to over the past four years. Well, as close as one can get to people that have been dead more than a century!

I know it is not a *real* goodbye. I have never met any of the characters in this twisted drama, but I have come to know them quite well. I have obsessed over details of their lives and tried crawling into their minds to figure out what made them tick. This was only enhanced once I had focused on completing the research and writing this book.

I also know that the completion of this book isn't even close to being an authentic goodbye, because my eyes and ears will always be open for more information and facts. I know there is more information out there. It may be buried in a historical society archive, or in an old collection of government documents, or even tucked away in a family Bible. I suppose all I am really saying goodbye to is the research for this first edition. I am confident that there will be future editions with updated information.

As this book was ready to go to press, I had an interesting conversation with my wife, Renee. While she was looking over a chapter for me, she said she was amazed that they didn't even try to hide the body. The police officer in me said in return that that was because most people that commit these crimes don't think them through and make mistakes. This conversation inspired me, though, to look beyond the facts that I have written. Here is my take on the crime and my own opinions.

First off, this was a poorly planned and even more poorly executed crime. And I am not convinced that this was even planned out in advance, as Jack Hodges had stated. The fact that there was no effort to conceal the body, to me hints at a more spontaneous act. If four men had spent so much time and energy to devise a plan to rid the world of Richard Jennings, then why wouldn't they go to more lengths to prevent the discovery of the crime? It was common knowledge that the penalty for murder was death, so they had a very good reason to cover their tracks. Leaving the battered and bloody body in nearly plain view is either a very bad mistake or evidence that the crime was not premeditated.

Another troubling aspect of the case is the selection of Jack Hodges as the man to kill Jennings. On the surface, he seems a logical choice. He was an intemperate former sailor who could be easily manipulated with the right amount of whiskey, and he was loyal to his employer (David Conkling). So in a sense, Jack seems like a good candidate to commit murder. But would three white males in 1818 stake their lives on the actions of Jack Hodges (who was African American)? Again, the penalty for murder was death on the gallows, so conspiring with a drunkard to kill a man was not a great idea. Of course, neither is murder!

Alcohol is a depressant and lowers inhibitions, which certainly may have led to Jack committing the act at the prodding of the other men. Those same inhibitions, however, can also mean that Jack would have developed a case of *loose lips*. We have to believe that Teed, Dunning, and Conkling trusted Jack enough to believe he would not speak of the crime or plot. That is a bit of a stretch for me. Then again, looking at it from a different point of view, perhaps they felt that even if Jack implicated them, no one would ever believe him.

More troubling is the fact that Jack goes to Teed's home before the murder and agrees with Dunning to commit the crime. So the plotters leave it to Jack to discuss the actual details with Dunning? Is this really a well thought-out plan? Why wasn't Dunning included in the secret meeting at the hovel when the plan was made?

These are brief overall impressions:

- Testimony was given that placed Dunning in the Teed home at the time of the murder.
- Testimony was given that described Richard Jennings walking alone into the disputed lot where he was murdered.
- There was testimony that there were two sets of tracks in the snow leading to where Jennings was murdered, and only one set leaving.
- When Jack testified about conversations he had with the other men regarding the crime, he always pointed out that no one else was around to hear it.
- He, at one point, described Conkling making the offer of money (with Teed possibly chipping in), then described the exact same thing, but attributed it to Teed having made the offer.
- The plotters themselves did not seem to get along very well. Conkling and Dunning were engaged in a lawsuit while in jail awaiting trial for murder! Dunning had his own dispute with Teed over fence rails. These are unlikely allies in a murder plot.
- Why David Dunning? He had no issue with Richard Jennings, and was, according to the available records, on friendly terms with him.
- Dunning maintains that he did not beat Jennings with the gun right up until the moment of his death on the gallows.
- If there had been a plot, why didn't any of the others try to save themselves and come clean?

Jack tells a rather consistent story after his confession, and as pointed out during the trials, it really wasn't hard for him to do so. Most of the events were a given: Jennings was dead, it was done on Monday the 21st, he had been shot and beaten to death and left in a field. Jack needed to only include some details of the plot to make it a believable and consistent story.

But looking at his confession, I go back to his initial apprehension by Charles Durland. Jack denied any involvement in the crime – and Durland certainly prodded him to confess. Durland also provided Jack with the necessary details of the crime scene and condition of the body. Did Durland inadvertently give Jack all of the information needed to devise an elaborate lie? Durland told Jack that Dunning had informed on him, so was this Jack's motive? Essentially, if he was going to hang, they all would hang.

After confessing and being convicted at his own trial, was Jack made a promise that if he testified against the others, and gained convictions, then he would be pardoned? This was denied during the trials, but I suspect – no, I believe - that it was very likely that a promise had been made. For the prosecution to admit that such a promise had been made would have cast serious doubt on Jack's credibility. The jury may have dismissed his testimony and acquitted the other men. If a pardon was promised – and I believe that it was – then this would have been a well-guarded secret.

Do I have evidence of a promise? I have the words of Judge Van Ness who, in his March 31, 1819, letter to Governor DeWitt Clinton requesting a pardon for Hodges, wrote:

I find it to be a settled rule in the criminal law, that an accomplice who is received and used as a witness; who fully and truly discloses the joint guilt of himself and his companions; who answers honestly to all questions that are put to him, and appears to have acted a fair and ingenuous part, by giving a faithful relation of all the facts within his knowledge, is equitably entitled to the favor and mercy of the government.[1]

I believe that this is evidence that the court had a pardon in mind throughout the trials. Hodges was, after all, a key element of the charges against the others. Again, we can look to Judge Van Ness's own words for evidence:

As the accessories could not by law be tried, until after one of the principles had been convicted, Hodges was first brought to trial, and being found guilty, the public prosecutor next proceeded against the accessories, who were separately indicted, and made use of Hodges as a witness against them, as he also did against Dunning.[2]

The promise of a pardon would have given Jack an excellent motive to lie: his life. Often when someone lies or fabricates an incident they go into elaborate detail. It is not enough to make a simple, false statement. It has to be an elaborate, false statement! Jack's story about the plot and offer of a thousand dollar reward for the murder could have been that elaborate, false statement. It wasn't enough to say that he had been hired to kill Jennings – he had to create an intricate fabric of deceit and ruthlessness – and show how he was manipulated by the others with whiskey and constant prodding. Was this complicated story evidence of deceit?

The problem with a lie is keeping the story straight and there may be evidence that Jack did have some trouble in that area. In the "Second Convict's Story," Jacob Abbott wrote about a prisoner named "W" (it was Jack Hodges) and his conversion in prison. Abbott wrote that Jack explained that he had been supplied with alcohol, but that it was not enough to intoxicate him, but rather to "destroy what little conscience he had" and that on the day of the murder, after drinking, he went and "laid down in the skirts of a wood where they expected to commit the murder."[3]

Jack then told Abbot that the other man who was to assist him woke him up and said, "If we mean to do anything, we had better do it now." They went out and found their victim – Jack shot him, and the other man beat him to the head with the gun.[4]

Did you catch that? This is a strikingly different version of the crime than that which Jack had testified to (recall Jack said that he had been eating breakfast when Jennings was seen walking past the Teed residence). Did Jack Hodges misstate a portion of the story that he had fabricated? It certainly raises doubt in my mind as to the authenticity of Jack's initial testimony.

If Hodges lied, then David Dunning and James Teed died on the gallows as innocent men. David Conkling spent a good number of years in state prison. Countless other lives were affected. The thought that two innocent men may have been wrongly executed troubles me. And maybe it troubled Hodges – that could explain his religious conversion.

Did Hodges immerse himself in religion out of guilt and remorse? Was his miraculous transfiguration in Auburn Prison inspired by the realization that two men had died because of his false testimony? His words had already done their damage, so there would be no point in admitting his deceit. In fact, he would most likely have feared additional punishment if it were exposed. So perhaps religion was his only means of coping with an irreversible situation.

During the trials, it was proposed that Jack had acted alone out of a sense of devotion and dedication to Conkling, and his own potential losses associated with Jennings's repossession of the disputed land. Conkling and Teed may have wanted Jennings dead, but they never intended to actually kill him, so Jack took it upon himself to do what the other men were unable to do for themselves. This would support Jack as the lone assassin of Richard Jennings. This is a very plausible scenario.

In this scenario, Jack retaliated against Dunning for informing on him and dragged the others in to create a conceivable plot. Everyone knew Teed and Conkling had a feud with Jennings, so he would be believed. He testified against the others knowing, or at least understanding, that he would be spared the gallows if he helped gain convictions.

Or, Jack Hodges was telling the truth. He was a pawn used by wicked men to achieve a dastardly end, who confessed his role in the crime and, without any hope of a pardon, testified against the others. He found a deep and meaningful redemption in prison and lived a pious life for the remainder of his years of freedom.

Jack Hodges is either a shrewd, cunning, master manipulator or, as he had been often described in the press during the trials, was a vile ex-sailor and a drunken, ignorant man with no religion or moral compass. Two very different views of one very interesting man.

Four years after beginning this journey, I have doubts about Jack's story. It's too neat and convenient, and for the reasons I have mentioned in this epilogue, it just doesn't add up. As I write this, I have a terrible feeling that two men may have unjustly died at the end of a rope for a crime they did not commit. Unfortunately, the only people that can tell us what really happened are long gone. Jack Hodges took the truth with him to the grave. Everyone involved in this twisted affair did. So we can only look back with the information available to us and draw our own conclusions.

I would like to know what you think.

JACK HODGES

APPENDIX: TIMELINE OF KEY EVENTS

1806

--- - *James Teed dies; his estate is left to his widow, Phoebe Allison Jennings, with a clause giving the young James Teed a 50 acre parcel upon Phoebe's death.*

---- - *At some point, James Teed enters an agreement with his mother to obtain title to the 50 acre parcel. Richard Jennings intercedes and gains legal rights to the land*

---- - *A protracted court fight begins with Teed and Jennings; Teed eventually deeds the property to his brother in law, David Conkling; Conkling begins his own protracted legal battle with Jennings.*

JUNE 1818

23 - *Phoebe Jennings Teed dies.*

FALL 1818

---- - *Richard Jennings serves noticed on David Conkling that he is suing him at the fall term of the Circuit Court; he is awarded title of the land but will not be able to take possession until after the new year.*

DECEMBER 1818

17 - *Teed, Conkling & Hodges meet at the hovel and devise a plan to murder Jennings.*

19 - *Conkling gives Hodges loaded musket; Teed leaves for New York; Hodges leaves for Teed's home where he meets Dunning and they discuss the details of how they plan to kill Jennings.*

20 - *Hodges and Dunning confer about the plot.*

21 - *Jennings is seen walking by the Teed home; Dunning catches him and walks to the lot, Hodges shoots Jennings, but doesn't kill him; Dunning beats Jennings to death with the breech of the gun.*

22 - *Hodges collects the broken pieces of the gun and returns to Conkling's. Tries to tell Conkling the details of the crime, but Conkling stops him.*

23 - *Conkling tells Hodges to leave because he may be detected.*

24 - *Conkling offers Jack money to leave.*

25 - *Christmas Day. Hodges and Conkling are busy with work during the day, and Hodges spends the evening at the home of a Mr. Howell.*

26 - *The absence of Richard Jennings has become an issue in the village; rumors swirl that he has been murdered by Jack Hodges. Teed & Conkling prevail upon Jack to leave and give him a letter addressed to Mr. James Adair. Hodges departs and spends the night in Chester.*

27 - *Hodges travels to New Windsor and Newburgh where he is met by Teed. Teed is upset that Hodges has not gotten further away.*

28 - *Teed accompanies Hodges to the Ferry landing and Hodges crosses the North River.*

29 - *Search is organized to find Jennings. Samuel Pitts and Noble Howell discover the body; a coroner's inquest is convened; Dunning and Conkling are arrested and sent to the county jail; Hodges boards a sloop at Cold Spring bound for New York; Charles Durland & three other men set out in pursuit of Hodges.*

30 - *Hodges arrives in New York; James Teed is examined and makes a statement.*

31 - *Durland arrests Hodges at the wharf in New York & they begin the journey back to Orange County.*

JANUARY 1819

1 - *On board the sloop, Hodges confesses to Durland and reveals the details of the crime.*

2 - *Hodges is committed to the county jail; he makes a full written confession.*

4 - *Hannah Teed is arrested & remanded to the county jail.*

FEBRUARY 1819

23 - *A Grand Jury is convened & hears the evidence.*

24 - *Indictments handed up for the Teeds, Hodges, Conkling, and Dunning; they are arraigned in court.*

25 - *Court in recess.*

26 - *Trial of Jack Hodges begins & ends; the jury renders a guilty verdict; Trial of James Teed begins.*

27 - *People v. Teed continued.*

28 - *People v. Teed continued.*

MARCH 1819

1 - *People v. Teed continued. People rest / Defense begins.*

2 - *People v. Teed continued.*

3 - *People v. Teed. Last day of testimony.*

4 - *3:00 AM - Verdict – People v. Teed – guilty; Trial of David Conkling begins at 9:00AM.*

5 - *People v. Conkling continued. People rest / Defense begins.*

6 - *People v. Conkling continued.*

7 - *Sunday – no court.*

8 - *People v. Conkling continued.*

9 - *Verdict – People v. Teed – Guilty. Hannah Teed pleads guilty to accessory after the fact. Trial of David Dunning begins.*

10 - *Verdict - People v. Dunning – guilty.*

11 - *Hannah Teed sentenced to 30 days in jail; Teed, Dunning, Hodges, and Dunning sentenced to death.*

31 -   *Judge Van Ness writes a letter to Governor DeWitt Clinton seeking a pardon for Jack Hodges; the Governor forwards the letter to the Legislature for consideration.*

APRIL 1819

6 -   *The New York State House of Assembly considers a bill to pardon Jack Hodges; Hodges and Conkling make the first draft of the pardon; The inclusion of James Teed in the pardon is defeated.*

10 -   *During continued debate in the House of Assembly, James Teed is approved for inclusion in the pardon; the proposed bill granting a pardon to James Teed, David Conkling, and Jack Hodges is sent to the New York State Senate for consideration; the Senate rejected the pardon with the inclusion of James Teed, and after reconsideration in both houses of the Legislature, the pardon is passed sparing only Jack Hodges and David Conkling from the gallows. David Conkling is sentenced to hard labor for life in prison, Jack Hodges to 21 years of hard labor in prison.*

15 -   *David Conkling (aware of his pardon) meets with Jack Hodges (who is unaware of his pardon) in the prison to confront Jack about Dunning's persistent denials. Hodges maintains that he has told the truth; James Teed and David Dunning are baptized by the Rev. Richard F. Cadle from the St. James Protestant Episcopal Church in Goshen. Both men make written confessions.*

16 -   *Before nearly 15,000 people, James Teed and David Dunning are publically executed on a scaffold just south of Goshen; David Dunning dies denying that he had struck Jennings with the gun; an unidentified gentleman confronts Jack at the county jail about Dunning's dying declaration and Jack maintains that he has told the truth; later that day, David Dunning is buried by friends.*

18 -   *James Teed is laid to rest by his family.*

20 -   *David Conkling and Jack Hodges are taken from the Orange County Jail and transported to the state prison known as Newgate in New York.*

27 -   *Rumors that David Dunning was revived after the execution prompt a group of men to exhume his body and verify that it is still in the grave.*

---- -   *Pamphlets are published: A Report of the Trials of the Murderers of Richard Jennings, and an Account of the Murder of Richard Jennings.*

AUGUST 1819

16 -   *Nathaniel and Deborah Knapp write to John Teed and Phanny Teed about the death of James Teed; the letter indicates that the Knapps claimed Teed's body.*

OCTOBER 1819

---- -   *The sermon delivered on the scaffold by Rev. Fisk, Sin Finds out the Criminal, is published.*

JANUARY 1820

8 - *Julia Ann Teed writes to John Teed and Fanny Teed.*

MARCH 1820

8 - *Julia Ann Teed writes to John Teed and Fanny Teed.*

JULY 1823

30 - *Hannah Teed is last seen entering the North River at Newburgh, New York.*

AUGUST 1823

2 - *Hannah Teed's lifeless body is pulled from the North River; her death is ruled a suicide.*

APRIL 1825

--- - *Jack Hodges is transferred to the new state prison at Auburn, New York; he becomes very religious and forms a close bond with the Rev. Louis Dwight of the Prison Discipline Society, and the Rev. Jared Curtis. Hodges learns how to read and is an exemplary inmate.*

MID 1820s

--- - *David Conkling is transferred to the new state prison named Mt. Pleasant (later to be called Sing Sing).*

AUGUST 1827

3 - *In People v. Elsie Whipple, Albany, NY, Judge William Duer cites the Jennings case in a legal decision prohibiting Whipple's co-defendant from testifying against her. Duer was a member of the legislature at the time Hodges was pardoned.*

FEBRUARY 1829

26 - *Jack Hodges is pardoned and released from prison; he lives in Auburn for the first two years of his freedom and works at the Auburn Theological Seminary; Jack eventually relocates to Canandaigua, New York, and joins the First Congregational Church. He will end up living and working in the home of a widower named Harriet Martin.*

JANUARY 1834

16 - *David Conkling receives a pardon and is released from prison*

\--- - *The Record of Crimes in the United States is published and contains a chapter on the Jennings murder. It is essentially plagiarized from the pamphlet, An Account of the Murder of Richard Jennings.*

1836

\--- - *United States Criminal History is published and contains a chapter dedicated to the Jennings murder. Like the 1834 book, it is plagiarized from the original 1819 source document (An Account...).*

1840

\--- - *The United States Criminal Calendar is published with a chapter devoted to Richard Jennings. It is, like the books of 1834 and 1836, plagiarized.*

DECEMBER 1840

13 - *David Conkling dies and is buried in what is now known as Monroe Community Cemetery, Monroe, NY.*

LATE 1841

\--- - *Future Governor of New York Myron Clark purchases Harriet Martin's home and Jack Hodges is kept on as an employee and continues to reside in the home.*

JANUARY 1842

\--- - *Towards the end of the month Jack Hodges becomes ill.*

FEBRUARY 1842

16 - *At 6:00 PM, Jack Hodges dies. He is later laid to rest at a well attended funeral in what is now referred to as the Old Pioneer Cemetery in Canandaigua, NY.*

\--- - *About one week after his death, rumors persist that Hodges had not been buried and that his body had been sent to the anatomists to be dissected. His body is exhumed to verify that it is still in the grave.*

JUNE 1875

\--- - *In an appeal in a first degree murder case (People v. Lindsay), the Jennings case is mentioned in a court decision.*

JANUARY 1954

21 - *The Chester Observer prints an article by Samuel Levy titled, "The Imperfect Crime or How The Murderers of Richard Jennings Were Brought to Book in 1818."*

1955

--- - *Bruce Sherwood, a descendant of Frances Teed (James Teed's sister) attempts to obtain files from the New York Historical Society and is told that the files are 'restricted' – he subsequently obtains them with the assistance of a family matriarch, Elizabeth Teed.*

1975

--- - *Donald M. Barrell's book Along the Wawayanda Path From Old Greycourt to Chester to Sugar Loaf is published. A chapter on the Richard Jennings murder is included. This account appears to be the first source to print many of the local legends.*

JULY 1975

16 - "Old Warwick Valley and the Ways of Its People," by Donald M. Barrell is printed int *Warwick Valley Dispatch*, July 16, 1975.

2005

--- - *The Richard Jennings murder is included in Hudson Valley Faces & Places by Patricia Edwards Clyne.*

FALL 2009

--- - *Michael Worden begins research into the Richard Jennings murder.*

OCTOBER 2013

--- - *Worden's book on the Richard Jennings murder is released.*

NOTES

Chapter 1

1. Sally Teed Foust. "James Teed Dies on Gallows in 1819 at Goshen, New York, After Intra-Family Conspiracy Murder," *The Teed Tree – A Genealogical Exchange for the Teed Family and Allied Families,* Issue No. 15, Fall, 1997, 156-157.
2. Ibid.
3. *Report of the Trials of the Murderers of Richard Jennings. At a Special Court of Oyer and Terminer for the County of Orange, Held at the Court House in the Village of Goshen on Tuesday, February 23rd, 1819: With Arguments of Counsel,* (Newburgh: Benjamin F. Lewis and Co., 1819), iii.
4. Foust, *The Teed Tree,* 157; Report, iii.
5. *Report of the Trials,* iii-iv.
6. Ibid; Foust, *The Teed Tree,* 157.
7. *Report of the Trials,* iv.
8. Ibid.
9. "Shocking Murder," *The Orange County Patriot; or The Spirit of Seventy-Six,* (Goshen, NY), January 5, 1819.
10. *Report of the Trials,* iv.
11. "Shocking Murder."
12. *Report of the Trials,* iv.
13. *An Account of the Murder of Richard Jennings; Together with the Confessions of Teed & Dunning,* (Newburgh: Benjamin Lewis, & Co., 1819), 17. This was a statement that Jennings allegedly had made to Dunning in the months prior to the murder. Dunning had asked if Jennings would indemnify Conkling, and of course, Jennings said that he wouldn't and made this quoted statement. It goes to demonstrate the level of animosity that existed between the parties involved.
14. *Report of the Trials,* 80.
15. Ibid.
16. Ibid.
17. Ibid, 81.
18. Ibid, 32. Note that the statements, which Hodges attributed to James Teed, are very similar to those Hodges attributed to David Conkling. With the discrepancies between Dunning and Hodge's accounts of the crime, this certainly raises a question as to Hodges's integrity.
19. Ibid, 15.
20. The hovel was most likely a small, open shed on Conkling's property.
21. *Report of the Trials,* 14. This description of the plot comes from a statement Jack Hodges made to Justices of the Peace and the Coroner. I find it very interesting that the plot included the portion where Dunning was to walk with Jennings. How could the plotters guarantee that there would be sufficient opportunity for Dunning to observe Jennings walking, then walk with him, and have Jack Hodges ready and waiting with a loaded gun? Was Jack being honest, or was he taking liberties with the truth?
22. *Report of the Trials,* 39, 111.
23. Ibid, 14-15.
24. Ibid, 51.
25. Ibid, 14-15.
26. Ibid, 15.
27. Ibid.
28. Ibid, 27.
29. Ibid, 14, 34.
30. Ibid.
31. Ibid, 27.
32. Foust, *The Teed Tree,* 157; "Shocking Murder;" *Report of the Trials,* 34, 64: Ira Jennings, son of the deceased, testified that his father had left on the morning of the 21st to check on the lot.
33. *Report of the Trials,* 34. A discrepancy in Jack's story arises here. He testified at Dunning's trial that on the morning of the murder, he and Dunning had agreed to go into the woods to chop wood, as this would draw

Jennings to the wood lot. This conversation is missing from his voluntary statement as well as testimony against Teed at that trial.

34. Ibid.
35. Ibid, 15.
36. Ibid, 110. The distance from the road is given as "eight or nine rods." A rod was a unit of measurement equal to sixteen and a half feet; see *Report of the Trials*, 34.
37. Ibid, 12-13, 15-16, 34-35.
38. Ibid, 35.
39. Ibid, 12-13, 15-16, 26-27, 34-35.
40. Ibid, 16, 35.
41. Ibid, 12-13. See testimony of Dr. Samuel S. Seward.
42. Ibid, 16, 35.
43. Ibid, 16, 35.
44. Ibid, 27. See testimony of Noble Howell.
45. Ibid, 35-36.
46. Ibid, 36
47. Ibid.
48. Ibid.
49. Ibid, v.
50. Ibid, 36. David Conkling was telling Hodges that Teed have informed him that people suspected Jennings was dead and that Hodges had killed him.
51. Ibid, 17, 36-37.
52. Ibid, 37.
53. Ibid.
54. Ibid, 17, 37-38, 44.
55. Ibid.
56. Ibid, 25-27. See testimony of Samuel Pitts and Noble Howell.
57. Ibid, 26.
58. Ibid.
59. Ibid, 27.
60. Ibid, 111-112. Coroner Curtice read Dunning's testimony into the record at Dunning's trial..
61. Ibid, 12. See testimony of Dr. Samuel S. Seward.
62. Ibid, 79.
63. Ibid, 111-112.
64. Ibid, 12-13.
65. "Shocking Murder."
66. *Report of the Trials*, vi.
67. *Report of the Trials*, vi; "Shocking Murder."
68. *Report of the Trials*, vi, 17.
69. Ibid, 13. See testimony of Charles B. Durland; "Shocking Murder."
70. Ibid, 13-14.
71. Ibid.
72. Ibid, 42-43.
73. Ibid.
74. D. T. Valentine, *Manual of the Corporation of the City of New York for 1855,* (New York: McSpedon and Baker, 1855), 486-487.
75. *Report of the Trials*, 43; "Shocking Murder."
76. *Report of the Trials*, 43.
77. Ibid, 13-14, 43-44; "Shocking Murder."
78. *Report of the Trials*, 14.
79. "The Murder," *The Orange County Patriot; or The Spirit of Seventy-Six*, (Goshen, NY), January 12, 1819.
80. Ibid.

Chapter 2

1. Oyer and Terminer literally means, "to hear and determine."

2. *Report of the Trials*, 2; "Special Court of Oyer & Terminer," *The Orange County Patriot; or The Spirit of Seventy-Six*, (Goshen, NY), March 2, 1819.
3. *Report of the Trials*, 2; "Special Court of Oyer & Terminer."
4. "Special Court of Oyer & Terminer."
5. Walter C. Anthony, *Sketches of Some of the Prominent Members of the Orange County Bar*, (Newburgh: News Printing & Publishing, Co., 1917), inside front.
6. Anthony, *Sketches of Some of the Prominent Members*, 15; Louise Hasbrouck Zimm, comp., et al., *Southeastern New York. A History of the Counties Ulster, Dutchess, Orange, Rockland and Putnam*, vol 1, (New York: Lewis Historical Publishing Company, Inc., New York, 1946), 490.
7. Edgar L. Murlin, *The Red Book. An Illustrated Legislative Manual of the State, Containing the Portraits and Biographies of its Governors and Members of the Legislature, Also the Enumeration of the State for 1892, with Election, Population Statistics, and List of Postmasters*, (Albany: James B. Lyon, 1893), 24.
8. *Report of the Trials*, 10-11.
9. Ibid, 11-13.
10. Compiled from People v. Hodges: *Report of the Trials*, 10-23.
11. *Report of the Trials*, 12-13.
12. Ibid, 14.
13. Ruttenber, E. M. and Clark, L. H. comp, *History of Orange County, New York, with Illustrations and Biographical Sketches of many of the Pioneers and Prominent Men*,(Philadelphia: Everts & Peck, 1881), 20-25.
14. *Report of the Trials*, 14-18.
15. Ibid, 18-19.
16. Ibid, 20.
17. Ibid, 21.
18. Ibid.
19. Ibid, 21-23.
20. Ibid, 23.
21. Ibid.
22. Ibid. 24.
23. "Special Court of Oyer & Terminer."
24. *Report of the Trials*, 24-25.
25. Anthony, *Sketches of Some of the Prominent Members*, 6-7.
26. *Report of the Trials*, 25.
27. Ibid. The quote has long been attributed to having been uttered by Martin Van Buren in the opening of the trials. But as is now known, the statement was actually made by Samuel R. Betts at the commencement of James Teed's trial.
28. Ibid, 25-27.
29. Compiled from People v. Teed: *Report of the Trials*, 24-77.
30. *Report of the Trials*, 27-28.
31. Ibid, 29.
32. Ibid, 29-30.
33. Ibid, 30.
34. "Special Court of Oyer & Terminer."
35. *Report of the Trials*, 31-32.
36. Ibid, 32-42; "Special Court of Oyer & Terminer."
37. *Report of the Trials*, 39-41. Jack was either testifying that the conversations referenced were on different days – one before the murder, one after, or was making generic statements about Dunning's pre-murder knowledge. If his testimony was simply about what Dunning had known about the plot in general, then that is a major inconsistency and raises some question as to his credibility.
38. Ibid, 42-46.
39. Ibid, 46-47.
40. Ibid, 47.
41. "Trials for Murder," *The Orange County Patriot; or The Spirit of Seventy-Six*, (Goshen, NY), March 9, 1819.
42. *Report of the Trials*, 50.

43. Ibid, 50-52.

44. Ibid, 52-53.

45. Ibid, 54.

46. Ibid, 54-55.

47. "Special Court of Oyer & Terminer."

48. *Report of the Trials*, 55.

49. Ibid, 55-58.

50. Ibid, 58; "Special Court of Oyer & Terminer."; "Trials for Murder."

51. William Raymond, *Biographical Sketches of the Distinguished Men of Columbia County, Including an Account of the Most Important Offices They Have Filled, State and general Governments, and in the Army and Navy*, (Albany: Weed, Parsons and Company, 1851), 21-31

52. Ibid, 58-61.

53. Ibid 68.

54. Anthony, *Sketches of Some of the Prominent Members*, 26-27.

55. *Ex parte* generally means a legal proceeding involving only one party: the other party to the action is not present in court at the proceeding.

56. *Report of the Trials*, 69.

57. Anthony, *Sketches of Some of the Prominent Members*, 26-27.

58. *Report of the Trials*, 69.

59. Ibid, 73.

60. Ibid.

61. Ibid, 94-96.

62. Ibid, 73.

63. Ibid 73-74.

64. Ibid, 75-76.

65. Ibid, 77; "Trials for Murder."

66. *Report of the Trials*, 78-79.

67. Ibid, 79-81.

68. Compiled from People v. Conkling: *Report of the Trials*, 78-107.

69. *Report of the Trials*, 80-81.

70. Ibid, 81.

71. Ibid, 83.

72. Ibid, 84.

73. Ibid.

74. Ibid, 85; During Teed's trial, Charles was introduced as being nine years of age and it is noted that he was examined by the court and had demonstrated a belief in God and the consequences of providing false testimony. As such, he was sworn in as a witness. See *Report of the Trials*, 65.

75. *Report of the Trials*, 65.

76. Ibid, 86

77. "Settling Differences by Law," *Westchester Herald*, (Mount Pleasant, NY), February 23, 1819; "Settling Differences by Law," *Spectator*, (New York, NY), February 16, 1819.

78. We learn that Lewis Dunning was David Dunning's son from the testimony of Charles Teed. See trial of James Teed. (*Report of the Trials*, 66.)

79. *Report of the Trials*, 86.

80. Ibid, 86.

81. Ibid, 86-87.

82. Ibid, 87.

83. Ibid, 62.

84. Ibid, 88.

85. Anthony, *Sketches of Some of the Prominent Members*, 15.

86. Evidence supporting the location of the court house is found in E. M. Ruttenber and L. H. Clark, comp., *History of Orange County, New York, with Illustrations and Biographical Sketches of many of the Pioneers and Prominent Me,* (Philadelphia: Everts & Peck, 1881), 29.

87. *Report of the Trials*, 89.

88. Ibid, 90.

89. The *Report of the Trials* (page 91) indicates that Edward Ely began the closing argument for the defense. The account of the trial reported in the March 9, 1819, Orange County Patriot (see "Trials for Murder.") indicates that it was Jonathan Fisk.

90. *Report of the Trials*, 91.

91. Ibid, 92.

92. Ibid.

93. Ibid, 93-94.

94. "Trials for Murder."

95. *Report of the Trials*, 94-96.

96. Ibid, 97

97. Ibid.

98. Ibid, 97-99. According to the source, some of Duer's argument had been unavailable to them at the time the pamphlet went to press.

99. Ibid, 107.

100. "Trials for Murder," *The Orange County Patriot; or The Spirit of Seventy-Six*, (Goshen, NY), March 16, 1819.

101. "Trials for Murder." (March 16, 1819); *Report of the Trials,,* 107; "Poetry," *The Orange County Patriot; or The Spirit of Seventy-Six*, (Goshen, NY), April 13, 1819.

102. *Report of the Trials*, 108.

103. *Report of the Trials*, 108; "Trials for Murder." (March 16, 1819).

104. *Report of the Trials*, 108. *Nolle prosequi* literally means to be unwilling to prosecute or pursue.

105. Ibid, 108.

106. Ibid.

107. Ibid, cover.

108. Ibid, 109.

109. Ibid.

110. Compiled from People v. Dunning: *Report of the Trials*, 109-128.

111. *Report of the Trials*, 110; "Trials for Murder." (March 16, 1819).

112. *Report of the Trials*, 111.

113. Ibid, 112.

114. Ibid, 112-113.

115. Ibid, 113-114.

116. Ibid, 114-115.

117. Ibid 115-116.

118. Ibid, 117.

119. Ibid, 117-119.

120. Ibid, 119-126.

121. Ibid, 126.

122. Ibid, 126-128.

123. Ibid, 128; "Trials for Murder." (March 16, 1819). There is a discrepancy in the sources regarding the amount of time spent in deliberations. The *Report of the Trials*, identifies it as one hour, and the newspaper article as five hours.

124. "Trials for Murder." (March 16, 1819).

125. Ibid.

126. "Trials for Murder." (March 16, 1819); Report, 128-129.

127. "Trials for Murder." (March 16, 1819); Report, 128-129. In Barell's 1975 account of the case, erroneously includes Hannah Teed as also having been sentenced to death. See Barrell, Donald Barrell, *Along the Wawayanda Path From Old Greycourt to Chester to Sugar Loaf*, (Middletown: T.E. Henderson, 1975), 170.

128. *Report of the Trials*, 128.

129. Claudius Smith and members of his gang were hanged in Goshen on January 22, 1779.

130. "Trials for Murder." (March 16, 1819).

131. *Report of the Trials*, 130.

132. Ibid, 129-132.

133. Barrell, *Along the Wawayanda Path*, page 170. The convicts had not been harangued for hours – the text of the sentencing speaks for itself (see *Report of the Trials*, 129-132).

134. *Report of the Trials*, 132.

135. "Jack Hodges," *The Orange County Patriot; or The Spirit of Seventy-Six*, (Goshn, NY), March 23, 1819.

136. *Report of the Trials*, 132.

137. Ibid.

138. "Poetry," *The Orange County Patriot; or The Spirit of Seventy-Six*, (Goshen, NY), April 13, 1819; "We are Under the Necessity of Omitting this Week, the Lines," *The Orange County Patriot; or The Spirit of Seventy-Six*, (Goshen, NY), March 23, 1819.

139. "Poetry."

140. *An Account of the Murder of Richard Jennings*, cover.

Chapter 3

1. Claudius Smith and members of his gang were hanged in Goshen on January 22, 1779. Smith was a British Loyalist and terrorized the Hudson Valley. Legends of his life – and execution – grew and I think in some ways the hanging of Claudius Smith has become confused, in part, with that of Teed and Dunning. During my research I located an 1898 book titled *Chronicles of Monroe in the Olden Time* by Rev. Daniel Niles Freeland (The De Vine Press, New York). On page 60, details of the hanging of Smith include the "sermon … preached on the scaffold by the Pastor of the Presbyterian Church, the Rev. Ezra Fisk, D.D., in the presence of 50,000 spectators." This is an obvious error: Rev. Fisk was not born until 1785!

2. "Notice," *The Orange County Patriot; or The Spirit of Seventy-Six*, (Goshen, NY), April 6, 1819.

3. Charles Z. Lincoln, ed., *State of New York. Messages from the Governors Comprising Executive Communications to the Legislature and other Papers relating to Legislation from the Organization of the First Colonial Assembly in 1683 to and Including the Year 1906. With Notes. Volume II 1777-1822*, Vol. II (Albany: J.B. Lyon Company, State Printers, 1909), 996.

4. Ibid, 997.

5. Ibid. Specifically, the conclusion of the letter affirms that Van Ness was satisfied with justness of the conviction. While he has recommended a pardon – his recommendation seems to be limited more towards a pardon from the gallows, not from punishment: "Whether the pardon, however, ought to be absolute or conditional, is worthy of serious consideration. Sound policy, and a due regard to the public safety, would seem to require, that so dangerous a man should not, at lease for some time to come, be set at liberty."

6. Ibid.

7. "House of Assembly. April 6," *The Orange County Patriot; or The Spirit of Seventy-Six*, (Goshen, NY), April 13, 1819.

8. Ibid.

9. Ibid.

10. "House of Assembly. April 10," *The Orange County Patriot; or The Spirit of Seventy-Six*, (Goshen, NY), April 20, 1819.

11. Ibid.

12. *Laws of the State of New York Passed at the Forty-Second, Forty-Third and Forty-Fourth Sessions of the Legislature. From January 1819 to April 1821*, Vol. V. (Albany: William Gould & co. Law Book Seller; and Gould & Banks, Law Booksellers, 1821), 180.

13. *Laws of the State of New York Passed at the Forty-Second Session of the Legislature, Begun and Held at the City of Albany, The Fifth day of January, 1819*, (Albany: J. Buel, Printer to the State, 1819), 180; "House of Assembly. April 10."

14. Edgar L. Murlin, *The Red Book. An Illustrated Manual of the State, Containing the Portraits and Biographies of its Governors, State Officials and Members of the Legislature, with Portraits of Congressmen, Judges and Mayors, Also the New Constitution of the State, Election and Population Statistics, and General Facts of Interest*, (Albany: James B. Lyon, 1895), 35.

15. "The Execution," *The Orange County Patriot; or The Spirit of Seventy-Six*, (Goshen, NY), April 20, 1819.

16. Ibid.

17. Conclusion based upon research and review of descriptions of the location, and conversations and communications with Ginny Privitar, who kindly provided information she had developed based upon descriptions and review of old maps.

18. "The Execution."

19. Ibid.

20. "Goshen, (Orange County,) April 17," *Evening Post*, (New York, NY), April 21, 1819.

21. "The Execution."

22. According to David Conkling's Combined Military Service Record he served in the 1st Regiment of Belknap's New York Militia. Is this the same regiment that was identified as being present at the executions? If it is, one can appreciate the irony that Conkling narrowly escaped being hanged before his former regiment. Combined Military Service Record, David Conkling, Detached Militia 1st Regiment New York, War of 1812, Record Group 94, Records of the Adjunct General's Office, National Archives, Washington, DC.

23. Ibid.

24. Ibid.

25. Gertrude A Barber, comp., *St. James Protestant Episcopal Church Records, Goshen, Orange County, New York*, (1932), 6.

26. "The Execution."

27. Ibid.

28. "Execution Sermon," *The Orange County Patriot; or The Spirit of Seventy-Six*, (Goshen, NY), October 19, 1819.

29. "The Execution."

30. Time estimates are:

    "...almost three hours..." [Donald Barrell, *Along the Wawayanda Path*, 171.]

    "...two long hours..." [Patricia Edwards Clyne, *Hudson Valley Faces & Places*, (Woodstock: Overlook Press, 2005), 161.]

    An eyewitness account puts the time of the hanging at 2:05 P.M. ["Goshen, N.Y. April 17," Spooner's Vermont Journal (Windsor, VT), May 3, 1819.]

    Another newspaper account documented the time of hanging at 2:30 P.M. ["Execution" *Spectator*. (New York, NY), April 23, 1819.]

31. "The Execution;" "Execution," *Spectator*. (New York, NY), April 23, 1819.

32. "The Execution;" "Execution," *Spectator*.

33. "The Execution." Interestingly, accounts of the execution printed in several other papers are nearly verbatim from this source, however some omit the line, "I hope this will be a warning to all never to keep company with black people."

34. *An Account of the Murder of Richard Jennings*, cover.

35. "The Execution."

36. Wener U. Spitz, Daniel J. Spitz, and Russell S. Fisher, eds., *Spitz and Fisher's Medicolegal Investigation of Death. Guidelines for the Application of Pathology to Crime Investigation*, 4th ed. (Springfield: Charles C. Thomas Publisher, LTD., 2006), 788.

37. "Escape from Prison," *Berkshire Star*, (Stockbridge, MA), April 22, 1819.

38. "Execution of Teed and Dunning," *Berkshire Star*, (Stockbridge, MA), April 29, 1819.

39. Barrell, *Along the Wawayanda Path*, 171.

40. "Execution, &c.," *The Orange County Patriot; or The Spirit of Seventy-Six*, (Goshen, NY), April 27, 1819.

41. Barrell, *Along the Wawayanda Path*, 171.

42. Ralph Birdsal, *The Story of Cooperstown*, (Cooperstown: The Arthur H. Crist Co., 1917), 174-182.

43. The case of Stephen Arnold is fascinating and worthy of further study. As with so many other aspects of my research, I found myself easily pulled in the direction of yet another historical event and easily distracted by the details of the crime, trial and drama on the scaffold. The brief paragraphs I have written here are merely a general synopsis of the case in order to prevent making the chapter confusing. The connection between Stephen Arnold, and Teed and Dunning, however, can't be overlooked.

44. *Portrait and Biographical Record of Orange County New York Containing Portraits and Biographical Sketches of Prominent and Representative Citizens of the County. Together with Biographies and Portraits of all the Presidents of the United States*, (New York and Chicago: Chapman Publishing Co., 1895), 705.

45. Barrell, *Along the Wawayanda Path*, 170-171. There is no explanation in the text on how this number of 4000 people was estimated or determined.

46. The estimate range of 15,000 to 20,000 is presented in various newspaper accounts, which are nearly verbatim, indicating they originated with a single source article. The original may have been the *Newburgh*

Gazette of April 20, 1819. The April 21, 1819 edition of the *Commercial Advertiser* (New York, NY), and the April 23, 1819, edition of the *Spectator* (New York, NY) are among two of the papers, which credit Newburgh as the original source. Upstate newspaper the *Rochester Telegraph* (Rochester, NY), in the May 11, 1819 edition, credits the *Lansingburgh Gazette* as their source. The estimates of 12,000 people originates with a single source, which is an eyewitness account published in multiple newspapers. The eyewitness is never identified by name. See the New York, NY, *Evening Post*, of April 21, 1819.

47. "The Execution." Also, the same article is reprinted in the May 25, 1819, edition of the *Carlisle Republican* (Carlisle, PA).

48. "The Execution."

49. The National Archives, National Archives and Records Service, *National Archives Microfilm Publications. Microcopy No. 33. Population Schedules of the Fourth Census of the United States 1820 New York, Roll 64 New York Volume 3*, (Washington: National Archives, 1959).

50. "From the Newburgh Political Index of April 20. To Moses D. Burnet, Esq. Sheriff of Orange," *The Orange County Patriot; or The Spirit of Seventy-Six*, (Goshen, NY), April 27, 1819.

51. *Northern Christian Advocate*, (Syracuse, NY), September 16, 1886.

52. "Execution &c." The identity of the gentleman who spoke to Jack immediately after the executions is not made known, although it can be speculated that the person must have been of high standing in the community and was most likely a prominent citizen.

53. "Substance of a Conversation between David Conkling and Jack Hodges," *The Orange County Patriot; or The Spirit of Seventy-Six*, (Goshen, NY), April 27, 1819.

54. Ibid.

55. Barrell, *Along the Wawayanda Path*, 165-166; Foust, *The Teed Tree*, 156-159. The newsletter version of the case seems largely drawn upon Clyne's account. There is mention in the article that a Teed family descendant (Bruce Sherwood) had been writing a paper while at Cornell University and had felt that the discretionary legal decisions in the Teed case were significant, especially the decision of the guilty verdict against James Teed. Apparently, Sherwood had felt that the decision was discretional and based upon the "wealth, prestige and political connections of Richard Jennings – Sherwood's 5-x great-grandfather." This is known to be inaccurate because the verdict was not delivered by a judge, but rather a jury, and Teed was part of the Jennings family, so above all, he should have been spared if wealth and political connections were in play. The article also states that Sherwood had attempted to obtain court records on the trials from the New York State Historical Society in 1955 but was told that the records were restricted. The records were apparently unsealed when a Teed family matriarch went and demanded to see them. From my research I can find no such records to exist in the collection of the New York Historical Society.

56. The crime books published in the 1830s and 1840s containing the Richard Jennings murder are:

    P. R. Hamblin, comp., *United States Criminal History; Being a True Account of the Most Horrid Murders, Piracies, High-way Robberies, &c. Together with the Lives, Trials, Confessions and Executions of the Criminals. Compiled from the Criminal Records of the Counties*, (Fayetteville: Mason & De Puy, Printers, 1836), 151-161.

    Henry Clair, comp., *The United States Criminal Calendar: Or an Awful Warning to the Youth of America Being a True Account of the Most Horrid Murders, Piracies, High-way Robberies, &c. &c. Compiled From the Best Authorities*, (Boston: Printed and Published by Charles Gaylord, 1840), 185-198.

    The Record of Crimes in the United States; containing a Brief Sketch of the Prominent Traits in the Character and Conduct of Many of the Most Notorious Malefactors Who Have Been Guilty of Capital Offences; and Who Have Been Detected and Convicted. Compiled From the Best Authorities, (Buffalo: H. Faxon & Co., 1834), 316-333.

57. Robert Bruce Clark, *The First Presbyterian Church, Goshen, New York, 1720-1895*, (New York: Anson D. F. Randolph and Co., 1895), between 28-29.

58. Ezra Fisk, *Sin Finds Out the Criminal. A Sermon Delivered at the Execution of James Teed and David Dunning for the Murder of Richard Jennings, April 16, 1819*, (Goshen: T. B. Crowell, 1819), 30.

59. Clark, *The First Presbyterian Church*, 30.

60. Fisk, *Sin Finds Out the Criminal*, cover.

61. *An Account of the Murder of Richard Jennings*, 15-16.
62. Ibid, 16-20.

Chapter 4

1. Sugar loaf cemetery is located on a hill where Kings Highway turns towards Sugar Loaf (if you continue on the King's Highway Bypass you have missed it.) An approximate address for GPS is to use 1415 King's Highway, Chester, NY, 10918. This should bring you to the firehouse opposite the hill.
2. Barrell, *Along the Wawayanda Path*, 172; Clyne, *Hudson Valley Faces & Places*, 161; The Orange County Genealogical Society, *Orange County, New York, Cemetery Series Cemeteries of Chester, New York*, (Monroe: Library Research Associates, 1977), 81-82; Donald M. Barrell, "Old Warwick Valley and the Ways of Its People," *Warwick Valley Dispatch*, July 16, 1975.
3. The main sources of Orange County History are:

   Portrait and Biographical Record of Orange County New York Containing Portraits and Biographical Sketches of Prominent and Representative Citizens of the County. Together with Biographies and Portraits of all the Presidents of the United States, (New York and Chicago: Chapman Publishing Co., 1895). On Page 29 is a reference to Teed and Dunning having been executed south of the courthouse about a mile outside of town in a field.

   Samuel W. Eager, *An Outline History of Orange County, With An Enumeration of the Names of the Towns, Villages, Rivers, Creeks, Lakes, Ponds, Mountains, Hills and Other Known Localities, and Their Etymologies or Historical Reasons Therefor; Together with Local Traditions and Short Biographical Sketches of Early Settlers, Etc.*, (Newburgh: S.T. Callahan, 1846-47). On Page 225 is a reference to the death of Hannah Teed, and pages 437-441 contain information on the Richard Jennings murder, albeit with incorrect dates (February 1818 for the murder as opposed to the correct date which is December 1818).

   E. M. Ruttenber and L. H. Clark, comp., *History of Orange County, New York, with Illustrations and Biographical Sketches of many of the Pioneers and Prominent Men*, (Philadelphia: Everts & Peck, 1881). The small account on page 575 repeats the erroneous dates found in Eager's *An outline History*, and also places the location of the trials in Warwick. It is also erroneously reported that all four men had been "tried, condemned, and executed."

   Russel Headley, ed., *The History of Orange County, New York*, (Middletown: Van Deusen and Elms, 1908). There is no mention of the Jennings case at all in this source.
4. "Execution, &c."
5. Nathaniel and Deborah Knapp to John Teed and Phanny Teed, August 16, 1819, *Teed Family Letters Collection*, Delaware County Historical Association, Delhi, NY.
6. Ibid. The spelling and grammatical errors were transcribed without correction.
7. Ibid.
8. Ibid.
9. See: "Execution &c." and Nathaniel and Deborah Knapp to John Teed and Phanny Teed, August 16, 1819.
10. Nathaniel and Deborah Knapp to John Teed and Phanny Teed, August 16, 1819.
11. Julia Ann Teed to John Teed and Fanny Teed, January 8, 1820, *Teed Family Letters Collection*, Delaware County Historical Association, Delhi, NY; Julia Ann Teed to John Teed and Fanny Teed, March 8, 1820, *Teed Family Letters Collection*, Delaware County Historical Association, Delhi, NY.
12. Orange County Genealogical Society, *Cemeteries of Chester*, 81-82, 86.
13. Ibid, 81-82.
14. "Execution &c."
15. Henry R. Robinson, "A Galvanized Corpse," From Library of Congress Prints and Photographs Online Catalog, http://hdl.loc.gov/loc.pnp/cph.3b17055.
16. "Execution &c." Full sentence reads: "We hear a report from abroad that Dunning was restored to life."

"David Dunning," *The Orange County Patriot; or The Spirit of Seventy-Six,* (Goshen, NY), May 4, 1819. This article contains several of the rumors, including "that he had been seen and conversed with" since the execution and "if he were dead his body had never been buried."

Columbian (New York, NY), May 7, 1819. Refers to the body having been dug up and dissected, and also references the body having been restored to life and Dunning heading towards the west.

For an interesting account of an attempt to revive a executed criminal in November of 1818, see "Foreign Articles. From the Baltimore Telegraph., March 15," *The Orange County Patriot; or The Spirit of Seventy-Six,* (Goshen, NY), March 30, 1819.
17. See: "David Dunning," *The Orange County Patriot,* and *Columbian.*
18. "Execution &c."

Chapter 5

1. "Death of Mrs. Teed," *The Orange County Patriot; or The Spirit of Seventy-Six,* (Goshen, NY), August 11, 1823.
2. Ibid.
3. Eager, *An Outline History of Orange County,* 225.
4. "Death of Mrs. Teed."
5. Barrell, *Along the Wawayanda Path,* 172.
6. "Death of Mrs. Teed."

Chapter 6

1. Barrell, *Along the Wawayanda Path,* 172; Clyne, *Hudson Valley Faces & Places,* 161.
2. Barrell, *Along the Wawayanda Path,* 165.
3. Ibid, 168.
4. Ibid, 172.
5. D. T. Valentine, *Manual of the Corporation of the City of New York for 1853,* (New York: McSpedon and Baker, 1853), 461.
6. "Execution, &c."
7. "Sing Sing Prison, New York", *Ballou's Pictorial* IX , no. 20 (1855), 309.
8. W.A. Coffey, *Inside Out, or, An Interior View of the New-York State Prison: Together with Biographical Sketches of the Lives of Several of the Convicts,* (New York: J. Costigan, 1823), 77-80.
9. Barrell, *Along the Wawayanda Path,* Pg 172; Clyne, *Hudson Valley Faces,* 161.
10. New York State Senate, "No. 8. Annual Report of the Inspectors of the State Prison at Mount-Pleasant," *Documents of the Senate of the State of New York, Fifty Eighth Session, 1835. Volume I From No. 1 To No. 26 Inclusive,* vol. I (Albany: E. Croswell, Printer to the State, 1835), 15.
11. New York State Assembly, "No. 288. Report of Robert Wiltse, Agent of the State-Prison at Mount-Pleasant, Pursuant to a Resolution Passed 26th February Last," *Documents of the Assembly of the State of New York, Fifty-Seventh Session, 1834. Volume IV. From No. 251 to 401 Inclusive,* vol. IV (Albany: E. Croswell, Printer to the State, 1834), 14.
12. Ibid.
13. Eager, *An Outline History of Orange County,* 441.
14. Ibid, 437. Eager writes that "Richard Jennings . . . was missing from his house on the 21st of Feb., 1818, and on the 28th was found on his farm dead." The dates are obviously incorrect, as is the location where Jennings was found. Otherwise, Eager's text on the trials (pages 437-441) seem to be extracted directly from newspaper accounts of the time.
15. Barrell, *Along the Wawayanda Path,* 172. The complete sentence is, "He changed his name to Daniel Conklin, was taken home and cared for by his faithful wife, but died soon after, and as a further effort to disguise the identity of this man, the date of his death was recorded as 1810, instead of 1832 to 1834 as his actual death."
16. *Report of the Trials,* 85.
17. Pension Application File 4227, David Conklin, War of 1812, Record Group 15, Records of the Veterans Administration, National Archives, Washington, DC.

18. Edgar L. Murlin, *The Red Book. An Illustrated Manual of the State, Containing the Portraits and Biographies of its Governors, State Officials and Members of the Legislature, with Portraits of Congressmen, Judges and Mayors, the New Constitution of the State, Election and Population Statistics, and General Facts of Interest*, (Albany: James B. Lyon, 1897), 41.

19. Pension Application File 4227.

20. My first task was to ensure that the grave of David Conklin located in Monroe's Community Cemetery is that of the same David Conklin convicted of the murder of Richard Jenning. To make an accurate conclusion I established certain facts which, when put together, provided an abundance of evidence to support that I had located the correct grave: Conklin was married to Fanny Knight; Conkling served in the War of 1812 in Capt. Hallocks Co. N.Y. Militia; he was 50 years of age upon discharge from state prison in 1834; and that he died December 13, 1840 (making the time frame between release and death consistent), and he is buried next to Fanny Knight, who is identified as his [David Conklin's] wife on Fanny's gravestone. This information was gathered from numerous sources, including the government pension file, service file, and transcript of the trial.

21. Gravestone of Sandford Roberts who died 1843, Monroe Community Cemetery, Monroe, New York.

22. The cemetery is located off of Route 17M, Monroe, New York, opposite 573 Rte. 17M. The old section of the cemetery is to the left when you enter. The Conklin graves are about 2/3 of the way into this older section. Look for Fanny Knight's gravestone as hers is very easy to discern.

23. Gravestone of Sandford Roberts.

24. Pension Application File 4227.

25. "Masonic," *The Orange County patriot; or The Spirit of Seventy-Six*, (Goshen, NY), September 28, 1819. The same print notice appeared in the same publication on October 5, 1819 and October 12, 1819. Interestingly, the name is given as David Conklin as opposed to Conkling.

26. "Masonic."

27. *An Account of the Murder of Richard Jennings*, 20.

28. Ibid.

29. On March 31, 1819, Judge Van Ness wrote to Governor De Witt Clinton, recommending Jack Hodges as a "fit object of pardon." Conklin is never mentioned in the communication to the Governor, nor is Teed or Dunning. Clearly, the judge's intent was to secure a pardon for Hodges based upon his testimony at the trials against the other defendants. See: Lincoln, Charles Z., ed. *State of New York. Messages from the Governors Comprising Executive Communications to the Legislature and other Papers relating to Legislation from the Organization of the First Colonial Assembly in 1683 to and Including the Year 1906. With Notes. Volume II 1777-1822*, Vol. II (Albany: J.B. Lyon Company, State Printers, 1909), 997.

30. News accounts of the time show a division in the Legislature: Conklin's name is amended into the bill to pardon Hodges, and is at some point then removed by vote. There is also an attempt to amend the bill to include James Teed, however that failed. One source even erroneously reported that only Hodges was pardoned, with both Teed and Conkling having their pardons declined. See untitled article in the *Essex Patriot* (Haverhill, MA), April 17, 1819. See also: "House of Assembly," *The Orange County patriot; or The Spirit of Seventy-Six*. (Goshen, NY), April 13, 1819, and "Legislature of New York. In Assembly," *Watch-Tower* (Cooperstown, NY).

31. *An Account of the Murder of Richard Jennings*, 20.

32. See Conkling's trial transcript in *Report of the Trials*, pages 78-107.

Chapter 7

1. "Jack Hodges," *The Orange County Patriot; or The Spirit of Seventy-Six*, (Goshen, NY), March 23, 1819.

2. *Report of the Trials*, 32.

3. "Jack Hodges."

4. Records of the Department of Correctional Services, Auburn Prison – Inmate Records, Registers of Male Inmates Discharged, [ca. 1816]-1894, 1908-1942. B0068-77, New York State Archives, Albany, NY.

5. *Legislative Documents of the Senate and Assembly of the State of New York. Fifty-Third Session, 1830. Volume 1. From No. 1 to 68, Inclusive,* Vol 1, (Albany: E. Croswell, Printer to the State, 1830), 45-46.

6. Ansel D. Eddy, *Black Jacob, A Monument of Grace. The Life of Jacob Hodges, an African Negro, Who Died in Canandaigva, N.Y., February 1842,* (Philadelphia: American Sunday-School Union, 1842), 3.

7. Gravestone inscription of Jacob Hodges who died 1842, Old Pioneer Cemetery, Canandaigua, New York.

8. I have drawn this conclusion based upon the descriptions of Hodges in various sources, chiefly that of Ansel Eddy, and his age of discharge is given at about 70 when leaving Auburn in 1829.

9. Auburn Prison – Inmate Records, New York State Archives; *Seventeenth Annual Report of the Board of Managers of the Prison Discipline Society, Boston, May, 1842*, (Boston: Published at the Society's Rooms, 1842), 114; Eddy, *Black Jacob*, 3.

10. *Report of the Trials*, 38.

11. *Legislative Documents*, 45.

12. Eddy, *Black Jacob*, 4-5. Hodges in his trial testimony says he was eleven years of age (see *Report of the Trials*, 38-39).

13. Ibid, 5.

14. Ibid, 4-5.

15. Ibid.

16. *Report of the Trials*, 39.

17. N. Phelps Stokes, *The Iconography of Manhattan Island, 1498-1909. Compiled from Original Sources and Illustrated by Photo-Intaglio. Reproductions of Important Maps, Plans, Views, and Documents in Public and Private Collections*, (New York: Robert H. Dodd, 1915), plate 171.

18. Eddy, *Black Jacob*, 7-8.

19. *Report of the Trials*, 32.

20. "Execution, &c."

21. Eddy, *Black Jacob*, 23.

22. Ibid, 23-24.

23. "View of the State Prison and Railroad Buildings, Auburn, N.Y.," *Gleason's Pictorial*, III, no. 18, (1852), 280.

24. *Legislative Documents*, 45-46.

25. Eddy, *Black Jacob*, 26.

26. Ibid, 27.

27. Auburn Prison – Inmate Records, New York State Archives.

28. *Seventeenth Annual Report*, 113-119.

29. Ibid, 120.

30. Ibid, 117. As described by Rev. Louis Dwight, Secretary of the Prison Discipline Society. It is very fascinating to me that Hodges was compared to Washington, considering that Hodges was not only a convicted murderer, but also an African-American in pre-Civil War America.

31. Ibid, 121.

32. *Legislative Documents,* 45-46.

33. Eddy, *Black Jacob*, 41-45.

34. Ibid, inside cover. This illustration depicts Rev. Curtis and Jack Hodges during their first meeting in Jack's cell at Auburn Prison.

35. Ibid, 46.

36. Clyne, *Hudson Valley Faces & Places*, 161.

37. The story of Hodges residing with William H. Seward may also have been related to an 1881 article about the book *Black Jacob*, in which George W. Seward (brother of William H. Seward) is referenced along with the book. According to the article, George Seward felt that the book would be a "means of grace to many" if it were more widely available. The article also mentions that George recalls the scene in court when his father, Judge Seward passed the sentence of death upon Hodges (of course, this is inaccurate. Judge Samuel Seward was involved in the trial as a Commissioner of the Court of Oyer and Terminer, but it was Judge VanNess who passed the sentence of death). See "Interest In An Old Book Revived," *The Sunday-School World. A Magazine for Superintendents, Teachers, and Scholars* 21, no 1, (January 1881), 28.

38. John Quincy Adams, *A History of Auburn Theological Seminary. 1818-1819*, (Auburn: Auburn Seminary Press, 1918), inside cover.

39. Eddy, *Black Jacob*, 51; *Jacob Hodges*, Biography published by the Ontario County Historical Society, (Canandaigua: Ontario county Historical Society).

40. Eddy, *Black Jacob*, 72.

41. Ibid, 51.

42. Ibid, 55.

43. *Seventeenth Annual Report*, 130.

44. Printed documents on *Jacob Hodges* and *Ownership 29 Gibson Street,* Ontario County Historical Society, Canandaigua, N.Y.

45. Walter H. Cassebeer, photographer, "North East Elevation (Main Entrance) First Congregational Church, North Main Street, Canandaigua, Ontario County, NY," Photograph, March 15, 1937, From Library of Congress *Historic American Buildings Survey,* http://hdl.loc.gov/loc.pnp/hhh.ny0620/photos.121112p.

46. *Seventeenth Annual Report,* 133; Eddy, *Black Jacob,* 83; "Black Jacob –or- Jack Hodges," *Sailor's Magazine,* No. 56, August (1843), 230.

47. *Seventeenth Annual Report,* 133.

48. Eddy, *Black Jacob,* 83.

49. Ibid, 83.

50. *Seventeenth Annual Report,* 130-134.

51. Eddy, *Black Jacob,* 93.

52. Ibid, 92. The language used to describe Hodges and others of African descent is reflective of the time period in which it was written.

53. Eddy, *Black Jacob,* 92.

54. Printed documents, Ontario County Historical Society, Charlotte resided in the home with her father, Myron Clark, a future Governor of the State of New York; Curator to Charles W. Barrell, February 11, 1954, Ontario County Historical Society, Canandaigua, NY.

55. Charles C. Burleigh, *Thoughts on the Death Penalty,* (Philadelphia: Merrihew & Thompson, 1845), 17.

56. George B. Cheever and Tayler Lewis, *A Defence of Capital Punishment,* (New York: Wiley and Putnam, 1846), 341-342.

57. Joseph Adshead, *Prisons and Prisoners,* (London: Longman, Brown, Green and Longman, 1845), 128.

58. Edgar L. Murlin, *The Red Book. An Illustrated Manual of the State, Containing the Portraits and Biographies of its Governors, State Officials and Members of the Legislature, with Portraits of Congressmen, Judges and Mayors, Also the New Constitution of the State, Election and Population Statistics, and General Facts of Interest,* (Albany: James B. Lyon, 1895), 37-39.

59. Review of *Seventeenth Annual Report of the Board of Managers of the Prison Discipline Society. Boston. 1842, pp. 110, 8vo. The Monthly Miscellany of Religion and Letters* 8, no. 1, (January 1843), 47-48.

60. *Legislative Documents,* 46.

61. Eddy, *Black Jacob,* cover.

Epilogue

1. Lincoln, *State of New York. Messages from the Governors, 997.*

2. Ibid.

3. Abbot – 182-183. Abbott's interview is undated, but it had to predate Jack's release as Jack was still incarcerated at the time the story was written.

4. Ibid, 183. The same version of the crime is reported in "Second Conversation with Black Jacob," *Sailor's Magazine,* no. 58, October (1843).

BIBLIOGRAPHY

Books

Abbott, Jacob. *The Young Christian: or A Familiar Illustration of the Principles of Christian Duty.* New York: Published by the American Tract Society, 1832.

Adams, John Quincy. *A History of Auburn Theological Seminary. 1818-1819.* Auburn: Auburn Seminary Press, 1918.

Adshead, Joseph. *Prisons and Prisoners.* London: Longman, Brown, Green and Longman, 1845.

Anthony, Walter C. *Sketches of Some of the Prominent Members of the Orange County Bar.* Newburgh: News Printing & Publishing, Co., 1917.

Armistead, Wilson. *A Tribute for the Negro. Being a Vindication of the Moral, Intellectual, and Religious Capabilities of the Coloured Portion of Mankind; with Particular Reference to the African Race.* Manchester: William Irwin, 1848.

Barbour, Oliver L. *Reports of Cases in Law and Equity in the Supreme Court of the State of New York.* Vol. LXVII. Albany: W. C. Little & Co., Law Booksellers, 1878.

Barrell, Donald M. *Along the Wawayanda Path From Old Greycourt to Chester to Sugar Loaf.* Middletown: T.E. Henderson, 1975.

Birdsall, Ralph. *The Story of Cooperstown.* Cooperstown: The Arthur H. Crist Co., 1917.

Burleigh Charles C. *Thoughts on the Death Penalty.* Philadelphia: Merrihew & Thompson, 1845.

Cheever, George B., and Lewis, Tayler. *A Defence of Capital Punishment.* New York: Wiley and Putnam, 1846.

Clyne, Patricia Edwards. *Hudson Valley Faces & Places.* Woodstock: Overlook Press, 2005.

Coffey, W.A. *Inside Out, or, An Interior View of the New-York State Prison: Together with Biographical Sketches of the Lives of Several of the Convicts.* New York: J. Costigan, 1823.

Cowen, Esek. *Reports of Cases Argued and Determined in the Supreme Court; and in the Court for the Trial of Impeachments and the Correction of Errors, of the State of New York.* Vol. IX. 3rd ed. New York: Banks & Brothers, Law Publishers, 1859.

Eager, Samuel W. *An Outline History of Orange County, With An Enumeration of the Names of the Towns, Villages, Rivers, Creeks, Lakes, Ponds, Mountains, Hills and Other Known Localities, and Their Etymologies or Historical Reasons Therefor; Together with Local Traditions and Short Biographical Sketches of Early Settlers, Etc.* Newburgh: S.T. Callahan, 1846-47.

Eddy, Ansel D. *Black Jacob, A Monument of Grace. The Life of Jacob Hodges, an African Negro, Who Died in Canandaigua, N.Y., February 1842.* Philadelphia: American Sunday-School Union, 1842.

Edgar L. Murlin. *The Red Book. An Illustrated Manual of the State, Containing the Portraits and Biographies of its Governors, State Officials and Members of the Legislature, with Portraits of Congressmen, Judges and Mayors, Also the New Constitution of the State, Election and Population Statistics, and General Facts of Interest.* Albany: James B. Lyon, 1895.

Fifteenth Annual Report of the Board of Managers of the Prison Discipline Society, Boston, May, 1840. Boston: Published at the Society's Rooms, 1840.

Hamblin, P. R. comp. *United States Criminal History; Being a True Account of the Most Horrid Murders, Piracies, High-way Robberies, &c. Together with the Lives, Trials, Confessions and Executions of the Criminals. Compiled from the Criminal Records of the Counties.* Fayetteville: Mason & De Puy, Printers, 1836.

Headley, Russel. ed. *The History of Orange County, New York.* Middletown: Van Deusen and Elms, 1908.

Murlin, Edgar L. *The Red Book. An Illustrated Manual of the State, Containing the Portraits and Biographies of its Governors, State Officials and Members of the Legislature, with Portraits of Congressmen, Judges and Mayors, Also the New Constitution of the State, Election and Population Statistics, and General Facts of Interest.* Albany: James B. Lyon, 1895.

Portrait and Biographical Record of Orange County New York Containing Portraits and Biographical Sketches of Prominent and Representative Citizens of the County. Together with Biographies and Portraits of all the Presidents of the United States. New York and Chicago: Chapman Publishing Co., 1895.

Raymond, William. *Biographical Sketches of the Distinguished Men of Columbia County, Including an Account of the Most Important Offices They Have Filled, State and general Governments, and in the Army and Navy.* Albany: Weed, Parsons and Company, 1851

Ruttenber, E. M. and Clark, L. H. comp. *History of Orange County, New York, with Illustrations and Biographical Sketches of Many of the Pioneers and Prominent Men.* Philadelphia: Everts & Peck, 1881.

Seventeenth Annual Report of the Board of Managers of the Prison Discipline Society, Boston, May, 1842. Boston: Published at the Society's Rooms, 1842.

Sixteenth Annual Report of the Board of Managers of the Prison Discipline Society, Boston, May, 1841. Boston: Published at the Society's Rooms, 1841.

Spitz, Wener U. Spitz, Daniel J., and Fisher, Russell S. eds. *Spitz and Fisher's Medicolegal Investigation of Death. Guidelines for the Application of Pathology to Crime Investigation.* 4th ed. Springfield: Charles C. Thomas Publisher, LTD., 2006.

St. Clair, Henry. Comp. *The United States Criminal Calendar: Or an Awful Warning to the Youth of America Being a True Account of the Most Horrid Murders, Piracies, High-way Robberies, &c. &c. Compiled From the Best Authorities.* Boston: Printed and Published by Charles Gaylord, 1840.

Stokes, I. N. Phelps. *The Iconography of Manhattan Island, 1498-1909. Compiled from Original Sources and Illustrated by Photo-Intaglio. Reproductions of Important Maps, Plans, Views, and Documents in Public and Private Collections.* New York: Robert H. Dodd, 1915.

The 'Old Cemetery' at Canandaigua, N.Y. Canandaigua: The Ontario County Times Press, 1918.

The Record of Crimes in the United States; Containing a Brief Sketch of the Prominent Traits in the Character and Conduct of Many of the Most Notorious Malefactors Who Have Been Guilty of Capital Offences; and Who Have Been Detected and Convicted. Compiled From the Best Authorities. Buffalo: H. Faxon & Co., 1834.

Valentine, D. T. *Manual of the Corporation of the City of New York for 1853.* New York: McSpedon and Baker, 1853.

Valentine, D. T. *Manual of the Corporation of the City of New York for 1855.* New York: McSpedon and Baker, 1855.

Zimm, Louise Hasbrouck, comp., et al. *Southeastern New York. A History of the Counties Ulster, Dutchess, Orange, Rockland and Putnam.* Vol I. New York: Lewis Historical Publishing Company, Inc., New York, 1946.

Genealogical Resources

Barber, Gertrude A. Comp. *St. James Protestant Episcopal Church Records, Goshen, Orange County, New York,* 1932.

Clark, Robert Bruce. *The First Presbyterian Church, Goshen, New York, 1720-1895.* New York: Anson D. F. Randolph and Co., 1895.

Foust, Sally Teed. "James Teed Dies on Gallows in 1819 At Goshen, New York, After Intra-Family Conspiracy Murder." *The Teed Tree – A Genealogical Exchange for the Teed Family and Allied Families.* Issue No. 15. Fall, 1997.

Jacob Hodges. Biography published by the Ontario County Historical Society. Canandaigua: Ontario County Historical Society.

The Orange County Genealogical Society. *Orange County, New York, Cemetery Series Cemeteries of Chester, New York.* Monroe: Library Research Associates, 1977.

Government Documents & Sources

Combined Military Service Record, David Conkling. Detached Militia 1st Regiment New York. War of 1812. Record Group 94. Records of the Adjunct General's Office. National Archives: Washington, DC.

Laws of the State of New York Passed at the Forty-Second Session of the Legislature, Begun and Held at the City of Albany, The Fifth day of January, 1819. Albany: J. Buel, Printer to the State, 1819.

Laws of the State of New York Passed at the Forty-Second, Forty-Third and Forty-Fourth Sessions of the Legislature. From January 1819 to April 1821. Vol. V. Albany: William Gould & Co. Law Book Seller; and Gould & Banks, Law Booksellers, 1821.

Legislative Documents of the Senate and Assembly of the State of New York. Fifty-Third Session, 1830. Volume 1. From No. 1 to 68, Inclusive. Vol 1. Albany: E. Croswell, Printer to the State, 1830.

Lincoln, Charles Z., ed. *State of New York. Messages from the Governors Comprising Executive Communications to the Legislature and other Papers Relating to Legislation from the Organization of the First Colonial Assembly in 1683 to and Including the Year 1906. With Notes. Volume II 1777-1822.* Vol. II. Albany: J.B. Lyon Company, State Printers, 1909.

The National Archives, National Archives and Records Service. *National Archives Microfilm Publications. Microcopy No. 33. Population Schedules of the Fourth Census of the United States 1820 New York, Roll 64 New York Volume 3.* Washington: National Archives, 1959.

New York State Assembly. "No. 288. Report of Robert Wiltse, Agent of the State-Prison at Mount-Pleasant, Pursuant to a Resolution Passed 26th February Last." *Documents of the Assembly of the State of New York, Fifty-Seventh Session, 1834. Volume IV. From No. 251 to 401 Inclusive.* Albany: E. Croswell, Printer to the State, 1834.

New York State Senate. "No. 8. Annual Report of the Inspectors of the State Prison at Mount-Pleasant." *Documents of the Senate of the State of New York, Fifty Eighth Session, 1835. Volume I. From No. 1 To No. 26 Inclusive.* Albany: E. Croswell, Printer to the State, 1835.

Pension Application File 4227. David Conklin. War of 1812. Record Group 15. Records of the Veterans Administration. National Archives: Washington, DC.

Records of the Department of Correctional Services. Auburn Prison – Inmate Records. Registers of Male Inmates Discharged, [ca. 1816]-1894, 1908-1942. B0068-77. New York State Archives: Albany, NY.

Historical Society Collections

Printed documents on *Jacob Hodges* and *Ownership - 29 Gibson Street*. Ontario County Historical Society, Canandaigua, N.Y.

Letters written between Charles W. Barrell and the Curator of the Ontario County Historical Society. Ontario County Historical Society, Canandaigua, NY.

Teed Family Letters Collection, Delaware County Historical Association, Delhi, NY.

Images

Cassebeer, Walter H. Photographer. "North East Elevation (Main Entrance) First Congregational Church, North Main Street, Canandaigua, Ontario County, NY." Photograph, March 15, 1937. From Library of Congress *Historic American Buildings Survey,* http://hdl.loc.gov/loc.pnp/hhh.ny0620/photos.121112p.

"Execution Site." Photograph, undated. Chester Historical Society, Chester, NY.

Elliott, Charles Loring. *Moses DeWitt Burnet.* ca. 1835. Oil on canvas; *30⅛ x 24¾ in.* Accession #1953.34. New-York Historical Society, New York.

Jarvis John Wesley. *William Van Ness.* 1818. Oil on canvas; *33 x 26¾ in.* Accession #1871.2. New-York Historical Society, New York.

Robinson. Henry R. "A Galvanized Corpse." Lithograph on woven paper; 30.9x43cm. 1836. From Library of Congress Prints and Photographs Online Catalog. http://hdl.loc.gov/loc.pnp/cph.3b17055.

"Scene of the Jennings murder." Photograph, undated. Chester Historical Society, Chester, NY.

Newspapers

Barrell, Donald M. "Old Warwick Valley and the Ways of Its People." *Warwick Valley Dispatch,* July 16, 1975.

C. Boehm, Rosa. "Goshen Church Among County's Five Oldest." *Middletown Times Herald.* (Middletown, NY). November 20, 1937.

Columbian. (New York, NY), May 7, 1819.

"David Dunning." *The Orange County Patriot; or The Spirit of Seventy-Six.* (Goshen, NY). May 4, 1819.

"Death of Mrs. Teed." *The Orange County Patriot; or The Spirit of Seventy-Six.* (Goshen, NY). August 11, 1823.

"Escape from Prison." *Berkshire Star.* (Stockbridge, MA). April 22, 1819.

Essex Patriot. (Haverhill, MA). April 17, 1819.

Evening Post. (New York, NY). April 21, 1819.

"Execution." *Spectator*. (New York, NY). April 23, 1819.

"Execution, &c." *The Orange County Patriot; or The Spirit of Seventy-Six*. (Goshen, NY). April 27, 1819.

"Execution of Teed and Dunning." *Berkshire Star*. (Stockbridge, MA). April 29, 1819.

"Execution Sermon." *The Orange County Patriot; or The Spirit of Seventy-Six*. (Goshen, NY). October 19, 1819.

"Foreign Articles. From the Baltimore Telegraph., March 15." *The Orange County Patriot; or The Spirit of Seventy-Six*. (Goshen, NY). March 30, 1819.

"From the Newburgh Gazette, of April 20. Execution." *Commercial Advertiser*. (New York, NY). April 21, 1819.

"From the Newburgh Gazette, of April 20. Execution." *Spectator*. (New York, NY). April 23, 1819.

"From the Newburgh Political Index of April 20. To Moses D. Burnet, Esq. Sheriff of Orange." *The Orange County Patriot; or The Spirit of Seventy-Six*. (Goshen, NY). April 27, 1819.

"From the Orange County Patriot of the 20th inst. Execution." *Carlisle Republican*. (Carlisle, PA). May 25, 1819.

"Goshen, N.Y. April 17." *Spooner's Vermont Journal* (Windsor, VT). May 3, 1819.

"House of assembly. April 6." *The Orange County Patriot; or The Spirit of Seventy-Six*. (Goshen, NY). April 13, 1819.

"House of Assembly. April 10." *The Orange County Patriot; or The Spirit of Seventy-Six*. (Goshen, NY). April 20, 1819.

"Jack Hodges." *The Orange County Patriot; or The Spirit of Seventy-Six*. (Goshen, NY). March 23, 1819.

"Legislature of New York. *In Assembly,*" *Watch-Tower*. (Cooperstown, NY). April 19, 1819.

Levy, Samuel J. "The Imperfect Crime or How the Murderers of Richard Jennings were Brought to Book in 1818." *Chester Observer*. (Chester, NY). January 21, 1954.

"Masonic." *The Orange County Patriot; or The Spirit of Seventy-Six*. (Goshen, NY). September 28, 1819; October 5, 1819; and October 12, 1819.

Northern Christian Advocate. (Syracuse, NY). September 16, 1886.

"Notice." *The Orange County Patriot; or The Spirit of Seventy-Six*. (Goshen, NY). April 6, 1819.

"Poetry." *The Orange County Patriot; or The Spirit of Seventy-Six*. (Goshen, NY). April 13, 1819.

"Settling Differences by Law." *Spectator*. (New York, NY). February 16, 1819.

"Settling Differences by Law." *Westchester Herald*. (Mount Pleasant, NY). February 23, 1819.

"Shocking Murder." *The Orange County Patriot; or The Spirit of Seventy-Six*. (Goshen, NY). January 5, 1819.

"Substance of a Conversation Between David Conkling and Jack Hodges." *The Orange County Patriot; or The Spirit of Seventy-Six*. (Goshen, NY). April 27, 1819.

"The Execution." *Carlisle Republican.* (Carlisle, PA). May 25, 1819.

"The Execution." *The Orange County Patriot; or The Spirit of Seventy-Six.* (Goshen, NY). April 20, 1819.

"Trials for Murder." *The Orange County Patriot; or The Spirit of Seventy-Six.* (Goshen, NY). March 9, 1819.

"Trials for Murder." *The Orange County Patriot; or The Spirit of Seventy-Six.* (Goshen, NY). March 16, 1819.

"We are Under the Necessity of Omitting this Week, the Lines." *The Orange County Patriot; or The Spirit of Seventy-Six.* (Goshen, NY). March 23, 1819.

Pamphlets

An Account of the Murder of Richard Jennings; Together with the Confessions of Teed & Dunning. Newburgh: Benjamin F. Lewis and Co., 1819.

Fisk, Ezra. *Sin Finds Out the Criminal. A Sermon Delivered at the Execution of James Teed and David Dunning for the Murder of Richard Jennings, April 16, 1819.* Goshen: T. B. Crowell, 1819.

Report of the Trials of the Murderers of Richard Jennings. At a Special Court of Oyer and Terminer for the County of Orange, Held at the Court House in the Village of Goshen on Tuesday, February 23rd, 1819: With Arguments of Counsel. Newburgh: Benjamin F. Lewis and Co., 1819.

Periodicals

"Black Jacob –or- Jack Hodges." *Sailor's Magazine.* no. 56. August (1843).

"Black Jacob –or- Jack Hodges." *Sailor's Magazine.* no. 57. September (1843).

"From the New York Observor. Black Jacob, or Jack Hodges." *The African Repository and Colonial Journal* 18. no. 13. November (1842).

"Interest In An Old Book Revived." *The Sunday-School World. A Magazine for Superintendents, Teachers, and Scholars* 21. no 1. January (1881).

"Jacob Hodges The Sailor." *Sailor's Magazine* 14. no. 12. August (1842).

"Last Conversation with Jacob Hodges." *Sailor's Magazine.* no. 62. February (1844).

Review of *Black Jacob, a Monument of Grace. The Life of Jacob Hodges, an African Negro, Who Died in Canandaigua, New York, February, 1842. pp 96. By A. D. Eddy, London: Charles Gilpin. The Dublin Literary Journal* 2. no 22. January (1845).

Review of *Seventeenth Annual Report of the Board of Managers of the Prison Discipline Society. Boston. 1842, pp. 110, 8vo. The Monthly Miscellany of Religion and Letters* 8. no. 1. January (1843).

"Second Conversation with Black Jacob." *Sailor's Magazine.* no. 58. October (1843).

"Second Conversation with Black Jacob." *Sailor's Magazine.* no. 59. November (1843).

"Third Conversation with Black Jacob." *Sailor's Magazine.* no. 61. January (1844).

"Sing Sing Prison, New York." *Ballou's Pictorial* IX. no. 20, (1855).

Ure, Andrew. "An Account of Some experiments Made on the Body of a Criminal Immediately After Execution, with Physiological and Practical Observations." *The Electronic Repertory and Analytical Review.* 9. No. III. July (1819).

"View of the State Prison and Railroad Buildings, Auburn, N.Y." *Gleason's Pictorial* III, no. 18, (1852).

ACKNOWLEDGEMENTS

T his book would never have been possible without the assistance of so many people and organizations. I am grateful for their help in finding sources, confirming information, suggesting leads, and providing documents, images, and other information that was essential to the research behind this book. I sought nothing less than the most historically accurate account of this event, and I have a lot of people to thank for helping me achieve that. The risk in making such acknowledgements is, of course, that I will inadvertently forget someone. Considering that I have been working on this since the fall of 2009, that is entirely possible. So if I have forgotten anyone, my apologies in advance.

My special thanks to:

My loving wife, Renee, who has served as my editor, motivator, fact checker, and number one fan! She has been my constant companion at speaking engagements, helped me with research, and accompanied me on road trips to various places to further my work. Without her love and guidance, this book would not have been possible.

My sons, Ryan and Michael, who have patiently tolerated me dragging them to historical locations, cemeteries, and speaking engagements.

My good friends, Linda Zimmermann and Bob Strong, for their support, encouragement, and proofreading expertise! Linda has accompanied me to cemeteries, the NYS Archives, field visits, and has been a great source of inspiration.

A thank you to the following individuals who have helped in one way or another (in no particular order): Clifton Patrick, Ginny Privitar, Phil Enriquez, Ray LaFever, Kathy McConnell DeFoster, Jay Westerveld, Theodore Sly, Betsy Howard, Betty McMahon.

I also wish to extend my gratitude to the following organizations who have been of invaluable assistance (again in no particular order): New York State Historical Society, Orange County Genealogical Society, New York State Historical Association, New York State Library and Archives, Ontario County Historical Society, Chester Historical Society, Warwick Historical Society, Sugar Loaf Historical Society, Delaware County Historical Association, Syracuse University Library Special Collections Research Center, State Library of Arizona Genealogy Collection, Port Jervis Free Library, Minisink Valley historical Society.

I extend my gratitude to the many organizations and people in Orange County and beyond, who are dedicated to preserving and promoting local history.

INDEX

ABOUT THE AUTHOR

Michael J. Worden is an author and police detective who resides in Orange County, New York. When he is not solving crimes (either current or historical), he enjoys spending time with his family, reading, researching other topics of interest, dabbling in special effects makeup with his sons, and listening to music. Michael describes himself as being obsessed with the post-punk band, Joy Division, and all things Finnish. He is an avid traveler and has made numerous trips abroad, with his favorite country being, of course, Finland.

Michael is the author of the 2009 book *Ghost Detective,* and the new *Crime Scene* series of books. He is married and the father of twin sons.

Visit Michael on the web:
www.therealcrimescenes.com
www.paranormalpolice.com

www.ingramcontent.com/pod-product-compliance
Lightning Source LLC
Chambersburg PA
CBHW050642150426

42813CB00054B/1163